CASE STUDIES IN BUSINESS ETHICS

I Significant Facts
II Interested Parties
III Decision Makers
IV (Independant, dependant)
IV. Issues
V Options (≥2)
VI 1) Recomandations &
2) Justification (2 theories)

VII Primary Drawbacks:
1) Most likely
2) Most dangerous

CASE STUDIES IN BUSINESS ETHICS

Marianne M. Jennings
Professor of Legal and Ethical Studies In Business
Arizona State University College of Business

WEST PUBLISHING COMPANY
Minneapolis/St. Paul   New York   Los Angeles   San Francisco

West's Commitment to the Environment

In 1906, West Publishing Company began recycling materials left over from the production of books. This began a tradition of efficient and responsible use of resources. Today, up to 95 percent of our legal books and 70 percent of our college and school texts are printed on recycled, acid-free stock. West also recycles nearly 22 million pounds of scrap paper annually — the equivalent of 181,717 trees. Since the 1960s, West has devised ways to capture and recycle waste inks, solvents, oils, and vapors created in the printing process. We also recycle plastics of all kinds, wood, glass corrugated cardboard, and batteries, and have eliminated the use of styrofoam book packaging. We at West are proud of the longevity and the scope of our commitment to the environment.

Production, Prepress, Printing, and Binding by West Publishing Company.

COPYRIGHT ©1993   By WEST PUBLISHING COMPANY
                       610 Opperman Drive
                       P.O. Box 64526
                       St. Paul, MN 55164-0526

Printed in the United States of America

00 99 98 97 96 95 94 93   8 7 6 5 4 3 2 1 0

ISBN 0-314-01261-3

CONTENTS

INDIVIDUAL RIGHTS AND THE BUSINESS ORGANIZATION   39

BUSINESS AND ITS PRODUCT   203

PREFACE

In 1986, before Ivan Boesky was a household word and Michael Douglas was Gordon Gekko in *Wall Street*, I began teaching a business ethics course in the MBA program in the College of Business at Arizona State University. The course was an elective. I had trouble making the minimum enrollments. However, two things happened to change my enrollments and my fate. The American Association of Collegiate Schools of Business (AACSB) made its changes in the business curriculum for graduate and undergraduate programs. Those changes mandated the coverage of ethics in business degree programs. The other happening was actually a series of happenings. Indictments, convictions and guilty pleas by major companies and their officers from E.F. Hutton to Union Carbide to Beech-Nut brought national attention to the need for the incorporation of values in American businesses and business leaders.

Whether by fear, curiosity or the need for reaccreditation, business schools and students seized the concept of studying business ethics. My course went from a little-known elective to the final required course in the MBA program.

Application of ethical principles in a business setting is a critical skill. Real life examples are necessary. Over the past six years, I have collected examples of ethical dilemmas, poor ethical choices and wise ethical decisions from the newspapers, the business journals and my experiences as a board member. Knowing that other instructors and students were in need of examples, I have taken my experiences and readings and turned them into the cases in this book.

The cases come not only from six years of teaching business ethics, but also from my conviction that a strong sense of values is an essential management skill that can be taught. The cases apply theory to reality and hopefully nurture or reinforce that needed sense of values for future business leaders.

The book is organized according to the six areas listed by businesses as those of primary concern to them in resolving ethical dilemmas: individual values; individual rights; operations; competition; products; and stakeholders. A case can be located using the table of contents, the topical index, or the product index which lists both products and companies by name. An index for business disciplines is also provided to group the cases by accounting, management and the other disciplines in colleges of business.

This book is not mine. It is the result of the efforts and sacrifices of many. I am grateful to the reviewers for this project who took me from a proposal to a finished product with their detailed suggestions and helpful changes. Their patience, expertise, and service are remarkable. My thanks to Greg McCann, Stetson University; Robert Crowner, Eastern Michigan University; Kermit

Springstead, Jr., Florida Institute of Technology; Bob Waldo, University of Puget Sound; Jill Austin, Middle Tennessee State University; Lena Prewit, University of Alabama; Steve Payne, Eastern Illinois University; Steven Brenner, Portland State University; William Rhey, University of Tampa; J.P. Callahan, Florida Institute of Technology.

I love editors. They call you almost every day and make you feel needed. My thanks to Rick Leyh for recognizing not only the need for the book, but its potential. I am grateful to Jessica Evans for her daily efforts in dealing with everything from lost phone messages to the color orange in the original cover proposal. Barb Pavicic managed the production and ensured the book's high quality appearance.

I also love my family. They also love editors — they know them by name and by phone calls. I am grateful for their understanding, support and trips to Kinko's. I am most grateful for their values and the reminder their very presence gives me of what is truly important.

Marianne M. Jennings
Professor of Legal and Ethical
Studies in Business
College of Business
Arizona State University

INTRODUCTION

"There is no pillow as soft as a clear conscience."
—Kenneth Blanchard and Norman Vincent Peale
The Power of Ethical Management

A recent cover story from Fortune magazine was entitled, "The Payoff from a Good Reputation" (Fortune, February 10, 1992). A vice chairman of an advertising agency is quoted in the article as saying, "The only sustainable competitive advantage any business has is its reputation." The same statement could be made with respect to individual business persons. Reputation cannot be found in the required Securities Exchange Commission's annual 10K filing and won't be reflected in the net worth of the firm's balance sheet. But its loss can be so devastating that if it were quantifiable, the failure of a firm to disclose that its ethical values were waning would constitute fraud under the federal securities laws. A business lacking an ethical commitment will, eventually, bring about its own demise.

An examination of the fates of companies such as Union Carbide, Beech-Nut, E.F. Hutton, Salomon Brothers, Johns-Manville and others who experienced public exposure for ethical mishaps supports the notion that a lack of commitment to ethical behavior is a lack of commitment to a firm's success.

Many people have referred to the term business ethics as an oxymoron. Nonetheless, as with Fortune's observation, there are some compelling reasons for choosing ethical behavior. In courses in finance and accounting, we are taught that the primary purpose and obligation of a business is to earn a profit. The pursuit of the bottom line in the immediate time frame can occasionally distort the perspective of even the most conscientious of us. The fear of losing business and consequently losing profits can cause individuals and companies to make decisions, that while not illegal, raise concerns about fairness, equity, justice and honesty.

However, the pursuit of the positive figure for the bottom line must be made with a long-term perspective in mind. Running a successful and ethical business is not like a sprint, it is a marathon. Firms that perform better financially over time are those firms with a commitment to ethical behavior. For example, the Ethics Resource Center examined twenty-one companies with written codes of ethics. The center study found that if $30,000 had been invested in a Dow Jones composite thirty years ago, the investment would be worth $134,000 today. If that same $30,000 had been invested in the twenty-one companies, the investment would be worth $1,021,861 today. A study by the Lincoln Center for Ethics at Arizona State University demonstrated that a list of the U.S. corporations that have paid dividends for the past one hundred years coincides with the Center's list of companies that make ethics a high priority.

A 1988 Touche Ross (now Deloitte Touche) survey of companies with annual sales of $500 million or more found that 63 percent of the respondents indicated that ethical standards strengthen a business's competitive edge. Yet, 94 percent of the respondents felt that they were troubled by ethical issues.

There is a recognition of the value of ethics and a realization that the companies and their employees may not perceive or properly resolve ethical dilemmas that confront them. Many firms simply adopt a standard of complying with positive law. Positive law is any law enacted at any level of government that carries some sanction or punishment for noncompliance. While positive law promotes many ethical values and moral principles, there are many actions that comply with positive law but raise ethical issues. For example, several former border guards who once stood guard at the East German border have been tried for manslaughter for killing East Germans as they attempted to escape into West Germany. In their defense, the former guards raised the issue that they had been ordered to "shoot to kill." However, the judge, in sentencing the men noted that not all activity that is legal is right. Yet we have the former guards faced with the dilemma of obeying orders under similar threats or following their moral standards with respect to the value of human life.

The study of business ethics is thus not the study of what is legal, but the study of the application of moral standards to business decisions. Moral standards are canons of personal behavior that are neither legislated nor changed by legislation. For example, regardless of legislative and regulatory requirements, we all are committed to the safety of workers in the workplace. But what happens when several moral standards are at issue? A company that manufactures batteries is concerned that its female workers who are working at the production line near the battery acid may expose their unborn children to a debilitating or deforming hazard. The safety moral standard is the company's focus. However, these line positions offer a higher wage and the exclusion of women would violate another moral standard we hold about fair and just treatment in the workplace regardless of sex, age, race or national origin.

Employees hold moral standards of following instructions, doing an honest day's work for a day's pay and being loyal to their employers. But what happens when their employers are producing a product that, because of inadequate testing, will be harmful to its users? Other moral standards of not intentionally harming others and adequately testing products cause the employee to face a dilemma and decide the appropriate course of action.

There was a time when businesses, consumers and employees subscribed to the "what's good for GM is good for the country" theory of business ethics. Businesses have now begun to realize that, contrary to Sir Alfred Coke's allegation that a corporation has no conscience, the corporation must develop a conscience. That conscience is developed as individuals and firms develop guidelines for their respective conduct.

The remaining pages of this book illustrate ethical dilemmas faced by businesses and business people. The cases require critical examination of one's moral standards and the impact poor ethical decisions can have on individuals and companies. The cases are divided into categories developed from The Conference Board's groupings of ethical dilemmas in business. (The Conference Board is a private research and information group that focuses on corporate and business issues.) Each of these areas represents a grouping of the types of ethical dilemmas that were ranked most important by CEOs in a 1991 survey conducted by the Ethics Resource Center. The topics in each of the categories are listed below.

> Individual Values and the Business Organization
>> Employee Conflicts of Interest
>> Inappropriate Gifts
>> Security of Company Records
>> Personal Honesty
>> Government Contract Issues
>
> Individual Rights and the Business Organization
>> Corporate Due Process
>> Employee Screening
>> Employee Privacy
>> Sexual Harassment
>> Affirmative Action/Equal Employment Opportunity
>> Employment at Will
>> Whistle-Blowing
>> Employee Rights
>> Comparable Worth
>
> Business Operations
>> Financial and Cash Management Procedures
>> Conflicts Between the Corporation's Ethical Code and
>>> Accepted Business Practices in Foreign Countries
>> Unauthorized Payments to Foreign Officials
>> Workplace Safety
>> Plant Closures and Downsizing
>> Environmental Issues
>
> Business and Its Competition
>> Advertising Content
>> Appropriation of Others' Ideas
>> Product Pricing
>
> Business and Its Product
>> Contract Relations
>> Product Safety
>> Product Quality
>> Customer Privacy
>
> Business and Its Stakeholders
>> Shareholders' Interests
>> Executive Salaries
>> Corporate Contributions
>> Social Issues

Resolution of ethical dilemmas is difficult. As I teach my MBA students the value of good ethics, I encourage them to speak out and challenge ideas. There are, however, four things they are never permitted to say in my class: "Someone else will just do it anyway," "Everybody else does it," "We've always done it that way," and "I'll wait until the lawyers tell me it's illegal."

There are questions that managers should use in evaluating an ethical dilemma. The Blanchard and Peale model consists of three questions: "Is it legal?" "Is it balanced?" "How does it make me feel?"

As I say jokingly to my students, if the answer to the first question is "no," i.e., the activity is illegal, you need not proceed with your analysis. There are several cases in the book where you are asked to determine whether the activity is in fact legal or whether slight variations in the conduct would have made the actions illegal. Many ethical dilemmas involve no illegality. For example, the sale of tobacco is a legal activity. But, given the documented health damage to individuals, is it an ethical activity?

The second question of balance requires you to put yourself in the position of other parties affected by your decision. For example, as an executive, you might not favor a buy-out of your company because it means you will probably not have a job. However, a shareholder may stand to benefit substantially from the price paid for his or her shares in a buy-out. But, the employees of the business and their community may experience economic consequences if the purchaser decides to close the business or focus its efforts in a different product area.

The final question asks you to examine your comfort level with a particular decision. Many people find that after reaching a decision on an issue they still experience feelings of discomfort that may lead to loss of sleep or lack of appetite. Those feelings of conscience can serve as a guide in resolving ethical dilemmas.

Business ethicist and professor Laura Nash has a series of questions she has developed for resolving ethical dilemmas:

1. Have you defined the problem accurately?

Many students approach business ethics from an either/or perspective instead of seeking a balanced resolution of the problem. For example, many U.S. firms have international operations, and their safety standards, wage standards and environmental standards may be different from the required U.S. standards. They are not violating any laws in those countries, but they are operating with different standards in those countries. The problem is not a choice between operating competitively (by taking advantage of those countries) and not operating competitively. The problem is one of moving the company toward fair, responsible behavior in all the firm's operations.

2. How would you define the problem if you stood on the other side of the fence?

This question simply asks you to view the problem from others' perspectives and brings in the balancing approach of Blanchard/Peale. For example, you might rationalize the use of company time for personal items or your consulting business. However, your employer, who incurs costs when you are not 100% attentive to work needs, would have a different perspective on issues such as leaving early, making long distance calls at employer expense or taking home the company's laptop for consulting work.

3. How did this situation occur in the first place?

Many ethical dilemmas arise because there are no clear positions in a business about what is right and what is wrong. One of the cases in the text involves Sears, Roebuck Company and allegations by the California attorney general that Sears' auto repair centers were overcharging and "overrepairing" customers' vehicles. CEO Edward Brennan conceded that "mistakes" had been made in their auto repair operations because their sales incentive and compensation system imposed quotas on employees and pressured them into making decisions and recommendations to customers they would not have made under a different compensation system.

4. To whom and to what do you give your loyalty as a person and a member of the corporation?

In the cases on whistle-blowing and conflicts of interests, you will find employees who are torn between their personal values and their moral standard of loyalty to their companies and employers. For example, a Dow Corning scientist expresses concern about the safety of breast implants and no immediate action is taken. A Beech-Nut chemist talks with his plant manager and eventually the CEO to explain that the company's baby apple juice has no apple juice in it, but no changes are made. These individuals are faced with a choice between personal values and company loyalty, and, in effect, their jobs. Their struggles with their decisions provide insight into character and strength of conviction.

5. What is your intention in making this decision?

6. How does this intention compare with the likely results?

When Exxon corporation cut back its staffing on oil tankers, its intention was to cut costs, increase profits and maximize shareholder wealth. However, there was additional balancing that needed to be brought into the decision-making process on cutting costs: the issues of safety and environmental protection. The intention was a good one, but resulted in tired crews who made mistakes leading to the accident involving the oil tanker Valdez and the subsequent oil spill and damage to the Alaskan coast line, its wildlife and the economic base of the fishermen in the area.

7. Who could your decision or action injure?

With this question, you are examining possibilities and anticipating problems or injuries. For example, the Super Soaker squirt gun is a wonderful toy for children and adults as well. But, what if the gun is filled with chemicals and used on the streets? Your heavy milling equipment is an innocent product but, if sold to an aggressive nation it could be used for the development of military equipment. Such was the case of Toshiba's sales of heavy equipment to the Soviet Union at a time before the government had changed and its attitude on global war were different.

8. Can you engage the affected parties in a discussion of the problem before you make the decision?

Many managers force themselves into difficult ethical decisions without first discussing the problem with the affected parties. Often the affected parties can offer their own resolution. For example, rather than downsizing, some firms have approached employees with early retirement, bonus departure packages and consulting proposals that have enabled them to cut the payroll without damaging the economic well-being and security of their employees.

9. Are you as confident that your position will be as valid over a long period of time as it is now?

E. F. Hutton made its decision to maximize interest earnings by capitalizing on bank float available because some smaller banks were not computer linked and unable to tell whether or not checks were actually covered. The decision was one that was financially sound and earned extra funds. But as investigators checked into the float and the practice became public, E. F. Hutton experienced a setback in its earnings and significant damage to its reputation. The decision to build the Ford Pinto as economically and as quickly as possible without protective changes to the fuel tank, brought a small, fuel-efficient car to U.S. customers and sales for Ford. The litigation that resulted from the exploding gas tanks and the recall costs for repairing the fuel tanks cost Ford earnings, its reputation and brought a certain skepticism about its commitment to safety.

10. Could you disclose without qualm your decision or action to your boss, your CEO, the board of directors, your family, or society as a whole?

Many people feel comfortable with a decision they do not have to disclose. But once they discuss the decision with others, they are able to see a different perspective. For example, in a recent bidding process for a day care center at Arizona State University, the wife of a member of the University's Board of Regents was awarded the day care center contract. She may have had the best proposal. The bidding may have been open, objective and fair. But, others examining the decision would have doubts about the process given the results. Going back to the question of how the problem arose in the first place, the parties involved, by acknowledging the presence of a family relationship, could have arranged for an outside determination of the contract award to avoid even the appearance of impropriety. To those closely involved with the process, they knew they were being fair. To those outside the process, there would always be a question of fairness. Outside feedback helps make ethical dilemmas more obvious and often serves as a starting point for eliminating or resolving the dilemma.

11. What is the symbolic potential of your action if understood? If misunderstood?

Every action by a business is symbolic to employees, shareholders and communities. A company that switches, as Herman Miller did, from styrofoam coffee cups to mugs symbolically makes a statement about its commitment to the environment to employees, government agencies and communities. A company that has no diversity in its workforce also makes a symbolic statement about its commitment to equal opportunity in the workplace.

Of course, there are much simpler models for making ethical business decisions. One stems from Immanuel Kant's categorical imperative which is: "Do unto others as you would have them do unto you." There is the less-known, but certainly simple Jennings model which asks the question: "How bad could the newspapers make my actions look?" You should take the perspective here of an objective and critical reporter who would examine all sides of the issue. For example, William Aramony, the former head of the United Way, was paid as a CEO of a national firm and enjoyed the perks a CEO of a national firm would enjoy such as first-class flights and homes throughout the country. From the perspective of a successful CEO, his benefits were average. But, from the perspective of a wage earner who has pledged 5 percent of his or her wages to the United Way, the expenses were extravagant, and the newspapers reported that perspective as well as Aramony's.

Each case in this book requires you to examine different perspectives and analyze the impact of a resolution on the parties involved in the dilemma. Return frequently to these models to question the propriety of the actions taken in each case. Examine the origins of the ethical dilemma and explore possible solutions. As you work through the cases, you will find yourself developing a new awareness of values and their importance in making business decisions.

UNIT ONE
INDIVIDUAL VALUES AND THE BUSINESS ORGANIZATION

There are times when an individual who has become part of a larger organization feels that his personal values are in conflict with those the organization follows. Or there may be times when the interests of the individual are at odds with the interests of the organization. The types of ethical dilemmas that arise between the individual and his or her company are conflicts of interests and issues of honesty and fairness. An individual who negotiates contracts for an organization may find that those bidding on the contracts are willing to offer incidental benefits that may help the individual but also cloud judgment with respect to which vendor is best for the company. In other situations, an employee may find information that indicates a product has correctable dangers that are not being addressed. The individual must then confront the issue, pitting concerns about continuing employment and livelihood against moral standards and concerns about safety.

These individual dilemmas present the most common and the most difficult dilemmas business people face. Studying them, reviewing alternatives and carefully establishing values will prepare you for the dilemmas that we all must ultimately confront.

Section A
Employee Conflicts of Interest

Do you know when your personal gain is interfering with your objectivity or your loyalty? Can you avoid or resolve conflicts of interest?

1.1 The Realty with the Disguised Ownership

Algonquin Enterprises, Inc., was building a regional theme park in the southeastern corner of Utah. The location of the theme park was remote, and the traveling distance for workers from the closest town was fifty-five miles. Further, the labor force in the small communities within a one hundred-mile radius of the park was insufficient to meet the construction labor demands for the park. Algonquin executives concluded that they would need some form of housing for the labor force if the project was to proceed in a timely manner.

Algonquin decided to construct The Mining Camp Inn for this purpose. Algonquin executives felt the Inn could later be used for tourists once the park was open. Algonquin interviewed firms for the construction and management of the Inn.

Tonopah Realty was selected for the project. Algonquin and Tonopah entered into the contract in 1985 and agreed that it would run for five years unless the theme park was completed before that time. Algonquin agreed to pay Tonopah $7.1 million for construction, all operating expenses and a profit of $600,000 per year. Tonopah agreed to provide three meals a day for workers at the Inn as well as daily room cleaning and general facility upkeep. The contract provided that at the end of the contract term (after five years or upon park completion), Algonquin could elect to take title to the Inn. This election of title arrangement was negotiated by Algonquin for possible tax benefits.

Tonopah Realty's principals were Ellen Charkoff and Robert Owens. In the course of managing the Inn, Charkoff and Owens met with catering services for purposes of awarding the food service contract for the Inn. Charkoff and Owens met with two catering services. In both meetings, Charkoff and Owens indicated there would be a $100,000 retainer fee for the award of the food contract. The $100,000 retainer fee was to be paid to Elk Corp., Inc., a corporation owned by Charkoff. One catering firm, Bread and Butter, Inc., refused to pay the $100,000 fee, and the other firm, Meals-To-Go, Inc., agreed to do so and was awarded the contract by Charkoff and Owens. Meals-To-Go submitted a higher bid than Bread and Butter and, as part of its contract, required Tonopah to guarantee in the contract a minimum payment of three daily meals for 100 persons, regardless of the number of workers actually occupying the Inn. The contract with Meals-To-Go, Inc. provided for a penalty of $900,000 if the contract was terminated before 1990. On the other hand, Bread and Butter had proposed no minimum payment guarantee and an early termination fee of only $50,000.

Algonquin terminated the contract with Tonopah in 1988 because the theme park was completed ahead of schedule. Charkoff and Owens told Algonquin executives that there was a $1.8 million termination fee that would now be required for Meals-To-Go's early termination. Algonquin paid the $1.8 million to Tonopah. Charkoff and Owens paid Meals-To-Go $900,000 and kept the remaining $900,000.

Tim Horne was the vice president of Bread and Butter who negotiated with Charkoff and Owens. When Horne learned of the $100,000 retainer fee, he debated discussing the matter with Algonquin. Tim concluded such a discussion was not in his or Bread and Butter's best interests. Tonopah is a powerful company that issues many catering contracts and Tim felt he needed to stay on Charkoff's and Owens' best side. Tim then learned of the termination of Tonopah's contract through a friend who is also an Algonquin executive, Bob Ward. Ward also stated, "Yes, and we had to pay an early termination fee of $1.8 million for Meals-To-Go." Tim listened carefully because he knew from his failed negotiations with Tonopah that Meals-To-Go's termination fee was $900,000. Tim is now faced with the issue of whether he should disclose to his friend the information he has about Meals-To-Go and Tonopah.

Discussion Questions

1. Did Tonopah violate any moral standards?
2. Would you classify Tonopah as an agent of Algonquin or did their ownership of the Inn prior to termination make them an independent entity?
3. Should Tim have discussed the kickback issue with Algonquin when Charkoff and Owens first demanded it?
4. Should Tim disclose what he knows to Bob Ward?
5. Will Tim harm himself and his company by disclosing what he knows?

1.2 THE CITY COUNCIL EMPLOYEE

Bimini Outdoors is an outdoor advertising firm that is experiencing the crunch of environmental controls on the number and type of billboards the city of Wikieup will permit it to have. The mayor of Wikieup has discussed what she calls the signs, "gigantic litter," with James Houston, Bimini's CEO. The mayor has told Houston that one of her goals for her four-year term is to eliminate completely billboard advertising.

Houston recognizes that Bimini has not diversified and that with no outdoor advertising permitted in Wikieup, Bimini will be a defunct firm. Houston is a member of the city's public relations trade group and the issue of the billboards has been debated many times at the group's luncheons. Some members see the billboards as eyesores and environmental disasters. Other members offer figures to support their notion that the signs are safety hazards for drivers. Still another faction in the group calls them effective and "environmentally sound" because they don't produce the waste of flyers or newspaper ads.

There is a city council election in three months. Three of the five seats on the council are up for re-election. Houston has noticed that Jake Gilbert, one of the candidates, is very vocal about the need to retain billboard advertising. Gilbert has referred to the billboards as a "clean, efficient and effective" means of advertising.

Gilbert is a graphic artist and a well-respected member of the community who has served on the school board. He is a board officer for the symphony and a key fund raiser for the city's Child Crisis Center.

One month before the election, Houston is told by Ralph Dewey, one of his managers, that Jake Gilbert was the victim of a downsizing at his firm. Because of his loss of employment and resultant financial constraints, Gilbert is considering withdrawing from the race. Coincidentally, Bimini has sent out requests for proposals to several graphic artists for upcoming projects. Houston tells Ralph Dewey, "Why don't we get an RFP (request for proposal) to Gilbert and tell him to freelance until he gets another job? I'd even be willing to take graphics in-house if Gilbert would take the job."

Ralph Dewey is concerned about the appearance of having a potential city council member with a pro-billboard position as an employee of Bimini. James Houston's response is: "We need a graphic artist. He's a graphic artist. Get the RFP to him and let him know we've got a job if he's interested."

Discussion Questions

1. Why would Dewey be worried if Houston needs graphic art work?
2. If Gilbert were hired, how would the story be reported in the newspaper?
3. Would you feel differently if Houston helped Gilbert get a job with one of the members of his public relations club?
4. What if Gilbert submits a bid that is the best in terms of cost, proposal and quality? Should he be hired?
5. Should Gilbert run for office on a platform for keeping billboards if he accepts the position with the company?

1.3 THE FIRM WORKOUT AND THE FONDA PHD

The FIRM is a company based in Columbia, South Carolina, that produces exercise videos. The series of six videos have been well-received and the FIRM has advertised by using direct comparative ads as follows:

> I used to exercise with Fonda videos and belong to a gym. Not any more. Now I brag to my friends that I own the best set of exercise videos in the world. Thank you for a workout that suits me perfectly. Congratulations on winning *Self* magazine's "Best All-Around Workout" award for Volume 4! P.S. Your music is wonderful and never boring.

Susan L., Ronkonkoma, New York

Shape magazine reviews all exercise tapes annually. *Shape* did not give Volume III of the FIRM exercise tapes a flattering review in December 1990 and stated that one of the tapes was not an aerobic workout. A reader wrote into *Shape* magazine with the following comment regarding The FIRM videotape evaluation:

> I'd like to see you use the videotapes you rate. I had a tremendous amount of respect for your magazine until you said The Firm videotape was "not aerobic." I may not be dancing around when I do The Firm tapes, but my heart rate is definitely in the aerobic range. This misstatement caused me to question your other ratings.

In the August 1991 issue of *Shape*, the editor responded with the following remarks:

> Mark Henriksen, a medical writer for The Firm, also contacted our office, suggesting that we may have misinterpreted the ACSM guidelines regarding continuous aerobic training requirements: "All the research we found indicates that interval training boosts aerobic capacity much faster than traditional, continuous, steady-state aerobics."

Barbara Harris, *Shape* editor in chief, also responded:

> Dan Kosich, Ph.D., exercise physiologist and a member of the review panel, affirms after a second review that the tape's workout is not of sufficient intensity and duration to induce a significant cardiovascular training effect. What is described as interval training is undefined in nature, with no specific work-recovery intervals. It would be more accurately described as variable-intensity training.
>
> We do not dispute the effectiveness of interval training, however, we do question its application in The Firm Volume 3 and its validity as a superior training measure as applied in this videotape. When we monitored the heart rate of an exerciser of average cardiovascular fitness by heart-rate telemeter while she did the tape, we found that the cardiovascular effects of The Firm Volume 3's variable-intensity program were not adequate to cause a training effect.
>
> The subject's heart rate did not stay in the target zone for sufficient duration and, in fact, reached the target zone (65 to 90 percent of maximum heart rate) only twice during the workout.

While the workout may be fun and popular, we rate a tape according to the claims made and its overall effectiveness, as well as on its foundation or basis in current scientific research.

The FIRM ran the following response:

Shape Magazine Video Review: Fonda's Insider Influence

How did a frequent employee of Jane Fonda get a job reviewing exercise videos for *Shape* magazine? *Shape* has yet to explain, but the resulting review (12/90) was suspiciously predictable: the only unflattering review ever written about any FIRM workout. The same two FIRM videos given the highest-possible ratings by *Self, Ladies Home Journal* and *Mirabella* were not only slammed but slandered — accused of false advertising claims! Meanwhile, *Shape* gave Jane Fonda's entry a perfect score of "5" for "excellence." Coincidence?

Shape's unethical conflict of interest came to light slowly:

First, Dan Kosich, Ph.D. — one of *Shape's* five review judges — claimed he had verified the magazine's false statement that FIRM Vol. 3 is "not an aerobic workout." Then we noticed Dan Kosich's name on the credits of Fonda's "Lean Routine" video. Then *Longevity* magazine (10/91) reported that Dan Kosich is "the fitness expert behind six Jane Fonda workout tapes!" (Meanwhile, *Shape* was proven wrong: conclusive verification that Vol. 3 is indeed aerobic came from an extensive test by Dr. Russell Pate, Ph.D., chairman of the American College of Sports Medicine guidelines committee).

Some who are familiar with the FIRM's direct, confrontational advertising may dismiss this incident as justifiable "tit for tat." No. Unlike *Shape's* review, our ads are never false or unscientific. Just the facts. Some say our ads show a personal dislike for our competitors. No. Harry S. Truman said it best: "I never give them hell. I just tell the truth and they think it's hell."

In its January 1992 Mailbag section, *Shape* magazine offered the following response:

In our August 1991 Mailbag, we responded to a controversy over our rating of The FIRM Volume 3 videotape workout in our December 1990 video review: In the review, we described The FIRM Volume 3 as "good conditioning exercises, but not an aerobic workout" and rated the tape "average."

In Mailbag, we clarified the review, describing the tape's workout as "not of sufficient intensity and duration to induce a significant cardiovascular training effect." To further clarify: The primary reason for the average rating was the tape's inability to fulfill the claims used to market it, including "aerobic workout with weights ... for beginner and advanced ... rated among thousands of users 'the most effective video they've used.' "

These claims indicate that the tape's exercise program will be highly effective for both cardiovascular and muscular development in beginner, intermediate and advanced exercisers.

A University of South Carolina study recognized that the workout is aerobic; however, it also reports that the tape would be most highly recommended for those who are at a moderate fitness level or below. The study, performed on subjects who were moderately fit, concluded that the average intensity that subjects achieved during the program was not quite 48 percent of their maximum aerobic capacity.

To enhance aerobic endurance, the American College of Sports Medicine (ACSM) recommends that one perform exercise at a level of intensity that is between 40 percent and 85 percent of her maximum aerobic capacity. Therefore, makers of the FIRM Volume 3 are clearly misleading the public when implying that the tape provides a highly effective aerobic workout for advanced exercisers.

On one point, we stand corrected: The FIRM Volume 3 does meet standards for aerobic conditioning. However, we also stand by our average rating of the tape, because that claim can only be applied to exercisers who are at a low to moderate level of fitness and because those who are moderately fit are exercising at the low end of the intensity range recommended by the ACSM for developing aerobic endurance. Thus, the impact of this workout in the aerobic fitness of advanced exercisers would be, at best, marginal.

It is important to note that *Shape's* video review panel evaluates all tapes not only on their overall effectiveness but also in accordance with the manufacturer's claims, including the validity of such claims for the audience to whom they are directed.

Discussion Questions

1. Should *Shape* magazine have disclosed Dr. Kosich's affiliation?
2. Are the readers' letters with direct comparisons misleading?
3. If you were Dr. Kosich, would you have participated in *Shape's* exercise video review?
4. Is this type of direct response advertising helpful to consumers?

SOURCES

FIRM Brochure.
"Mailbag." *Shape* August 1991, 18–19.
"Mailbag." *Shape* January 1992, 16.

1.4 THE CHAIN OF COMMAND AND PURCHASING

Frank Hoffman is the CEO of Triple Plus, Inc., a group of four successful restaurants in the southwest. One of the members of the Triple Plus board of directors, Sam Wasson, has a daughter, Chelsea Wasson, who has just started a business that supplies restaurant linens, Chelsea's Cloths. Wasson has approached Hoffman to explain Chelsea's business. Chelsea's Cloths has adopted an environmental emphasis in its operations as a way of countering the industry trend toward use of paper products in restaurants. Sam Wasson initially recruited Hoffman as CEO, was instrumental in having the board select Hoffman, and is one of Hoffman's strong supporters. Wasson has been helpful to Hoffman at times when other board members were impatient with his new procedures, policies and changes.

Ordinarily when someone approaches Frank Hoffman with information on a new supplier, he takes the information and refers it to the purchasing/supply area or refers them directly to the manager of purchasing. In this case, Frank went to present the information himself to Triple's purchasing manager, Deidre Hall. Frank offered Deidre the Chelsea Cloth's brochure and card and explained, "She is Sam Wasson's daughter. She just graduated in marketing from State University last June and now has her own firm. See what you can do. Our contract with Lila's Linens is up for renewal. Maybe we can do something."

Deidre evaluated both Chelsea's and Lila's proposals as well as one of an additional firm, in making the purchasing decision. Although the pricing is equivalent between Chelsea's and Lila's, Chelsea's is such a young firm that a track record is not available and Deidre is not convinced Chelsea's has the ability to handle Triple's large account. Deidre is confused about what recommendation to make because of Mr. Hoffman's interest.

Discussion Questions

1. Should Deidre recommend Chelsea's firm or offer her true recommendation?
2. Would it be ethical for Hoffman to change Deidre's decision?
3. What if Wasson had requested bid information so that his daughter could be competitive? Should Deidre supply it? Should Hoffman direct Deidre to supply it?
4. Can you solve the conflict without offending the director?

1.5 Conflicts of Interest in Referrals

Tina Reese is the administrator of a large metropolitan hospital that is private and nonprofit. Tina has discovered that many of the physicians with privileges at the hospital are shareholders in the corporations that provide the hospital with the following services or are post-release care providers:

- Radiology Center
- MRI Facility (MRI = Magnetic Resonance Imaging, a diagnostic tool)
- Home Health Care and Nurse Services
- Medical Equipment Leasing and Sales
- Physical Rehabilitation Centers
- Nursing Homes
- Radiation Therapy Facilities.

In most instances, there are no outside investors in these facilities and annual returns for the physician shareholders are significant. Indeed, in many cases, the physician investors are courted for investment and ownership in these supplemental service and diagnostic areas because of the referrals they will bring to the providers.

A Blue Cross study (1983) has shown that physician ownership leads to increased referrals for testing and post-release care and increased prices. Further, some testing facilities owned by physicians with privileges at Tina's hospital are competing successfully with hospital services and testing centers. Because of ease of access and physician referrals, the hospital testing facilities are now being used less and less. A 1991 study by Public Citizen Health Research Group showed that physicians in Florida who engaged in self-referral are twice as likely to order tests.

The areas of physician-owned services and testing facilities and physician self-referrals has become controversial over the past few years and brought the attention of both the public and regulators. The Department of Health and Human Services' (HHS) regulations prohibit self-referral if a doctor owns more than 40 percent of an x-ray or other diagnostic lab. HHS covers Medicare and Medicaid insurance programs. Some states currently have disclosure requirements for physicians who refer patients to their own facilities. Those disclosure statutes require physicians to reveal to patients any ownership interests they may have in referred facilities and services prior to the time the patient commits for the services. However, the American Medical Association, in its 1992 annual meeting, endorsed physician referrals of patients to labs and other facilities in which they have a financial interest. Florida bans self-referral and bills to curb self-referral are pending in two dozen state legislatures.

Discussion Questions

1. Should Tina implement a disclosure requirement for the physicians? Why or why not?
2. If you were a patient, would you want to have the ownership interest of your physician disclosed?

3. Is there a conflict between physician ownership and referrals that are self-serving?
4. Would a newspaper story on physician-ownership of facilities and services be favorable?

SOURCES

Burton, Thomas M. "Doctor-Owned Labs Earn Lavish Profits In a Captive Market." *Wall Street Journal* March 1, 1989, A1, A6.

Burton, Thomas M. "Doctors May Refer Patients to Labs Owned by Doctors, Doctors' Group Says." *Wall Street Journal* June 24, 1992, B6.

1.6 DONATIONS AND VENDORS

As CEO of a large hotel in Chicago, you and your purchasing manager are in the midst of the annual review of several vendors' contracts. One of the suppliers is Sherman Distributors, a restaurant supply company that furnishes straws, salt, pepper, condiments, and other similar items for the restaurants and room service in your hotel. Your spouse, an associate dean at one of the local university's business schools, has informed you that Sherman's CEO serves on the school's council of advisors and has mentioned Sherman's supply contract and a willingness to endow a scholarship fund. Your spouse's primary area of responsibility for the school is fund raising.

Discussion Questions

1. What ethical issues are raised?
2. Does it make a difference that Sherman's bid is the lowest?
3. If Sherman's contract is renewed, would there be an appearance of impropriety?
4. Are there ways to avoid negative perceptions?

1.7 The Quality Kickback

Caremark, Inc., is a home health care provider with eighty offices around the United States. Its services include the administration of pain medication, chemotherapy, intravenous feedings and antibiotic treatment to home-bound patients.

Caremark serves 3,500 patients, 600 of whom are Medicare or Medicaid patients. With $600 million in annual revenues, Caremark is the leading firm in the home health care industry.

Caremark has established a quality control system whereby physicians who are not involved in the treatment of Caremark clients are paid to monitor the treatment of Caremark patients by reviewing medications and lab results. Under this system, Caremark has contracted with over 800 doctors across the nation for their monitoring program. The doctors are paid between $12 and $150 for their participation.

Other home health care providers rely on the patient's own physician for monitoring and do not employ independent physicians for review of cases. In some cases, it is not clear whether Caremark is actually receiving services from the doctors or whether the fees simply offer incentives for the contracting physicians to refer patients to Caremark.

Under Medicare laws, kickbacks to physicians for referrals are prohibited, but there are certain payments to physicians from providers that are considered a "safe harbor." The "safe harbor" exception would include those cases where the physician actually does perform a service for the fee.

The president and CEO of Caremark has summarized the motivation for the physicians' payments: "We believe strongly that physicians should be involved in home health care."

Discussion Questions

1. Evaluate the ethical propriety of the physician-monitoring payment arrangement. How important is the company's motivation in the arrangement?
2. Is anyone really harmed by the arrangement?
3. Does a patient need monitoring beyond his/her actual physician's follow-up?

Source

Siler, Julia, and Susan Garland. "Just What Baxter Didn't Need: A Payola Probe." *Business Week* Oct. 7, 1991, 110.

1.8 THE LOAN OFFICER AND THE DEBTORS

Ben Garrison is a senior loan officer with First National Federal Bank. First National Federal is the second largest financial institution in Wyoming. Ben handles loan applications from all over the state and has been with First National Federal Bank for ten years.

Following the savings and loan debacle of the late 1980s, First National Federal implemented many changes in its operations. Some of the changes were operational, and others were made in the area of lending policy. A change that Ben found fundamental was an increasing emphasis on ethics. Ben complained to one of his loan officers, "I don't get this ethics stuff. If it's legal, I'm ethical." One of the loan officers, Shelby Grant, a recent graduate of the University of Wyoming School of Business replied, "Well, sometimes doing what's ethical helps you avoid legal problems." Ben replied, "Sometimes doing what's ethical just costs you more money!"

Later that morning, following the discussion between Shelby and Ben, Ben appeared in Shelby's office and explained that he had a loan application from a rancher in the northwestern part of the state and that they needed to take a trip to evaluate the proposed collateral for the loan. An on-site evaluation of the collateral is one of the required procedures for First National Federal's loan processing. Ben added, "Doug Whitton is the rancher who has applied for the loan, and he's paying our way up there for the evaluation." Shelby asked, "Shouldn't the bank pay our way up there since we may not make the loan and we don't want to be obligated to Whitton?" Ben responded, "Now why in the hell would I want to pay our way up there and increase my costs when he's offering to pay?" Shelby was uncertain about the propriety of the proposal.

Ben added that First National Federal's annual fundraiser picnic was coming up and that they were planning to have the usual drawings for prizes. "So," he told Shelby, "just get on the phone to all the customers whose loans you handle and see what prizes they are willing to donate for this year's drawings." Shelby asked, "Isn't it wrong for us to pressure our customers into donating prizes?" Ben replied angrily, "These prizes are not for us! The money is not for us! This is charity! What could be unethical about that?"

Shelby went home that evening to prepare for the trip to the ranch. She hadn't called any of her customers for donations and she didn't want to go on the trip unless the bank paid. She was also $20,000 in debt from school and it had taken her four months after graduation to find this job. "I guess this is just the way business is done," she concluded.

Discussion Questions

1. Is Shelby correct? Are both these issues just the way business is done?
2. Is the appearance of impropriety an important ethical constraint?
3. What problems arise in having the potential borrower pay for the collateral evaluation trip?
4. What problems arise in soliciting donations from loan customers?
5. Would it be different if a merchant offered to donate items without being asked?

1.9 INCIDENTAL BENEFICIARIES OF THE PHILANTHROPISTS'S ESTATE

Peggie Jean Gambarana was a real estate investor in the Las Vegas area whose substantial holdings enabled her to become one of the community's most generous philanthropists. Upon her death, her will provided that $1.5 million in cash and property be given to the University of Nevada at Las Vegas Foundation to benefit the James R. Dickinson Library. The testate donation was the largest ever for the library.

The $1.5 million donation included $350,000 in cash, three properties and a leasehold interest on a downtown Las Vegas souvenir shop. However, by the time the funds and properties were converted to permanent library endowments, their value had been reduced by one-third. The reduction in value was the result of three real estate deals that involved some members of the foundation.

The three donated properties were all sold below appraised values. The sale of the Gambarana family home was to Arthur Nathan who was moving from New Jersey to become the human resources director for the Mirage Hotel. The UNLV Foundation's chairwoman, Elaine Wynn, is an executive in Mirage Resorts, Inc., and her husband, Steve Wynn, is the corporation's chairman. Nathan purchased the home for $157,500 and it was appraised for $170,000. Golden Nugget, Inc., which later became Mirage Resorts, Inc., loaned Nathan the funds for the purchase of the Gambarana home. Wynn said she did not get involved in the negotiations:

> It's possible for me to represent both interests without ... creating a conflict of interest in this, especially since I didn't benefit personally nor did Mr. Nathan benefit personally.[1]

Ms. Wynn signed the sale documents for the property transaction.

The second property the foundation sold was appraised at $270,000 and sold for $206,628. A third property was appraised at $490,000 and sold for $320,000. After real estate commissions were paid, the foundation received $296,200 for the property. The real estate commission was paid to Madison Graves, a candidate for university regent in 1992 and a long-time friend of the foundation's director, Lyle Rivera. Rivera is also a broker for Graves' Flamingo Realty, the agency that handled the sale. Rivera saw no conflict of interest because Graves probably lost money on the sale, because it took so long to sell the property:

> We always ask them to do it at a lesser commission than standard so most of these guys don't relish doing business with the foundation.[2]

One of the purchasers of the third property was Shelli Lowe, who had also performed the appraisal on the property. The foundation lost $235,000 on a lease because it failed to exercise the option to renew the lease on the souvenir shop located at Fremont and Fourth Streets in downtown Las Vegas.

---

1. John Gallant, "UNLV's Gift Fails to Meet Projections," *Las Vegas-Review Journal* (June 26, 1992): 1A and 3A.

2. *Ibid.*

Discussion Questions

1. Was there a conflict of interest in the Nathan sale?
2. Would you have handled the Nathan sale differently?
3. Was there a conflict in having Madison Graves as the listing broker for the property appraised at $490,000?
4. Is there a conflict when an appraiser purchases a property for which she has furnished the appraisal?
5. Did the foundation manage the funds as if they were their own personal funds? Is this right or wrong?
6. What things would you have done differently if you had been a foundation member responsible for managing the gift?

SECTION B
INAPPROPRIATE GIFTS

A form of conflicts of interest, taking gifts from vendors or compensation from outside interests, can cloud your perspective no matter how objective you profess to be. As you review these cases, think of ways a company's code of ethics could help employees when presented with gifts.

1.10 THE PURCHASING AGENTS' WONDER WORLD TRIP

Paul Backman is the head of the purchasing department for LA East, one of the so-called "baby bells" or regional phone companies that came into existence in 1984 after the divestiture of AT&T. Backman's department is responsible for purchasing everything from wire for equipment lines to napkins for the head-quarter's cafeteria.

S. C. Rydman is an electronics firm and a major LA East supplier. S. C. Rydman is also a co-sponsor of an exhibit at Wonder World in Florida. LA East has used Rydman as its major supplier since 1984. Contract decisions are made on the basis of bids submitted by Rydman and others in response to requests for proposals. Paul Backman has final say on the electronics contracts because of the significant amounts involved.

S. C. Rydman's vice president and chief financial officer, Gunther Fromme, visited Backman in his office on April 3, 1992. Rydman had no bids pending and was awarded a six-month contract by LA East on March 1, 1992. Fromme explained to Backman, "Look, I'm just here for goodwill. But Rydman does have a block of rooms with room service at one of the hotels in Wonder World. If you like, you and your staff could go down there and use them. We also get free passes to the park. You could go to the park and see the good work we've done on our exhibit there. You and your families would just have to pay air fare. If you're interested just let me know when and how many."

Paul Backman explained the offer at the next staff meeting and it was warmly received by everyone except Sheila Tate. Sheila raised a concern at the meeting, "Should we accept the free rooms and passes from a supplier?" Backman responded, "I could understand your concern if Rydman had a bid pending, but there won't be anything for Rydman to even bid on for at least three months. If we go now, it is just a friend's favor."

All the purchasing agents except Sheila Tate signed up for the trip. Backman and the agents and their families planned a five-day excursion to Wonder World. As her co-workers discussed their plans, Sheila wondered whether someone should be told about the trip.

Discussion Questions

1. Should Sheila Tate talk with someone outside her department about the planned trip?
2. Is it enough for Sheila simply to forego the trip?
3. Suppose that after the trip, the CEO of LA East learns of it and takes disciplinary action. Should Sheila be disciplined for her acceptance of the conduct?

1.11 PHARMACEUTICAL HONORARIUMS TO RESEARCHERS: RETIN-A

The aging process has become one of increasing concern as the United States approaches a time when 50 percent of its population will be over fifty-five. Currently, Americans spend $1.2 billion a year on cosmetic creams and moisturizers and $1–2 billion on cosmetic surgery.

For the past twenty-five months, the focus in spending has been on all-trans-retinoic acid or tretinan or Retin-A. Retin-A was introduced in the market by Ortho Pharmaceutical as an acne cream. Ortho is a $600-million subsidiary of the $9 billion Johnson & Johnson. The drug not only treats the symptoms of aging but appears to reverse the aging process. The *Los Angeles Times* called it a "medical milestone," *Business Week* named it "one of the best scientific innovations of 1988" and *U.S. News & World Report* described it as a "facelift out of a tube."

The $20 twenty-gram tubes of Retin-A have been sold primarily as a wrinkle cream but the FDA has not yet given approval for such use as safe and effective. Ortho's profits for 1988 on the drug were $20 million. Doctors are permitted to prescribe drugs for purposes other than those specifically designated by the FDA without violating any laws or ethical canons. After the introduction of Retin-A, Johnson & Johnson's stock price increased from $79.86 a share to $87.13 a share.

Dr. Albert Kligman, the man who developed Retin-A, has been disqualified from FDA drug investigations for violating FDA testing rules. While working for drug-testing labs in the 1960s, Kligman's findings were reviewed by the FDA and there were discoveries of discrepancies between lab reports and the records of the prisons where the drugs were being tested. Kligman reported he had tested DMSO on three groups of prisoners, while the prison reported that only two groups were tested. When questioned about his more recent Retin-A testing, Kligman replied, "That was probably the one time in life where we did not exaggerate." Kligman, who has earned a royalty of 3 percent of net sales of Retin-A, has donated the royalty earnings to the University of Pennsylvania dermatology department where he conducts his medical research.

A review of the studies on Retin-A showed that the studies were not "double-blind" (meaning the researchers knew which patients were using Retin-A and which were using placebo creams). Also, the studies were conducted at the University of Pennsylvania which was given the 3 percent of net sales as royalties by Kligman and which stood to gain more if the product did well.

In a separate study conducted at the University of Michigan by researchers not funded by Ortho, fourteen of forty patients using Retin-A withdrew because of skin irritation or had to be treated to calm a resulting skin inflammation. The Michigan study did find significant reduction of skin wrinkles in eleven patients and photos were released to the popular press of these transformations. These photos were so dramatic that all three networks reported on Retin-A the same day as the press conference. Subsequent experiments have been unable to produce the dramatic types of photos released with the initial studies. Some researchers maintain that Retin-A simply causes inflammation of the skin causing puffiness that gives the appearance of wrinkle reduction.

However, within a month after the photo releases (February 1988), 1,162,000 tubes of Retin-A were sold compared with 217,000 tubes in February 1987. Total sales for 1987 were $62.3 million. In 1988, sales jumped to $115 million.

Dr. Barbara Gilchrest, a retinoid researcher and chair of the dermatology department of Boston University, was paid $3,000 by Ortho to appear at an educational symposium in 1986 to kick off Ortho's public campaign for Retin-A. Gilchrest had "an eight-year working relationship with Ortho" and organized the symposium. Also, Gilchrest helped organize a speakers' tour comprised of eight dermatologists who were paid $500 a day plus air fare and hotel for discussing Retin-A with the media and others.

The complexities of the relationships between the Retin-A researchers and Ortho are not unusual. Medical researchers are increasingly dependent on pharmaceutical companies to fund their research and potentially compromise their objectivity by accepting fees from drug companies for consulting them on public-information events. The close relationships between researchers and drug companies are rarely disclosed to the public. Neither Kligman's nor Gilchrest's relationship to the drug company was disclosed to the public.

The Retin-A campaign by Ortho is indicative of a trend in the pharmaceutical industry in which companies increasingly bypass clinical physicians and promote new prescription drugs directly to consumers through the popular press, leaving the explanation of limitations and dangers to the doctors. Press coverage is an integral part of this strategy, but press releases are not scrutinized by the FDA prior to their release due to FDA staffing limitations. Some publicity efforts take place before a drug has been approved by the FDA.

In March of 1988, the FDA warned Ortho that it was illegal to promote Retin-A for the unapproved use of fighting wrinkles. Later that year, the head of the FDA called Ortho's Retin-A campaign "an expensive therapeutic gamble."

Research on Retin-A continues, but the FDA has not approved the drug for combating aging. A study in the *New England Journal of Medicine* in 1992 disclosed that the cream can also lighten skin discolorations. The research was conducted at the University of Michigan. The same researchers who conducted the studies on wrinkles conducted the study on liver spots and freckles. An unusual footnote in the Journal noted that Johnson & Johnson had funded the liver spot research, but "had no part in the design or conduct of the study or in the analysis, interpretations or reporting of the results." The note also included the disclosure that two of the researchers had been paid consultants to Johnson & Johnson during part of the research.

Discussion Questions

1. Assume that you are a vice president for marketing for Ortho Pharmaceutical. Do you face any ethical dilemmas? Describe them if you do.
2. As a vice president for Ortho, would you take any action at this time? Would you continue your advertising program as it stands? Would you verify Kligman's results?

3. Assume that you are a university administrator in a university with a medical school that has an active research program. Would you adopt any policies with respect to your professors who conduct research for pharmaceutical firms?
4. If Retin-A works for individuals and they are pleased with it, is there any harm in the advertising campaign?
5. If Retin-A works for individuals and they are pleased with it, are there really any concerns about not disclosing the information on Dr. Kligman's history and the sponsorship of the symposium?

SOURCES

Waldholz, M. "Johnson & Johnson's Retin-A Can Ease Problem of Liverspots, Researchers Say." *Wall Street Journal* Feb. 6, 1992, B6.

Vreeland, Leslie N. "The Selling of Retin-A." *Money* April 1989, 75–87.

Repinski, Karyn. "Age-Spot Fade-Outs Another Coup for Retin-A." *Longevity* April 1992, 20.

SECTION C
SECURITY OF COMPANY RECORDS

Information is a powerful business tool and often a competitor's edge. Inside information released too early to the press can be harmful to the company and employees. Employees must recognize the value and ownership of company information.

1.12 THE SALE OF SAND TO THE SAUDIS

Joe Raymond's position as sales manager for Granite Rock and Sand was in jeopardy. His unit was the low performer for sales for the past seven quarters. Joe's supervisor, vice president Tom Haws, told Joe that he had the next quarter to pull his unit from last place. Tom Haws also told Joe that Joe would have to be replaced if the change in performance did not occur.

Joe and his wife had just purchased their first home. Facing mortgage payments of $1,100 per month, the loss of Joe's salary would mean the loss of their home.

Following Tom's warning, Joe began a series of interviews for filling a vacant sales position in his unit. Joe interviewed three candidates and the final candidate, Jessica Morris, arrived. During the interview with Ms. Morris, Joe learned that she was a victim of a layoff by a competitor, Silt, Sand and Such. Joe was not terribly impressed with Ms. Morris, but just before she left, she opened her briefcase and offered Joe a sheet of paper. On the sheet of paper was the name of an official in the Saudi Arabian government. Ms. Morris explained:

> When I was with Silt, Sand and Such, we started a program for finding innovative markets for our products. You know, we wanted to tap markets no one ever thought of. After a lot of research, we discovered the Saudi desalinization plants needed a particular type of sand they didn't have over there, but we have here.

We're the only firm that knows about this. If you hire me, I can see the sale through for Granite.

Ms. Morris then added:

Look, I need this job. You need your sales up. Think about it and call me.

After Ms. Morris left, Joe sat in his office and felt his problems were solved. Or were they?

Discussion Questions

1. If you were Joe, would you hire Ms. Morris?
2. Is anyone harmed if you do hire Ms. Morris?
3. What long-term problems could you foresee if Ms. Morris is hired?
4. Is there anything illegal about using the information Ms. Morris would bring?

1.13 THE EMPLOYEE AND THE REPORTER

Jim Lamb is an employee of Uintah Power and Light, one of two major utilities in the State of Colorado. Jim is employed in the rate department of the company. Jim and his co-workers develop data necessary for presentation to the regulatory commission when Uintah applies for a rate increase.

Like most utilities around the country, Uintah is experiencing competition from natural gas companies and the threat of customer competition from co-generation. Many municipalities within Colorado are studying proposals for city buy-outs of Uintah facilities for the purpose of operating city-owned utilities.

In this intensely competitive environment, Uintah's management hired a consulting firm to conduct a study of Uintah for downsizing, reorganization and operations consolidation.

Jim, along with many other employees, was apprehensive about the study and its results because of feared cutbacks. Jim has always been friends with Gary Larsen, a reporter for the *Denver Post Gazette.* Larsen has relied on Jim for explanations and clarifications of figures and information in Uintah's rate cases. Jim and his supervisors have agreed that Jim's efforts with Larsen have produced fair newspaper accounts of the rate cases and the evidence presented.

No one outside the company was aware of the presence of the consulting firm or its purpose. Uintah recently had a rate case decision, and no regulatory hearings are expected for three years. However, Gary Larsen phoned Jim to ask if anything is new. Jim told Larsen about the management consultants and their purpose.

After the disclosure, Larsen ran a story about Uintah's downsizing. Uintah's CEO was furious and threatened to "fire anyone who discloses anything more to the press."

Jim was feeling betrayed because Uintah's CEO promised last year that no further reductions in force would be necessary. Now six months later, rumors were flying that nearly 10 percent of Uintah's labor force would be laid off. Jim continued to feed Larsen information daily, hoping that pressure from the media would soften the amount of the reduction.

When the management consultant made its final recommendation, Jim obtained a copy of the proposal. Uintah's CEO asked that the plan be kept private until he had a chance to talk with the affected employees and refer them to an outplacement service set up by the consultant.

Jim still gave the proposal to Larsen who broke the story. As employees left the building the day of the story, Larsen and other journalists confronted them with questions about their layoffs. Most of the employees were unaware of the plan and its impact on them.

Uintah's public relations vice president hastily called a press conference to discuss details and confirmed Uintah's CEO's disappointment with the leak to the press and the hardship for the affected employees.

Jim was not part of the group of employees to be laid off. The discussion of the leak continued for some time at staff meetings. Jim's supervisor commented in one meeting, "There were a lot of hurt people because of that leak. The officers will fire anyone who was responsible."

Discussion Questions

1. Was it ethical for Jim to disclose the information to Gary Larsen?
2. If Jim hadn't disclosed the downsizing to Larsen, wouldn't he have discovered it some other way, given that Uintah is one of the state's largest employers?
3. Should Jim do anything now?

Section D
Personal Honesty

Is your resume accurate, or does it cross the line of demarcation in exaggeration ? How far would you go to win a prestigious office in a college club? Is it acceptable to "puff" when you are a reference? Personal standards of behavior often come into play as we confront dilemmas of qualifications and landing that important job or title.

1.14 The Rigged Election

The Finance Club at Harvard University is a prestigious organization for Harvard MBA students. The student members have the opportunity to interact with public officials like Senator William Proxmire and business executives such as Bruce Wasserstein. The Finance Club also serves as a network for job hunting.

Each spring, the club holds elections for its officers, including two co-presidents. In the spring of 1992, after initial balloting, there was a tie between two teams of two co-presidents. Murry Gunty was one member of one of the teams and busily recruited students to vote in a run-off election. The new votes gave Mr. Gunty his victory. However, two of the votes were from students who were not members of the club, but used someone else's name to vote.

After an anonymous tip, the elections were set aside and the runners-up installed as co-presidents. Mr. Gunty was required to write a paper on ethics.

Discussion Questions

1. In the words of the school newspaper publisher, "Why would anyone do this? It's just a club."
2. Was anyone really hurt by the conduct?
3. Would you have reported the conduct anonymously or disclosed it publicly?

SOURCES

Fuchsberg, Gilbert. "Harvard Has Some Crimson Faces Over a Lesson in Practical Politics." *Wall Street Journal* Apr. 9, 1992, B1.

"Harvard Student Rigging Election Must Write Paper." *Wall Street Journal* April 24, 1992, A3.

1.15 PUFFING IN THE RESUME

The resume is the door opener for the job seeker. What's on the paper can get you in the door or cause the door to be slammed shut. With that type of pressure, it is not surprising to learn that one 1988 study by Equifax, a credit-reporting agency often used for background checks on potential employees, showed that one third of all resumes have misstatements on them. The study by Equifax also found the following:

11 percent of all applicants lie about their reasons for leaving a previous job;

4 percent fudged job titles on their resumes;

3 percent listed fake employers;

3 percent fabricated jobs;

3 percent pretended to have a college degree.

Vericon Resources, Inc., a background check firm, has found that in 2 percent of their cases, a criminal past is hidden. Vericon has found that the lying about previous employment is easily discovered by requests for W-2s from previous employers.

In one resume "puffing" case, Michael Oliver, a former executive recruiter and now Director of Staffing for Dial Corporation, said that a strong candidate for a senior marketing management position said he had an MBA from Harvard, four years experience at a previous company and had been a vice president of marketing. Actually, Harvard had never heard of him, he had only worked for the firm for two years, and he was a senior product manager, not a vice president.

In a wrongful firing case by a former employee against Honeywell, a federal court permitted Honeywell to use the defense that the employee had lied on her resume (over eight years ago) by stating she had a college degree when she had only taken six courses (two as audits) and that she had managed property during a time when she owned no property and was unemployed. The discharge had nothing to do with the resume puffing, but the court ruled that "an employer may defend a wrongful discharge claim on the basis of facts unknown at the time of discharge."

Discussion Questions

1. Would it be wrong to engage in resume puffing and then disclose the actual facts in an interview?
2. Suppose that you had earned a college degree but it was never formally awarded because there was a hold on the degree due to unpaid debts. Would you state on your resume that you had a college degree?
3. Suppose that, in an otherwise good career track, you were laid off from your previous job because of an economic downturn and remained unemployed for thirteen months. Would you attempt to conceal the thirteen-month lapse in your resume?
4. Won't complete candor prevent you from ever getting a job?

1.16 THE GLOWING RECOMMENDATION

Jake Spacek is a credit manager for a medium-sized electrical supply business. He has a full staff of analysts, collectors and clerical employees who report to him. One of Jake's analysts, Bob Guthrie, has just come to Jake and said, "I've got a great job offer from Edison Electric Supply in Cleveland. But it is contingent on a background check and a good reference from you, Jake."

Jake would classify Bob as an average and conscientious employee who reports to work on time and puts in a full day. However, Bob has made a number of errors that Jake has caught over the years and saved the firm great expense and embarrassment. Jake has not objected to the errors because Bob is a pleasant fellow and a good friend. Jake has thought often of replacing Bob but has been hesitant because of their friendship.

If Jake gives a good recommendation, Bob will get the job and a new hire can be brought in to help Jake with his workload.

Discussion Questions

1. If you were Jake, what kind of recommendation would you give?
2. Should Jake have done something about Bob's work prior to the time he was placed in this dilemma?
3. Was Jake being more loyal to his friend than he was to his employer?
4. Is this type of recommendation commonly given to get rid of employees?

SOURCE

Jennings, Marianne. "How Ethical Are You?" *Business Credit* April 1992, 32–33.

1.17 THE GOOD BUSINESS REFERENCE

You supply paper for a printing business that is a slow pay. It is clear that the business is struggling, but one major contract, if managed properly, would bring the printing business through. As a new business, the printer has experienced difficulties with printing errors and missed deadlines. A major corporation has called for a reference for the printer because it is thinking of transferring all of its financial printing to them. An ink supplier has called for a credit reference as well.

Discussion Questions

1. What type of picture will you paint as a business reference?
2. Is that picture different from the one you would paint for the potential creditor (ink supplier)? Why or why not?
3. Will honesty cost your firm money?

SOURCE

Jennings, Marianne. "How Ethical Are You?" *Business Credit* April 1992, 32–33.

1.18 THE UNOFFICIAL GOVERNMENT CONTRACT AND THE ACCOUNT SALE

You are a credit manager for a large, interstate equipment supplier. You have had collection difficulties on an account worth approximately $50,000. The customer/debtor no longer has a line of credit with your firm, and you have simply been trying to collect the balance due. You are negotiating the sale for the account. Given the history of the account, the assets of the customer, and its existing debt structure, sale of the account should bring about $10,000. Your cousin's firm, in which you are a stockholder, is interested in buying the account. You have disclosed your relationship to the buyer to your company. Your company is just happy to get the cash and be rid of the account. Just before the sale takes place, you learn, unofficially, that the customer/debtor has won a substantial government contract that will run for five years.

Discussion Questions

1. Will you go through with the sale? (Assume no binding contract as yet.)
2. Will you make additional disclosures?

SOURCE

Jennings, Marianne. "How Ethical Are You?" *Business Credit* April 1992, 32–33.

1.19 RADAR DETECTORS AND THE LAW

Just recently the state of Connecticut legalized the use of radar detectors, reversing a previously passed statute that permitted state police to fine motorists for using the devices. Some legislators objected to the legalization of the devices, such as Representative Alex Knopp, who stated, "The bottom line is that speeding kills and that radar detectors will cause more speeding in the state of Connecticut."[1]

Discussion Questions

1. Are radar detectors a means of breaking the law and avoiding getting caught?
2. Is it morally wrong to speed?
3. Is it morally wrong to use a radar detector?
4. Is it possible that speeding laws constitute positive law but do not reflect any ethical or moral standard?

---

1. Kirk Johnson, "Connecticut Lawmakers Legalize Radar Detectors," *New York Times* (June 23, 1992): A6.

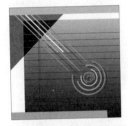

SECTION E
GOVERNMENT CONTRACT ISSUES

Often we see unlimited sources of funds as a means of justifying behavior. In government contracts, the supply of funds seems endless, and the competition is stiff. These benefits and pressures often cause poor resolutions of dilemmas. Pay particular attention to the impact of media coverage in the cases.

1.20 BATH IRON WORKS

Bath Iron Works, located in Maine, is the country's largest shipbuilding firm and Maine's largest employer. A Navy consultant left a confidential report at the Bath Iron Works' office while visiting there in May 1991. The file contained cost information on the Aegis guided-missile destroyer program and also included information about the competition's costs.

Bath Iron Works' Chairman William Haggett found the file and had it photocopied. Haggett then concluded he had made "an inappropriate business-ethics decision."[1] The file was returned to the Navy and while the Navy was investigating, Haggett resigned because he "failed to set a strong moral example."[2]

Discussion Questions

1. What pressures caused Mr. Haggett to use the confidential file?
2. Was anyone really harmed by Mr. Haggett's use of the file and his acquisition of the information?
3. Was Mr. Hagget's resignation necessary?
4. Would you have used the file? Why or why not?

---

1. "Unbecoming An Officer," *Time* (Sept. 30, 1991): 52.

2. *Ibid.*

1.21 STANFORD UNIVERSITY AND GOVERNMENT OVERHEAD

Government research funds to universities include indirect cost payments. This rate is paid to the university as part of the research fund or grant to compensate the university for its overhead: the use of its facilities by the grant investigators as they do their research.

Stanford University receives approximately $240 million in federal research funds annually. The funds are disbursed as actual research funds ($75 million), and then Stanford bills the federal government for its overhead ($85 million or 20 percent of its operating budget). An audit of Stanford's research program in 1990 by U.S. Navy accountant, Paul Biddle, revealed that the federal government was billed for a $3,000 cedar-lined closet in then- president Donald Kennedy's home, $2,000 in flowers, $2,500 for refurbishing a grand piano, $7,000 in bedsheets and table linens, a $4,000 reception for trustees following Kennedy's 1987 wedding and $184,000 in depreciation for a seventy two-foot yacht as part of the indirect costs for federally funded research.

In response to the audit, Stanford withdrew $1.35 million submitted for reimbursement as unallowable and inappropriate costs. Stanford's federal funds were cut by $18 million per year.

Kennedy issued the following statements as the funding crisis evolved.

December 18, 1990:

"What was intended as government policy to build the capacity of universities through reimbursement of indirect costs leads to payments that are all too easily misunderstood.

"Therefore, we will be re-examining our policies in an effort to avoid any confusion that might result.

"At the same time, it is important to recognize that the items currently questioned, taken together, have an insignificant impact on Stanford's indirect-cost rate ...

"Moreover, Stanford routinely charges the government less than our full indirect costs precisely to allow for errors and disallowances."

— From a university statement

January 14, 1991:

"We certainly ought to prune anything that isn't allowable — there isn't any question about that. But we're extending that examination to things that, although we believe are perfectly allowable, don't strike people as reasonable.

"I don't care whether it's flowers, or dinners and receptions, or whether it's washing the table linen after it's been used, or buying an antique here or there, or refinishing a piano when its finish gets crappy, or repairing a closet and refinishing it — all those are investments in a university facility that serves a whole array of functions."

— From an interview with *The Stanford Daily*

January 23:

"Because acute public attention on these items threatens to overshadow the more important and fundamental issue of the support of federally sponsored research, Stanford is voluntarily withdrawing all general administration costs for operation of Hoover House claimed for the fiscal years since 1981. For those same years, we are also voluntarily withdrawing all such costs claimed for the operations of two other university-owned facilities."

— From a university statement

February 19:
"I am troubled by costs that are perfectly appropriate as university expenditures and lawful under the government rules but I believe ought not be charged to the taxpayer. I should have been more alert to this policy issue, and I should have insisted on more intensive review of these transactions."

— From remarks to alumni

March 23:
"Our obligation is not to do all the law permits, but to do what is right. Technical legality is not the guiding principle. Even in matters as arcane as government cost accounting, we must figure out what is appropriate and act accordingly. Over the years, we have not hesitated to reject numerous lawful and attractive business proposals, gifts, and even federal grants because they came with conditions we thought would be inappropriate for Stanford. Yet, with respect to indirect-cost recovery, we pursued what was permissible under the rules, without applying our customary standard of what is proper ...

"The expenses for Hoover House — antique furniture, flowers, cedar closets — should have been excluded, and they weren't. That the amounts involved were relatively small is fortunate, but it doesn't excuse us. In our testimony before the subcommittee I did deal with this issue, but I obviously wasn't clear enough. I explained that we were removing Hoover House and some similar accounts from the cost pools that drew indirect-cost recovery because they plainly included inappropriate items. What came out in the papers was that Stanford removed the costs because it was forced to, not because it was wrong ... That is not so. To repeat, the allocation of these expenses to indirect-cost pools is inappropriate, regardless of its propriety under the law."

— From remarks to alumni[1]

By July 1991, Mr. Kennedy announced his resignation, effective August 1992 stating, "It is very difficult ... for a person identified with a problem to be a spokesman for its solution."[2]

Discussion Questions

1. Did Mr. Kennedy's ethics evolve during the crisis?
2. Contrast his March 23 ethical posture with his December 18th assessment.
3. Is legal behavior always ethical behavior?

1. Karen Grassmuck, "What Happened at Stanford: Key Mistakes at Crucial Times in a Battle with the Government Over Research Costs," *The Chronicle of Higher Education* (May 15, 1991): A26.

2. "Embattled Stanford President to Quit," *Mesa Tribune* (July 30, 1991): A6.

SOURCES

McWilliams, Gary. "Less Gas for the Bunsen Burners." *Business Week* May 20, 1991, 124–26.

Cordes, Colleen. "Universities Review Overhead Charges; Some Alter Policies on President's Home." *The Chronicle of Higher Education* Apr. 3, 1991, A1.

AP. "Stanford's Chief Resigns Over Billing Controversy." *Arizona Republic* July 30, 1991, A8.

Shao, Maria. "The Cracks in Stanford's Ivory Tower." *Business Week* Mar. 11, 1991, 64–65.

1.22 THE DEGREES FOR GRANTS PROGRAM

Professor Walter Frost was a professor at the University of Tennessee in the field of aerospace-related sciences. Professor Frost was part of the University of Tennessee Space Institute, a specialized campus for graduate studies in the aerospace industry. The Institute is located in Tullahoma, 135 miles from the University of Tennessee's main campus in Knoxville. Also the Institute is next to an Air Force Base and 50 miles from Huntsville, Alabama, where a large Army base and missile command center is located.

Professor Frost was an active researcher while at the Institute, and his work on wind shear and other hazards interested NASA. In 1975, Professor Frost established FWG Associates, Inc., a for-profit research firm. The University of Tennessee assisted FWG by providing cheap office space in a research park.

Professor Frost's energies and abilities were channeled into FWG and from 1981–1991, FWG earned $5.2 million from NASA on contracts. FWG also had contracts with the Army. Professor Frost was doing very well. He was driving a Porsche or Cadillac and had Christmas parties with dinner for one hundred at Nashville's Opryland Hotel.

A number of NASA, Army and other federal government employees became students of Professor Frost's in the master's and doctoral programs at the University of Tennessee. Leon Felkins, an employee at FWG began to notice similarities between drafts of documents FWG was preparing for government contracts and the master's theses and doctoral dissertations being completed by government employees. Felkins said, "He would get paid to do a study for NASA and he would do a study. Then one day the cover sheet on the report would change and it would become someone's dissertation."

For example, Dennis Faulkner, a civilian employee at the U.S. Army Space Center in Huntsville, was awarded a doctorate in May 1990. The following excerpts illustrate Mr. Felkins' point:

In addition to the spatial velocity and reflectivity fields of the JAWS microbursts, which were analyzed and reported by Frost, et al. (1985), JAWS data sets also provided turbulence information in the form of radar-measured pulse, wind, and total standard deviations (defined below).
 	
   'Development of a Microburst Turbulence Model' by H.P. Chang and Walter Frost, March 1987
	In addition to the spatial velocity and reflectivity fields of the JAWS microbursts, which were analyzed and reported by Frost, et al. (1985), JAWS data sets also provided turbulence information in the form of radar-measured pulse, wind, and total standard deviations (defined below).
	
	   Dennis A. Faulkner doctoral dissertation, May 1990

Peggy Potter, a NASA scientist, earned a master's degree in December 1989. The following excerpts were found by the University:

5.0 CONCLUSIONS

From the data set gathered at VAFB SLC-6 Tower 301 during the period from April 1975 to March 1982 the following concluding remarks may be made:

1. The most prevailing wind directions at Tower 301 are from north, northeast, southwest, and northwest especially in the spring and summer. Over 60 percent of the wind is from north. Significant diurnal variation of wind speeds occurs in the summer and fall months.

FWG Associates report to NASA by H.P. Chang and Walter Frost, February 26, 1987

5.0 CONCLUSIONS

From the data set gathered at VAFB SLC-6 Tower 301 during the period from April 1975 to March 1982 the following concluding remarks are made:

1. The most prevailing wind directions at Tower 301 are from north, northeast, southwest, and northwest especially in the spring and summer over 60 percent of the wind from north. Significant diurnal variation of wind speeds appeared in the summer and fall months.

Peggy S. Potter master's thesis, December 1989

John S. Theon, Chief of NASA's Radiation Dynamics and Hydrology Branch in Washington, D.C., entered the Ph.D. program at the Space Institute in 1983 and received his Ph.D. eighteen months later with a dissertation on the effects of orography. In 1984, NASA awarded FWG a contract on "Orographic Program Data." Eight pages of diagrams in the FWG reports are the same as diagrams in Mr. Theon's dissertation.

Upon the university's discovery of the similarities in FWG work and the theses and dissertations, Professor Frost retired. Two students were asked to return their degrees and one filed a lawsuit.

Discussion Questions

1. Was anyone really harmed by the degrees being awarded?
2. How would you have acted if you were an FWG employee aware of the similarities?
3. What if you were an army engineer with the opportunity to easily earn a Ph.D.? Would you have accepted the FWG work as a dissertation?
4. Is there a conflict of interest with the Institute and the University?

SOURCES

Putka, Gary. "A Professor Swapped Degrees for Contracts, University Suspects." *Wall Street Journal* July 12, 1991:A1.

UNIT TWO
INDIVIDUAL RIGHTS AND
THE BUSINESS
ORGANIZATION

In this section, the focus moves from how the individual treats the organization to how the organization treats the individual. How much privacy should employees have? What tests and screening are appropriate for pre-employment? What obligations does an employer have with respect to the workplace atmosphere? Should employees have job security? The conflicts between employer and employees rights take many different forms.

SECTION A
CORPORATE DUE PROCESS

Is fairness a criterion in employer decisions?

2.1 ANN HOPKINS, PRICE WATERHOUSE AND THE PARTNERSHIP

Ann Hopkins was a senior manager in the Price Waterhouse office of Government Services in Washington, D.C. She began her work there in 1977 and by 1982 was proposed as a candidate for partnership along with eighty-eight other Price Waterhouse employees.

Price Waterhouse is a nationwide professional accounting partnership. A senior manager becomes a candidate for partnership when the partners in her office submit her name for partnership status.

In 1982, Price Waterhouse had 662 partners, 7 of whom were women. Hopkins was responsible for bringing to Price Waterhouse a two-year $25 million contract with the Department of State.

All of the firm's partners are invited to submit written comments on each candidate. There are both "long" and "short" evaluation forms for the partnership candidates. Partners choose their forms according to their exposure to the candidate. All partners are invited to submit comments, but not every partner does so. Thirty-two partners submitted comments on Hopkins and one stated that "none of the other partnership candidates at Price Waterhouse that year had a comparable record in terms of successfully procuring major contracts for the partnership."

The firm's Admissions Committee makes recommendations on the partnership candidates after reviewing the comments. Those recommendations are made to the Policy Board and consist of accepting the candidate, denying the promotion, or putting the application on hold. The Policy Board makes the decision as to whether to submit the candidate to a vote, reject the candidate, or hold the candidacy.

There are no limits on the number of persons to whom partnership is awarded. There are no guidelines for evaluating positive and negative comments about candidates.

Of the eighty-eight candidates for partnership in 1982, Hopkins was the only woman. Thirteen of the thirty-two partners who submitted comments on Hopkins supported her; three recommended putting her on "hold"; eight said they did not have enough information; and eight recommended denial.

The partners in Hopkins' office praised her character as well as her accomplishments, describing her in their joint statement as "an outstanding professional" who had a "deft touch," a "strong character, independence and integrity." Clients appear to have agreed with these assessments. One official from the State Department described her as "extremely competent, intelligent," "strong and forthright, very productive, energetic and creative." Another high-ranking official praised Hopkins' decisiveness, broadmindedness, and "intellectual clarity"; she was, in his words, "a stimulating conversationalist." Hopkins "had no difficulty dealing with clients and her clients appear to have been very pleased with her work". She "was generally viewed as a highly competent project leader who worked long hours, pushed vigorously to meet deadlines and demanded much from the multidisciplinary staffs with which she worked."

On too many occasions, however, Hopkins' aggressiveness apparently spilled over into abrasiveness. Staff members seem to have borne the brunt of Hopkins' brusqueness. Long before her bid for partnership, partners evaluating her work had counseled her to improve her relations with staff members. Although later evaluations indicate an improvement, Hopkins' perceived shortcomings in this important area eventually doomed her bid for partnership. Virtually all of the partners' negative remarks about Hopkins — even those of partners supporting her — had to do with her "interpersonal skills." Both "[s]upporters and opponents of her candidacy, indicated that she was sometimes overly aggressive, unduly harsh, difficult to work with and impatient with staff."

There were clear signs, though, that some of the partners reacted negatively to Hopkins' personality because she was a woman. One partner described her as "macho", another suggested that she "overcompensated for being a woman"; a third advised her to take "a course at charm school." Several partners criticized her use of profanity. In response, one partner suggested that those partners objected to her swearing only "because it[']s a lady using foul language." Another supporter explained that Hopkins "ha[d] matured from a tough-talking somewhat masculine hardnosed manager to an authoritative, formidable, but much more appealing lady partner candidate." In order to improve her chances for partnership, Thomas Beyer, a partner, advised, Hopkins should "walk more femininely, talk more femininely, dress more femininely, wear make-up, have her hair styled, and wear jewelry."

Dr. Susan Fiske, a social psychologist and Associate Professor of Psychology at Carnegie-Mellon University reviewed the Price Waterhouse selection process and concluded that it was likely influenced by sex stereotyping. Dr. Fiske indicated some of the partners' comments were overly sex-based, while others that were gender-neutral were intensely critical and made by partners who barely knew Hopkins. Dr. Fiske concluded that the subjectivity of the evaluations and their sharply critical nature was probably the result of sex-stereotyping.

Of the group of eighty-eight candidates, forty-seven were admitted to partnership; twenty-one were rejected; and Hopkins and nineteen others were put on hold for the following year. Later, two partners withdrew their support for Hopkins, and she was informed that she would not be reconsidered the following year. Hopkins then resigned.

Discussion Questions

1. What ethical problems do you see with the partnership evaluation system?
2. Suppose that you were a partner and a member of either the Admissions Committee or the Policy Board. Would you have objected to any of the comments by the partners? Would it be difficult for you to object? Would it be more difficult if you were a female partner in that position?
3. Is the subjectivity of the evaluation troublesome? Would you change any aspects of it?
4. Would you say the partners had "mixed motives"? i.e., some of their points were legal factors while others were illegal?

SOURCES

Price Waterhouse v. *Hopkins*, 490 U.S. 228 (1989).
    Cohen, Cynthia. "Perils of Partnership Reviews: Lessons from Price Waterhouse v. Hopkins." *Labor Law Journal* Oct. 1991, 677–82.

AFTERMATH

Ms. Hopkins litigated the Price Waterhouse denial of her partnership as a violation of Title VII (U.S. antidiscrimination laws). The Supreme Court found for Ms. Hopkins. On remand, Ms. Hopkins was awarded her partnership and $350,000 in damages.

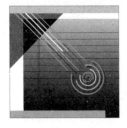

Section B
Employee Screening

What can an employer use to check an employee's background, personality and potential? How do we know the tests are accurate? Could these tests destroy opportunities?

2.2 Handwriting Analysis and Employment

Thomas Interior Systems, Inc., uses handwriting analysts to examine employment candidates' handwriting to develop a personality profile. President Thomas Klobucher says, "At first I thought (handwriting analysis) was hocus-pocus. But I've learned to depend on it."[1] "Handwriting is civilization's casual encephalogram," according to Lance Morrow.[2]

Graphology is used in two to three thousand U.S. organizations and is much more prevalent in Europe and Israel. Companies that have used graphology in personnel selection include Ford, General Electric, Mutual of Omaha, H & R Block, Firestone, USX Corp. and Northwest Mutual Life Insurance Company. Graphology was changed from an occult classification to psychology under the Dewey Decimal System in 1980 by the Library of Congress.

Views on the accuracy of handwriting analysis vary. Psychologist John Jones says, "No body of research shows that handwriting consistently predicts job behavior."[3] However, James Crumbaugh, a retired clinical psychologist, maintains that traditional personality tests, such as inkblots, are all hard to validate, but they continue to be used.

---

1. Michael J. McCarthy, "Handwriting Analysis as Personnel Tool," *Wall Street Journal* (Aug. 25, 1988): 19.

2. David L. Kurtz, et al., "CEOs: A Handwriting Analysis," *Business Horizons* (Jan.–Feb. 1989): 41–43.

3. *Ibid.*

Handwriting analysis is growing in popularity as a means of screening. A Honeywell manager explains, "I'm looking for any means that I think is credible to avoid a hiring mistake."[4]

The same manager adds, "I'm looking for any means that I think is credible to avoid a hiring mistake. I don't know if they're mass murderers or not; I simply learn if they'll operate well as sales representatives."[5]

Some samples of graphologists' analysis include:

The height of the signature. Those people with signatures above 1/4" in height, particularly when placed on the far right, are enterprising and motivated by prestige. They are good salespeople. Those with small signatures (less than 1/8" in height) are objective, cool, good listeners and negotiators. Those with medium signatures are team players. The dots on "i's", the bars on "t's", loops and hooks are all linked by graphologists to various personality traits. The absence of "i" dots, for example, can be indications of wandering attention and disregard for detail. Variances in pen pressure can demonstrate those same personality traits. A light pen pressure means the person is not aggressive. Rounded letters and variations in letter forms suggest listener more than persuader. Inconsistent legibility is linked with a lack of patience.

Graphologists charge between $150 and $500 for an analysis. Traditional areas of examination apart from size are slant, regularity, margin, pressure, lines, connection and work and line spacing.

Problems have developed with the use of handwriting samples. One truck driver applicant had his wife write his sample. Some applicants change their handwriting for the analysis sample. Some experts have raised the issue of discrimination in the use of the handwriting analysis tool. A test by the *Wall Street Journal* in which the same writing sample was submitted to three graphology firms yielded often conflicting results among the firms. Psychology Professor Richard Klimoski of Ohio State University says, "The better the studies (of handwriting analysis) have been, the less support they offer to proponents. My reading of the evidence is that there is nothing there that's worth your time and money."[6]

Discussion Questions

1. Would you have concerns about relevancy of the handwriting analysis?
2. Would you impose handwriting analysis as a requirement for employment?
3. Are you comfortable with the handwriting analysis test's level of accuracy?
4. One employer states that graphology has revealed so much to him that he feels as if the analysis is an invasion of privacy. Is this invasion the real concern or is it the accuracy?

---

4. Ibid.

5. McCarthy, 19.

6. Guy Webster, "Job Applicants' Fate Written in the Script," *Arizona Republic* (Sept. 1, 1991): F2.

SOURCES

Sackheim, Kathry K. *Handwriting Analysis and the Employee Selection Process.* Quorum Books: Westport, CT., 1990.

Kennen, William, Jr. "Handwriting Analysis — What Can It Tell You?" *Sales and Marketing Management* April 1990, 44–47.

2.3 HEALTH AND GENETIC SCREENING

During the past decade, significant strides have been made in the field of biology relating to genetics. Media attention has been focused on gene splicing, the creation of new forms of life, and the increase in agricultural products.

However, this new technology also means biologists have the ability to delve into complex genetic information. Tests of DNA will be able to provide full physical and mental profiles of individuals. Apart from the issues parents will face with in-utero testing, there are complexities that could develop in the workplace.

The Office of Technology Assessment of the House Committee on Science and Technology surveyed the five hundred largest U.S. industrial companies, fifty private utilities and eleven unions and found that seventeen had used genetic testing for the sickle-cell trait or enzyme deficiencies.

For example, genetic screening could reveal an individual's tolerance of or susceptibility to chemicals used in the workplace. With health insurance costs increasing exponentially, employers are now trying to improve employee health with routine medical screening, smoke-free environments and drug testing. Genetic profile tests could be used to hire only those individuals who meet certain minimum health requirements and are thus likely to keep health insurance costs down.

Insurers have used AIDS screening as a prerequisite for medical insurance coverage and genetic tests could predict heart disease and susceptibility to cancer. Genetic tests offer insurers the opportunity to screen and either deny coverage or create higher risk pools for those in high risk groups.

Scientist Robert Weinberg has stated:

A belief that each of us is ultimately responsible for our own behavior has woven our social fabric. Yet in the coming years, we will hear more and more from those who write off bad behavior to the inexorable forces of biology and who embrace a new astrology in which alleles rather than stars determine individuals' lives. It is hard to imagine how far this growing abdication of responsibility will carry us.

As a biologist, I find this prospect a bitter pill. The biological revolution of the past decades has proven extraordinarily exciting and endlessly fascinating, and it will, without doubt, spawn enormous benefit. But as with most new technologies, we will pay a price unless we anticipate the human genome project's dark side. We need to craft an ethic that cherishes our human ability to transcend biology, that enshrines our spontaneity, unpredictability, and individual uniqueness. At the moment, I find myself and those around me ill equipped to respond to the challenge.[1]

Starting in 1972, DuPont screened its black employees for sickle-cell anemia. Sickle-cell anemia affects one in every four to six hundred black Americans. Requested to do the genetic screening for sickle-cell disease by the Black DuPont Employees Association, DuPont administered the voluntary tests not to deny jobs, but to enable it to offer relocation to employees in chemical-free areas where the disease would not be triggered.

---

1. Robert Weinberg, "Genetic Screening," *Technology Review* (April 1991): 51.

Critics of DuPont said the testing allowed the company to transfer workers instead of cleaning up the work environment. DuPont's medical director responded,

> This is a very naive view. No one can operate at zero emissions, exposures — zero anything. There has to be an agreed-upon practical, safe limit. But there are some employees who are more susceptible to certain diseases than others. It's only common sense to offer them the opportunity to relocate.[2]

In the 1960s, certain workers at an Israeli dynamite factory became ill with acute hemolytic anemia. The walls of the red blood cells dissolve, thus making it difficult to get oxygen throughout the body. The workers were transferred to other parts of the plant, but genetic screening revealed that all of them had G-6-PD deficiency which causes hemolytic anemia upon exposure to chemicals. The information allowed the factory to place workers properly and reduce chemical levels in the plant.[3]

Discussion Questions

1. Is an employee's privacy violated by genetic screening?
2. Is genetic screening necessary for employers?
3. Is DuPont's sickle-cell anemia screening program justifiable?
4. Will genetic screening cause discrimination?
5. Will genetic screening help employers with safety in the workplace?

---

2. William P. Patterson, "Genetic Screening," *Industry Week* (June 1, 1987): 48.

3. Thomas H. Murray, "Genetic Testing at Work: How Should It Be Used?", *Personnel Administrator* (Sept. 1985): 90–92.

SECTION C
EMPLOYEE PRIVACY

Is there a line between my private life and my employment? How much can I be watched at work? Are mandatory drug tests a violation of my privacy or necessary for safety in my field?

2.4 THE SMOKING PROHIBITION

Janice Bone was a payroll clerk for Ford Meter Box, a small manufacturer in Wabash, Indiana. Ford Meter Box prohibited its employees from smoking and conducted urine tests to verify compliance.

Nicotine traces showed up in Bone's urinalysis and she was fired. Bone filed suit and the Indiana legislature passed a statute protecting workers who smoke outside the workplace from termination.

Ford Meter is one of many companies assessing the impact of their employees' health on their performance and the cost of insurance benefits. Twenty states now have laws in place that deal with employee activity off the job. Six of those states protect employees from being discriminated against for any legal off-the-job activity. The remaining states afford protection for off-the-job smoking only. Senator Carl Franklin, a supporter of Oklahoma's Off-The-Job Smoking Protection Statute says, "When they start telling you you can't smoke on your own time, the next thing you know they'll tell you you can't have sex but once a week, and if you have sex twice a week, you're fired."[1]

Some companies impose health insurance surcharges for smokers. Baker Hughes and Texas Instruments impose a $10 per month charge, and U-Haul International imposes a biweekly charge of $5 for health insurance of employees who smoke, chew tobacco or exceed weight guidelines. Turner Broadcasting will not hire smokers.

---

1. Z. Schiller, "If You Light Up On Sunday, Don't Come In On Monday, *Business Week* (Aug. 26, 1991): 68.

The American Civil Liberties Union is sympathetic to firms' positions on smokers because of the direct tie to health hazards and resultant health costs. However, the ACLU fears that the list of prohibitions will expand, as with U-Haul, to include weight, drinking, or as in Athens, Georgia — cholesterol-level tests for all city job applicants.

Discussion Questions

1. Would there be a more positive approach to accomplishing the goal of a healthier workforce? Would a reward system face fewer challenges?
2. Are the smoking prohibitions a justified invasion of privacy?
3. Will it be difficult to draw lines and balance employee privacy against employer risk as types of prohibited conduct grow?
4. Are hiring prohibitions on smokers discriminatory?
5. Would it be an invasion of privacy for an employer to refuse to hire employees who engage in hazardous activities (defined to include skydiving, riding motorcycles, piloting private aircraft, mountain climbing, motor vehicle racing)? What if the company cannot afford health coverage for its workers without this exclusion?

SOURCE

Stout, Hilary. "Paying Workers for Good Health Habits Catches On as a Way to Cut Medical Costs." *Wall Street Journal* Nov. 26, 1991, B1 and B5.

2.5 DUI AND DELIVERIES

John Lawn, the former director of the Drug Enforcement Administration (DEA), supported mandatory drug testing, calling it, "critical [i]n those occupations where either the public trust or public safety is involved." He listed doctors, lawyers, airline pilots, truck drivers and teachers as examples and urged the professions to develop their own rules and regulations for drug testing.

The Federal government has Supreme Court approval for 113 drug testing programs, but private employers are regulated by state law in the administration of their tests. Some states limit testing to safety-sensitive jobs; other states require probable cause as a prerequisite for testing employees. Courts continue to face the issues of employer need and employee privacy along with the added complexities of whether drug tests are reliable.

A Seattle equipment company worker complains:

I am so tired of hearing that I have a right to privacy. What about our right to safety?[1]

J. F. Spencer, a production manager for Pennwalt Pharmaceutical of Rochester, New York, expresses his feelings as follows:

People at work who are illegally using drugs are infringing on the rights of law-abiding individuals. It is an invasion of privacy, but until someone comes up with a better way to keep people on drugs out of high-risk jobs, I will put up with it."[2]

But a Boston executive maintains, "Individual rights are too precious to be compromised by this route. Other ways must be found to combat drug problems in the workplace."[3] New Jersey Superior Court Judge Donald A. Smith, Jr., wrote in a decision striking down a discharge of an employee who tested positive for marijuana and Valium, "Whether it be a private or public employer, a 'free-for-all' approach to drug testing cannot be tolerated."[4]

Kim Haggart, a quality-assurance manager at Dragon Valves, Inc., establishes the following position: "If the job is high-risk or safety-sensitive, testing should be required because impairment can affect the health and safety of others."[5]

You are the manager for a pizzeria that has no in-store business — it is simply a pizza delivery operation. As you evaluate the decision on drug testing for your drivers, consider the following questions.

Discussion Questions

1. Is there a safety issue involved with your drivers?
2. Will your testing be random?

---

1. "Test Workers for Drugs?" *Industry Week* (Dec. 14, 1987): 17.

2. *Ibid.*, 17.

3. *Ibid.*, 17.

4. Wayne A. Green, "Drug Testing Becomes Corporate Mine Field," *Wall Street Journal* (Nov. 21, 1989): B1.

5. *Industry Week*, 18.

3. Will you test all employees or just your drivers?
4. Will you test employees who are in an accident?
5. Should you test your employees?
6. Will you test only suspicious drivers?
7. What penalties will you impose when employees test positive?
8. Will you offer rehabilitation for employees who test positive?
9. How will you ensure the accuracy of the tests?
10. Will you let drivers know your policy on testing before hiring?

SOURCES

Hess, David. "Drug Tests Urged in Jobs Dealing With Public Trust." *Arizona Republic* Aug. 19, 1986, A1.

Eisen, Jerry. "Companies Increase Use of Testing to Determine Dishonesty, Drug Use." *Arizona Business Gazette* Feb. 29, 1988, 13.

Castro, Janice, et al. "Battling the Enemy Within." *Time* Mar. 17, 1986, 52–61.

Gary, Roderick. "Drugs in the Workplace." *Arizona Daily Star* Jan. 8, 1989, F1 and F5.

2.6 CORPORATE ANTHROPOLOGY: IS THE BOSS SPYING?

Thefts, liability for harm to customers, driving records and customer service are a few of the reasons businesses give for keeping a secret eye on employees. From the well-known secret shoppers of the retail industry to phone company monitoring of operator performance, employers are gathering data on employee performance and wrong doing.

Safeway Stores, Inc., a large multistore grocery chain, has dashboard computers on its 782 delivery trucks. The computers monitor speed, oil pressure, RPMs, idling and the length of stops. Safeway touts the program for its efficacy with regard to driver safety and truck maintenance.

In other businesses, high-tech developments enable employers to eavesdrop on employees' telephone and office conversations. Small cameras can be placed behind inconspicuous pinholes in walls to observe employee work habits and behavior.

The electronic surveillance of phone conversations has increased as employers seek to monitor productivity, accuracy and courtesy. Such monitoring is permissible if one party (the employee) consents. Some legislation has been proposed at state levels to require employers to sound a beeping tone when monitoring begins so that the employee is aware of the observations. But, an AT&T official notes that employers need the ability to monitor without notice, "Factory supervisors don't blow whistles to warn assembly-line workers they're coming."[1]

Barbara Otto, the director of 9 to 5, a national association of working women, maintains the monitoring affects personal calls, "Employers start catching non-work related information. They discover that employees are spending weekends with a person of the same sex or talking about forming a union."[2]

The American Civil Liberties Union raises objections to monitoring because of the lack of notice and also because of employees' lack of access to the information gathered about them via electronic means.

Discussion Questions

1. Is corporate spying necessary?
2. Is secret or electronic monitoring different from a manager's decision to, without notice, walk around an office to observe behavior and work?
3. Does an employee have a right to privacy in the workplace?
4. Would disclosure of monitoring activities lessen the invasion?
5. Is electronic surveillance different from going through an employee's desk?
6. Does the nature of the business affect your decision regarding surveillance?

---

1. Richard Lacayo, "Nowhere to Hide," *Time* (Nov. 11, 1991): 34.

2. *Ibid.*, 39.

SOURCES

Rothfeder, Jeffrey, et al. "Is Your Boss Spying on You?" *Business Week* Jan. 15, 1990, 74–75.

Garza, Christina E. "The Touchy Ethics of Corporate Anthropology." *Business Week* Sept. 30, 1991, 78.

2.7 THE HIV POSITIVE PHYSICIAN AND THE HOSPITAL'S LIABILITY

Dr. John Doe (a pseudonym) was an obstetrics/gynecology resident working at two medical centers: the Milton S. Hershey Medical Center at Pennsylvania State University and the Harrisburg Hospital.

On May 19, 1991, during the course of an invasive operative procedure, Dr. Doe was accidentally cut by the attending physician. No one can be certain whether there was an actual transfer of blood between Dr. Doe and the patient during the operation.

The following day, Dr. Doe voluntarily submitted to blood testing for the HIV virus. On May 21, 1991, Dr. Doe was informed that the test results were positive. At that time, Dr. Doe voluntarily withdrew from participation in further surgical procedures. An additional test called the Western Blot was performed on Dr. Doe's blood. The results, which were returned on May 28, 1991, confirmed that Dr. Doe was HIV positive. Dr. Doe informed the appropriate officials of his condition and pursued a voluntary leave of absence.

After investigation, Hershey Medical Center identified 279 patients who had been involved to some degree with Dr. Doe in the course of their medical treatment. Likewise, Harrisburg Hospital identified 168 patients who had been in contact with Dr. Doe since the time of his joint residency. Every patient who reasonably may have been exposed to Dr. Doe's condition was included.

Both medical centers then filed suit seeking approval for the compelling need to disclose information regarding Dr. Doe's condition to the identified patients as well as to certain staff members. The suit was filed under Pennsylvania's Confidentiality of HIV-Related Information Act. The Act was passed to promote voluntary blood testing to limit the spread of the Acquired Immune Deficiency Syndrome (AIDS). The Act provides, that in the interest of furthering public health, information gained from HIV testing will remain confidential. One of the exceptions to disclosure is consent, but Dr. Doe did not consent. Without Dr. Doe's consent, the medical centers needed a court order and filed suit to obtain that order under another exception to the Act which provides as follows:

(a) Order to Disclose — No court may issue an order to allow access to confidential HIV-related information unless the court finds, upon application, that one of the following conditions exists: [...] (2) The person seeking to disclose the information has a compelling need to do so.

In assessing compelling need for subsections (a) and (b), the court shall weigh the need for disclosure against the privacy interest of the individual and the public interests which may be harmed by disclosure.

In reaching its decision on disclosure, the court offered the following analysis:

Given the infectious nature of the HIV virus, coupled with the fact that full blown AIDS is in all cases fatal, there is no question that Hershey Medical Center and Harrisburg Hospital were faced with a grave dilemma. Unquestioningly, medical professionals have a duty to insure the health of their patients to the best of their capabilities. See THE HIPPOCRATIC OATH (providing, in part: "I will apply dietetic measures for the benefit of the sick according to my ability and judgment; I will keep them from harm and injustice."

In evaluating the hospitals' requests and allowing disclosure to patients and staff, the court discussed the following issues:

> Surely, when individuals visit their doctors, they do not expect to confront a risk of illness different from that which they already suffer. A hospital, which invites the sick and infirm, impliedly assures its patients that they will receive safe and adequate medical care. Thus, there is instilled public confidence in the health care system. It is understandable that Hershey Medical Center and Harrisburg Hospital were concerned about their obligations to their patients. At the same time, the Act in question affords confidentiality to those carrying the HIV virus.
>
> In this case, we have an added factor to consider. The physician who was infected by this potentially contagious and ultimately deadly virus, was involved in invasive surgical procedures where the risk of sustaining cuts and exposing patients to tainted blood was high. According to researchers, while the chances of transmitting the HIV virus via surgical procedures is very slim — one commentator has estimated the chances to be 1/48,000 — the potential is nevertheless there. When one begins to calculate how many individuals may be subjected to the same risk by the same medical worker, multiplied by the aggregate of infected health care professionals, the numbers become staggering. Surely, it is no consolation to the one or two individuals who become infected after innocently consenting to medical care by an unhealthy doctor that they were part of a rare statistic.
>
> Here, given the nature of Dr. Doe's residency and his involvement with the surgical teams at two hospitals, it is beyond dispute that the appellees demonstrated a compelling need for disclosure.

Dr. Doe strenuously argues that to allow future disclosures will be counterproductive and will discourage health professionals from seeking voluntary HIV testing. He contends that the facts here did not warrant the trial court's remedy and that if disclosure is permitted under the instant facts, the harm to the public interest in future like circumstances will be severe. Summarizing, Dr. Doe states:

> The public will be given a message that having an HIV-infected physician, *per se*, creates a risk of AIDS. Hospitals in the future will risk liability if they fail to follow through with similar unsubstantiated notifications to patients. The already high cost of medical care will be increased because of needless repetitious HIV testing. The high cost of medical malpractice insurance will be increased by imposing a notification standard which goes beyond a [sound] public health policy, and physicians and other health care workers will be discouraged from treating those infected with HIV.

Certainly, it is unfortunate that Dr. Doe will be made to suffer personally and/or professionally as a result of his illness and this case. At the same time, however, we must consider societal implications.

Dr. Doe presented a health risk to his patients and to the patients of others. It is admirable that he chose to withdraw from his residency program voluntarily. Indeed, he must have recognized the jeopardy involved, however slight. This Court does not deny Dr. Doe's right to privacy. Without question, one's health problems are a private matter to be dealt with by the individual in the way that s/he feels most comfortable and sees fit.

Additionally, Dr. Doe's name was not revealed to the public. The information disseminated to the patients was limited. In letters issued by the hospitals, the patients were informed that a resident physician who participated in their surgical procedure or obstetrical care is HIV-positive. They were then offered the opportunity to visit the hospitals for counseling and HIV testing. All efforts were made to keep Dr. Doe's identity confidential.

AIDS is not a disease that is, or that should be taken lightly by our society. Rather, many view it as a problem of epidemic proportion that knows no bounds and discriminates against no one. Although HIV has been extensively researched, the public, justifiably or not, is wary and frightened of its prevalence in our society. Acknowledging the public's perception, yet having become educated as to the facts and realities of HIV and AIDS, this Court has put public opinion aside and has attempted to balance the competing interests in this case carefully and thoroughly.

Discussion Questions

1. Was disclosure necessary for the hospitals to avoid lawsuits?
2. What rights did the court balance in reaching its decision?
3. Should a patient be told of his/her physician's health status before consenting to medical care by that physician?
4. Of what significance is the point that the chances a patient would have contracted AIDS from Dr. Doe are extremely remote?
5. Has Dr. Doe lost his medical career? If you were Dr. Doe, would you have consented to disclosure?
6. How are the reputations of the hospitals affected?

SOURCE

Excerpted from *In Re: Application of the Milton S. Hershey Medical Center of the Pennsylvania State University*, 56 EPD ¶ 40,904 (1991).

2.8 THE AFFAIR BETWEEN THE GATEKEEPER AND THE OPERATIONS VP

Deborah Shapiro earned a degree in accounting and began her professional career as a staff accountant for Worldwide Toys, Inc., a national toy firm headquartered in Irvine, California. Deborah enjoyed rapid advancement at Worldwide because of her intelligence, skills and diligence. She often arrived at the office at 7:00 A.M. and stayed until 7:00 P.M. or later. Within two years, she was the senior staff accountant.

As senior staff accountant, Deborah interacted frequently with the financial planning department, and in particular, Doug Thompson. The two worked long hours together and began seeing each other socially. Within a year, they were married.

Deborah's career continued to advance while Doug remained stagnant in his position. Through a series of promotions, Deborah reached officer status, that of treasurer/comptroller, within eight years from the time she joined Worldwide.

As treasurer, Deborah's long hours became a daily schedule and she was frequently required to travel to New York for meetings with shareholders and analysts. Deborah's work often involved the other officers of the company, and she worked particularly closely with Raymond Fercho, the vice president of operations. Together, Raymond and Deborah were responsible for the development of the annual operating and capital budgets. Deborah controlled the disbursements of the company.

Officers of the company were required to attend not only meetings together but various social, community and charitable functions as well. The officers also held two planning retreats during the year that involved three days at an isolated resort in Northern California.

Deborah and Raymond developed a close friendship that was obvious to the other officers. Worldwide's CEO, William Myers, talked privately with Deborah and said, "Careers can be made or broken by the way you conduct your private life and the moral standards you exhibit. Don't ever compromise your position of trust with the company." Myers had a similar conversation with Fercho.

Myers' secretary was in the John Wayne Airport on a Friday evening to pick up a relative when she saw Deborah and Raymond descend from a New York flight. They were holding hands and embracing frequently.

On Monday morning, Myers was told of the conduct by his secretary. Myers confronted both Deborah and Raymond independently. Both denied they were having an affair.

Deborah returned to her office after her discussion with Myers and talked with one of her friends who still served as a staff accountant. She fumed, "What business is it of his what I do on my own time? This is a private matter. My work is top notch and so is Raymond's. This is our private life. Myers had no right to question me."

It was just six weeks later that Ralph Verdi, the director of human resources, saw Deborah and Raymond leaving a motel as he returned to company headquarters from a luncheon speech. Verdi knew of Myers' concerns. All the other officers had discussed Raymond and Deborah's relationship. Myers had told

Verdi, "How can I be sure I have any effective internal control if those two are having an affair. I've got the gatekeeper fooling around with the guy who needs funds!" Verdi could see the problems but also worried about privacy. Myers said, "Privacy! These are two good people but I just can't have this. At this level in a company, we need people with far more control. And what about Doug? He doesn't have a clue. Who's going to tell him? He's the only person here who doesn't know!"

After he passed Raymond and Deborah at the motel, Verdi wondered whether he should tell Myers. He also wondered if he should tell Doug. "Maybe," he thought, "I should go to the Board Audit Committee. They could help."

Discussion Questions

1. Is the affair strictly a private matter, or one that concerns the company?
2. Should Verdi get involved? At any level?
3. Is Myers simply trying to impose his moral standards on employees?
4. Should there be a company policy on affairs between employees?
5. What would you do if you were Verdi?

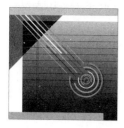

Section D
Sexual Harassment

The topic of the 90s, brought to the nation's attention by the Senate confirmation hearings of Justice Clarence Thomas, continues to present discussion issues. What is it? Can it be controlled? Is inaction a problem?

2.9 Ford v. Revlon

Leta Fay Ford was hired by Revlon Cosmetics in Phoenix in 1973 as a secretary. She was promoted several times during her ten years with Revlon and worked her way up to the position of buyer.

In 1979, Karl Braun was hired as the manager of the purchasing department and thus became Ford's supervisor. Braun invited Ford to dinner in 1980, and Ford accepted the invitation. During the dinner, Braun discussed the possibility of spending the night together and Ford left. Braun told her, "You will regret this."

Later in 1980, Braun fondled Ford at the company's Annual Service Awards Picnic while expressing his desire to have intercourse with her. Later at the picnic, Braun had Ford in a chokehold grip because she was refusing his advances. Another employee rescued Ford.

After the picnic, Ford reported her problems with Braun to the following people in the Phoenix offices: company comptroller, personnel manager for clerical and technical employees and the director of personnel. Ford expressed her feelings of fear and her need for help in dealing with Braun. Ford also called back to New Jersey (Revlon's headquarters) to report Braun's conduct to the human resource manager there. It was six months from the time of her first complaint before anyone from New Jersey talked with her.

While attempting to have the company act on her complaint, Ford developed high blood pressure, a nervous tic in her left eye, chest pains, rapid breathing and other symptoms of emotional distress. In 1981, Ford attempted suicide and Revlon issued a letter of censure to Braun. Ford also filed a complaint with the

EEOC in 1981 and filed suit in 1982 for intentional infliction of emotional distress resulting from sexual harassment and the failure of management to take action to stop the harassment.

Discussion Questions

1. Did Braun's conduct constitute sexual harassment?
2. Why didn't any of the Phoenix managers to whom Ford complained take action?
3. Suppose you had witnessed Braun's conduct at the company picnic. Would you have reported it?

SOURCES

Ford v. Revlon, 734 P.2d 580 (Ariz. 1987).

Adapted from Jennings, M. *Legal Environment of Business*. 2d ed. PWS-Kent Publishing: Boston, Ma., 1991, 317.

2.10 THE ATTORNEY AND THE LAW CLERK

Allan Heinze was the director of the Arizona Prosecuting Attorneys' Advisory Council from 1977 until early 1991. The Council was organized to provide training and technical assistance to the state's prosecutors.

Colleen "Kelly" Schallock was a law clerk hired to work in the Council offices in 1988. Ms. Schallock came forward with a complaint that Heinze sexually harassed her repeatedly while she worked in the offices and that eventually he raped her during the prosecutors' summer conference in Sedona in August of that same year.

When Ms. Schallock made her allegations, other former and current employees came forward to tell of fending off unwanted advances by Heinze. The witnesses testified to behavior such as Heinze dropping his pants in the office's reception area to show off his bikini underwear. According to the witnesses, Heinze also simulated sex acts behind women employees as they bent over, and unzipped his pants to facilitate waving his finger through his fly. Heinze reportedly touched himself and women in sexual areas. Heinze also kept a "bull's eye" on the ceiling above his desk for what he called "target practice" during solo-stimulated sex acts.

Eventually the case went to trial, and a jury awarded Ms. Schallock $2.38 million in damages. Heinze was ordered to pay $1.47 million and the Arizona Prosecuting Attorneys' Advisory Council was ordered to pay $908,000, which it paid in early 1992.

A judge required that the State of Arizona pay the $1.47 million assessed to Mr. Heinze. Judge Stanley Goodfarb stated:

> "There is no reason why the state or its treasury should not be responsible for the same type of act of its employees that Revlon or any bank would be responsible for ..."

Citing court cases, Goodfarb said:

> "Payment of substantial sums in damages is a very acceptable method of motivating employers to pursue active programs to stamp out sexual harassment. Can the government of this state ask for less?"[1]

There are four other sexual harassment lawsuits pending against Heinze, for which the state could be held liable.

Discussion Questions

1. How could the conduct described have continued for so long, and with so many people, without some disciplinary action being taken?
2. Is the Council morally responsible for Heinze's rape of Schallock? Is the Council financially responsible?
3. Is the state morally responsible for Heinze's rape of Schallock? Should the state be held financially responsible? Who will ultimately pay for the verdict?

---

1. Lynn DeBruin, 'State Liable in Harassment," *Mesa Tribune* (June 10, 1992): A1.

2.11 STROH'S SWEDISH BIKINI TEAM

Stroh's produces Old Milwaukee Beer. An advertising campaign for the beer features a dancing "Swedish Bikini Team" arriving at the campsite of some male campers with the slogan: "It just doesn't get any better than this."[1] *Playboy* has featured the Bikini Team in one of its issues.

Five women employees filed suit against Stroh's alleging that the ads produce, encourage and condone sexual harassment, discrimination and assault in their workplace. The attorney for the women, Lori Peterson says, "These ads tell Stroh's male employees that women are stupid, panting playthings."[2]

Law Professor Ronald K. L. Collins, Catholic University, describes the commercials as "the infrastructure of sexism" and suggests they be treated as legally equivalent to the behavior they encourage.[3]

Ms. Peterson maintains the employer should set an example: "Just as a kid looks to its parents as to what is appropriate behavior in the home, so does the employee look to the employer as to what behavior is appropriate in the work-place. Imagine our collective horror at seeing black men drop out of the sky to serve white men beer, tap-dance and shine shoes for them. Why is this scenario seen as horrible but similar caricatures of women (with oversized chests and undersized minds) still accepted?"[4]

Ms. Peterson alleges her clients have been taunted with lewd comments and shown pornography by their male co-workers. Stroh's officials say any link between the ads and the alleged conduct is preposterous. Further, Stroh's offi-cials have outlined the company's strong policies against sexual harassment.

Discussion Questions

1. If you were in charge of marketing for Stroh's, would you withdraw the ads?*
2. Would a victory in the suit for the five female employees be a form of censor-ship?
3. Should the conduct the women allege be addressed without linking it to the ad?
4. Would your opinion about the ads change if you knew they had a significant impact on sales?

*The ads were withdrawn by Stroh's.

---

1. "Battling the Bimbo Factor," *Time* (Nov. 25, 1991): 70.

2. *Ibid.*

3. G. Will, "Court Suit Against Beer Commercial Smacks of Censorship," *Mesa Tribune* (Dec. 1, 1991): A9.

4. *Ibid.*

2.12 TOP GUNS AND SEXUAL HARASSMENT

In September 1991, the Tailhook Association, a private group of retired and active-duty naval aviators, held their 35th annual convention at the Las Vegas Hilton in Las Vegas, Nevada. Over fifteen hundred current and former aviators attended the three-day meeting. Navy funds in excess of $190,000 were used to fly the officers on military aircraft to the Las Vegas meeting.

The Tailhook convention is known for its rowdiness. During the evenings, the officers occupied twenty hospitality suites on the third floor of the Hilton. Strippers and scantily clad bartenders worked the suites, and the alcohol bill for three days was estimated at $7,000 per suite. Pornographic films were shown in the suites, and the aviators travelled from suite to suite down a 140–foot hallway. One officer later noted that the hallway became so crowded that it took twenty minutes to go from one end to the other and described it as a "hot, drunken, messy mass of humanity."[1]

It was in the hallway that a pattern of sexual harassment developed over the three days. Groups of officers, in civilian clothes, shoved both female officers and civilians down the gauntlet, while grabbing at their breasts and buttocks and stripping off their clothes. Many of the women were ambushed at the elevator and shoved down the long hallway of arms. Two of the women, who were civilians, filed complaints with the Las Vegas police, but the complaints were dropped for a lack of evidence.

One of the women who was forced down the gauntlet was an admiral's aide who complained to her employer, Admiral John W. Snyder, who said, "That's what you get for going to a hotel party with a bunch of drunk aviators."[2] However, the Admiral did report the complaint and eventually the complaint went to then-Secretary of the Navy, H. Lawrence Garrett who launched (so to speak) an investigation.

The investigation encountered difficulties because of the officers' refusals to talk about the three-day gauntlet or identify any of the officers involved. However, Garrett ordered the scope of the investigation broadened to include senior officers who did not participate in the gauntlet but who were in the nearby suites and took no action to prevent the harassment of women. The investigation has now targeted seventy officers and identified harassment incidents involving twenty-six women. A video tape of the gauntlet discovered during the investigation shows a seventeen-year-old-girl being fondled and undressed.

In June 1992, the Navy announced the addition of sexual harassment training to its "Top Gun" training program and also started an awareness campaign for the prevention of sexual harassment. A poster on sexual harassment titled, "Not in Our Navy," is required to be placed on all bulletin boards of Navy bases.

At the end of June 1992, Navy Secretary H. Lawrence Garrett resigned abruptly. In his resignation letter to President George Bush, Garrett wrote that he

---

1. "Top Guns' Dogfight with Sex Scandal," *Arizona Republic* (June 14, 1992): A17.
2. *Ibid.*

accepted "full responsibility" for his "leadership failure" with respect to the incidents at the Tailhook convention.[3]

The Tailhook convention for 1992 was cancelled and acting Navy Secretary Daniel Howard vowed to purge the Navy of its "hard-drinking, skirt-chasing, anything-goes philosophy"[4] evidenced by Tailhook and imposed a requirement of one day of sexual harassment training for all officers and enlisted persons. Howard blamed Tailhook on a "decaying culture" and the "tolerance of Stone Age attitudes about warriors returning from the sea."[5]

Following Garrett's resignation, a party at the Miramar Naval Air Station Officers' Club included an annual review known as "Tomcat Follies." In the fliers for the review, there were pictures of scantily clad women holding a poster making reference to Representative Patricia Schroeder and oral sex. Schroeder is a member of the House Armed Services Committee who criticized the Navy for Tailhook and demanded an investigation. Two officers at Miramar were relieved of their command. Congressional hearings on sexual harassment of women in combat began and Sean O'Keefe, the Pentagon comptroller, was appointed Secretary of the Navy.

Shortly after Sean O'Keefe's appointment, Paula Coughlin, one of the twenty-six women sexually molested at the Tailhook Las Vegas convention, said that an agent of the Naval Investigative Service assigned to her case invited her to dinner and a drive in the country in November 1991. The agent, Laney Spigener, also called Ms. Coughlin "Sweetcakes" and pawed her as she sorted through photographs while attempting to identify the Tailhook officers. Spigener was removed from the case and suspended for three days.

In September 1992, four women sued both the Navy and Hilton Hotels for more than $2.5 million for their sexual assault in the hotel corridor gauntlet at the Las Vegas Hilton during the Tailhook convention.

Discussion Questions

1. Was the gauntlet sexual harassment or just "party fun"?
2. Do you "ask for" this type of treatment at a party in which drinking has been going on for three days?
3. Should the senior officers have taken action to stop the gauntlet?
4. Should hotel management have taken some action?
5. Would you be reluctant to identify your fellow officers if you had been involved or had witnessed the incidents? Why or why not?
6. Evaluate the conduct of Naval Investigator, Laney Spigener.

---

3. Andy Pasztor, "Garrett's Leaving Isn't Seen Protecting Administration from Scandal Fallout," *Wall Street Journal* (June 29, 1992): A14.

4. "Navy Orders Training on Sex Harassment," *Arizona Republic* (July 3, 1992): A8.

5. *Ibid.*

SOURCES

Stone, Andrea and Carol J. Castaneda. "Military Brass on Hill Today." *USA Today* July 30, 1992, 1A.

Stone, Andrea. "Military Sex Harassment Charged." *USA Today* Sept. 11, 1992, 3A.

Rohter, Larry. "The Navy Alters Its Training to Curb Sexual Harassment." *New York Times* June 22, 1992, A11.

Castaneda, Carol J. and Andrea Stone. "Girl's Ordeal Reignites Scandal." *USA Today* July 30, 1992, 4A.

Jolidon, Laurence. "Harassment Is on the Front Burner." *USA Today* July 8, 1992, 1A and 2A.

"Grounded." *Time* June 29, 1992, 31.

Schmitt, Eric. "Officials Say Navy Balked at Report." *New York Times* July 8, 1992, A1 and A10.

"Choppy Waters." *Time* July 6, 1992, 17.

"Swabbing the Deck." *Time* July 20, 1992, 15.

Smolowe, Jill. "An Officer, Not a Gentleman." *Time* July 13, 1992, 36.

Stone, Andrea. "Scandal Could be Agent of Change." *USA Today* July 30, 1992, 4A.

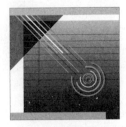

SECTION E
AFFIRMATIVE ACTIVE/EQUAL EMPLOYMENT OPPORTUNITY

Diversity in the workplace continues to be a stated goal, yet we still face difficult dilemmas such as danger to the fetus when a mother takes a higher-paying but exposure-risk job. When has an employer done enough? Are goals sufficient?

2.13 ON-THE-JOB FETAL INJURIES

Johnson Controls, Inc., is a battery manufacturer. In the battery manufacturing process, the primary ingredient is lead. Exposure to lead produces health risks and can cause harm to a fetus carried by a female who is exposed to lead.

Before the Civil Rights Act of 1964 was passed, Johnson Controls did not employ any women in the battery manufacturing process. In June 1977, Johnson Controls announced its first official policy with regard to women who desired to work in battery manufacturing, which would result in lead exposure:

> Protection of the health of the unborn child is the immediate and direct responsibility of the prospective parents. While the medical professional and the company can support them in the exercise of this responsibility, it cannot assume it for them without simultaneously infringing their rights as persons.
>
> Since not all women who can become mothers wish to become mothers (or will become mothers), it would appear to be illegal discrimination to treat all who are capable of pregnancy as though they will become pregnant.

The policy stopped short of excluding women capable of bearing children from jobs involving lead exposure but emphasized that a woman who expected to have a child should not choose a job that involved lead exposure.

Women who wished to be considered for employment in the lead exposure jobs were required to sign statements reflecting the fact that they had been told of the risks of lead exposure to the unborn child: "... that women exposed to lead have a higher rate of abortion … not as clear as the relationship between cigarette smoking and cancer … but medically speaking, just good sense not to run that risk if you want children and do not want to expose the unborn child to risk, however small."

By 1982, the policy of warning was changed to a policy of exclusion. Johnson Controls was responding to the fact that between 1979 and 1982, eight employees became pregnant while maintaining blood lead levels in excess of thirty micrograms per deciliter. This exposure level is in OSHA's critical level category. The company's new policy was as follows:

> It is Johnson Controls' policy that women who are pregnant or who are capable of bearing children will not be placed into jobs involving lead exposure or which would expose them to lead through the exercise of job bidding, bumping, transfer or promotion rights.

The policy defined women capable of bearing children as "all women except those whose inability to bear children is medically documented." The policy defined unacceptable lead exposure as the OSHA standard of thirty micrograms per deciliter in the blood or thirty micrograms per cubic centimeter in the air.

In 1984, three Johnson Control employees filed suit against the company on the grounds that the fetal-protection policy was a form of sex discrimination that violated Title VII of the Civil Rights Act. The three employees included: Mary Craig who had chosen to be sterilized to avoid losing her job that involved lead exposure; Elsie Nason, a fifty-year-old divorcee who experienced a wage decrease when she transferred out of a job in which she was exposed to lead; and Donald Penney, a man who was denied a leave of absence so that he could lower his lead level because he intended to become a father. The trial court certified a class action and included all past, present and future Johnson Controls' employees who have been or continue to be affected by the fetal protection policy implemented by Johnson Controls in 1982.

At the trial, there was uncontroverted evidence that exposure to lead affects the reproductive abilities of men and women and that the effects of exposure on adults are as great as those on the fetus, although the fetus appears to be more vulnerable to exposure than adults. Johnson Controls maintained that its policy was one that resulted from business necessity.

The employees argued that fertile men, but not fertile women are given the choice as to whether they wish to risk their reproductive health for a particular job. Johnson Controls responded that its policy was not based on any intent to discriminate, but rather upon its concern for the health of the unborn child. Johnson Controls also pointed out that more than forty states recognize a right for a parent to recover for a prenatal injury based on negligence or wrongful death, and its policy was designed to prevent its liability for such injury or death to fetuses. Johnson Controls maintains that just because it complies with Title VII does not mean it will be exempt from state tort liability for injury to the parent or the child.

Johnson Controls also maintains that its policy represents a bona fide occupational qualification and that it is requiring medical certification of non-childbearing status to avoid substantial liability for injuries.

Discussion Questions

1. If you were the director of human resources for Johnson Controls, would you support or change the policy on women performing in lead-exposure tasks?
2. Should women be given the choice to accept the risk of exposure?
3. Does the woman decide for the unborn child as well? Could the consent of the women or the acknowledgement of the danger mitigate liability? What if the born child with lead-induced birth defects sues? Does the consent of the mother apply as a defense?
4. The U.S. Supreme Court eventually decided the policy was discriminatory and a violation of Title VII (*International Union v. Johnson Controls, Inc.*). What steps would you take as director of human resources?
5. Are there times when issues of discrimination should be subordinate to other issues, such as the risk of danger to unborn children?

SOURCE

International Union v. Johnson Controls, Inc., 111 S.Ct. 1196 (1991).

2.14 WARDS COVE: SALMON CANNERY JOBS

Wards Cove Packing Company, Inc., operates salmon canneries in remote areas of Alaska. The canneries operate only during the salmon runs in the summer months. They are inoperative and vacant for the rest of the year. In May or June of each year, a few weeks before the salmon runs begin, workers arrive and prepare the equipment and facilities for the canning operation. Most of these workers possess a variety of skills. When salmon runs are about to begin, the workers who will operate the cannery lines arrive, remain as long as there are fish to can, and then depart. The canneries are then closed down, winterized, and left vacant until the next spring. During the off season, the companies employ only a small number of individuals at their headquarters in Seattle and Astoria, Oregon, plus some employees at the winter shipyard in Seattle.

The length and size of salmon runs vary from year to year and hence the number of employees needed at each cannery also varies. Estimates are made as early in the winter as possible; the necessary employees are hired; and when the time comes, they are transported to the canneries. Since salmon must be processed soon after they are caught, the work during the canning season is intense. Independent fishermen catch the salmon and turn them over to company-owned boats called "tenders," which transport the fish from the fishing grounds to the canneries. Once at the cannery, the fish are eviscerated, the eggs pulled, and they are cleaned. Then, at a rate of approximately four cans per second, the cans are filled with salmon. Next, the canned salmon are cooked under precise time-temperature requirements established by the FDA, and the cans are inspected to ensure that proper seals are maintained on the top, bottom and sides. For this reason, and because the canneries are located in remote regions, all workers are housed at the canneries and have their meals in company-owned mess halls.

Jobs at the canneries are of two general types: "cannery jobs" on the cannery line (unskilled positions) and "noncannery jobs," which fall into a variety of classifications. Most noncannery jobs are classified as skilled positions. Noncannery jobs include machinists and engineers who are hired to maintain the smooth and continuous operation of the canning equipment. Quality control personnel conduct the FDA-required inspections and recordkeeping. A variety of support personnel are employed to operate the entire cannery community, including cooks, carpenters, storekeepers, bookkeepers, beach gangs for dock yard labor and construction, etc. Cannery jobs are filled predominantly by nonwhites, Filipinos and Alaska Natives. The Filipinos are hired through and dispatched by Local 37 of the International Longshoremen Workers Union pursuant to a hiring hall agreement with the Local. The Alaska Natives primarily reside in villages near the remote cannery locations. Noncannery jobs are filled with predominantly white workers, who are hired during the winter months from the company's offices in Washington and Oregon. Virtually all of the noncannery jobs pay more than cannery positions. The predominantly white noncannery workers and the predominantly nonwhite cannery employees live in separate dormitories and eat in separate mess halls.

In 1974, a group of nonwhite cannery workers, both past and present employees, brought suit against Wards Cove for violation of the Title VII antidiscrimination laws because of their various employment policies, including nepotism, rehire preferences, a lack of objective hiring criteria, separate hiring channels and no promotions from within the organization.

The workers offered the following statistics:

17 percent of new hires for medical jobs were nonwhites;

15 percent of new hires for office workers were nonwhites;

Nearly all of the cannery workers are nonwhites; and

For 349 hires in four upper-level departments in 1970–75, 17 were nonwhites.

The court ruled that although there were significant disparities between the racial composition of the cannery workers and the noncannery workers, there was no indication of discrimination caused by specific, identifiable employment practices or criteria.

Discussion Questions

1. Although the court found no Title VII violations, would you, if you were the human resource manager for the canneries, change any hiring practices?
2. Would an affirmative action program be ethical in these circumstances?
3. Should an employer's workforce always mirror the general workforce's racial composition?
4. Do statistical matches require hiring on a basis other than qualifications?

SOURCE

Wards Cove Packing Co., Inc. v. Atonio, 490 U.S. 642 (1989).

Note: The Civil Rights Act of 1991 changed the law and *Wards Cove* might be decided differently today because of different standards and burdens of proof.

2.15 TWA AND ACCRUED VACATION TIME

In 1985, Trans World Airlines (TWA), a major domestic and international airline, was in dire financial straits. According to TWA's 1985 Annual Report, the airline suffered a pre-tax loss of $217.1 million and an operating loss of $62.4 million in 1985; had suffered a pre-tax loss each year since 1979 (with the exception of 1984); had suffered an operating loss each year since 1979 (with the exception of 1981 and 1984); and had seen its cash reserves decreased from $400 million in early 1985 to $50 million by year's end.

That same year, Carl Icahn and a group of investors began acquiring control of TWA with stock purchases. Icahn and his group gained control of TWA by January 1986.

At the time of the Icahn takeover, TWA was involved in significant efforts to reduce operating costs. For example, in 1984, TWA implemented a two-tier benefit and wage scale (the "B" scale) under which employees hired after March 1, 1984 received less in wages and benefits than employees hired previously. B-scale employees received fewer vacation days. The old policy is shown below and applied to all noncontract employees (agents, clerical employees and management).

Number of Full Years Active Service with Company Completed On or Before Jan. 15 of Year Vacation is Due to be Taken	Domestic Employees (Work Days)	U.S. Nationals Based Overseas (Work Days)
1 through 4 years	10	22
5 through 9 years	15	22
10 through 16 years	20	22
17 through 24 years	25	25
25 through 29 years	30	30
30 years and over	35	35

The new policy, for post-March 1, 1984 hires is shown below:

Number of Full Years Active Service with Company Completed On or Before Jan. 15 of Year Vacation is Due to be Taken	Vacation Allowance (Work Days)
1 through 5 years	10
6 through 15 years	15
16 through 25 years	20
26 years and more	25

Upon Icahn's takeover, he issued a directive for TWA to reduce employment costs by $300 million. In late August, 1985, Charles Glass, then TWA's senior vice president and controller, outlined for Richard Pearson, then TWA's president, a "possible reassessment of benefit programs to mitigate noncontract pay cuts" that included a *"rough* set of estimates of the annual effect of certain benefit reductions related to the noncontract work force".[1] Among the benefits Glass proposed for reduction were vacation days, floating and birthday holidays, management overtime, the medical and dental plans, and the thrift plan. According to Glass' estimates, imposing a four-week vacation cap would save TWA some $1.2 million in replacement costs and $4 million from a one-time favorable impact on TWA's income statement.[2] Glass also estimated the savings that could be realized from a three-week cap.

TWA announced its cost reduction plan to its noncontract employees in stages, beginning in October 1985. On October 18, 1985, Pearson announced that, effective November 1, 1985, TWA would reduce the wages for all salaried employees by 14 percent to a minimum of $1400 per month, or $6.90 per hour; reduce the number of management employees by 15 percent and the number of nonmanagement, noncontract employees by two percent; and undergo a departmental reorganization in order to move toward a "more cost-effective operation." In an accompanying statement, Icahn announced that all noncontract employees whose pay was being reduced would take part in a profit-sharing plan that was being developed.

On October 30, 1985, Pearson and Icahn announced that in addition to the previously announced cuts[3], cost reduction for noncontract employees would also include: (1) a 50 percent reduction in advertising for the remainder of 1985; (2) a hiring freeze for the remainder of 1985; (3) elimination of floating and birthday holidays; (4) revision of the medical and dental plans; and (5) the capping of vacation benefits at four weeks per year. In late 1985, TWA added one more element to its cost-reduction plan by establishing a voluntary termination program (VTP) for salaried employees who had been hired on or before December 31, 1976, and were either active or on an approved medical leave as of October 1, 1985.[4]

Although it considered several alternative methods of reducing vacation benefits, TWA ultimately decided to adopt the four-week vacation cap as part of its cost-reduction plan. Like the old vacation plan, employees would accrue vacation time over the course of one year for use during the next. Under the new plan, however, employees could accrue no more than four weeks vacation time — twenty work days — per year. The four-week cap, which went into effect on January 1, 1986, worked in the following manner:

---

1. While preliminary estimates indicated that employment cost reductions for noncontract employees would account for some $83 million of the reduction, TWA eventually determined that these costs would have to be cut by $93 million.

2. Reducing vacation benefits would enable TWA to enjoy savings on two fronts. First, TWA would reduce costs associated with paying replacement employees — either new hires or current employees working overtime — to fill in for vacationing employees. Second, because TWA carried the vacation benefits accrued by noncontract employees as a liability on its books, imposing the vacation cap would result in a one-time favorable impact on its profit and loss statement.

3. At this time, Pearson and Icahn announced that the previously announced 14 percent pay cut would be postponed to January 1, 1986.

4. TWA had offered voluntary termination programs in the past as well (Pearson Dep. at 37).

For employees hired after March 1, 1984:

Number of Full Years Active Service with TWA On or Before Jan. 15 of Year Vacation is Due to be Taken	Domestic Employees and U.S. Nationals Based Overseas (Work Days)
1 through 4 years	10
5 through 9 years	15
10 years and over	20

For employees hired after March 1, 1984:

Number of Full Years Active Service with TWA On or Before Jan. 15 of Year Vacation is Due to be Taken	Vacation Allowance (Work Days)
1 through 5 years	10
6 through 15 years	15
16 years and over	20[5]

Because they already had been accrued, the number of vacation days actually taken in 1986 was based on the former policy. Under the new policy, beginning January 1, 1986, noncontract employees began accruing the vacation days that would be taken in 1987.

Finally, TWA implemented a profit-sharing plan for noncontract employees under which TWA would return up to 20 percent of any annual "adjusted income" for 1986, 1987 and 1988. Under the plan, each employee would receive a profit share based upon the amount of his or her individual contribution, as a percentage of the total savings contributed by all noncontract and passenger service employees. The contribution for each employee was based upon the dollar value of his or her pay reduction, a $1260 credit for tax and benefit savings, and the dollar value of the amount of annual vacation time he or she had lost as a result of the four-week vacation cap. Because TWA suffered a $75.2 million operating loss in 1986, there was no profit-sharing distribution for that year. In 1987, however, TWA operated at a profit, and $2,488,000 was distributed to eligible employees.

Joan Finnegan, a TWA employee, filed a complaint with the EEOC regarding the action taken on vacation time. Finnegan maintained that the impact of the changes was a violation of the Age Discrimination in Employment Act (ADEA) because the effect was to deprive TWA employees with seniority of up to three weeks of accrued vacation time.

The EEOC found that the airline's vacation pay policy was a seniority system that was exempt from the ADEA. The EEOC also found that although the impact of the vacation plan was greater on older employees, the plan was validly based on years of service and not age.

---

5. TWA reduced vacation benefits for its part-time employees as well.

Discussion Questions

1. Although TWA had no legal obligation with respect to the employees who lost vacation time, did it have any moral obligation?
2. Was the financial health, or perhaps the survival, of TWA at stake? Are those interests more important than employee rights?
3. Are there any long-term consequences for TWA's policy changes?
4. Should legislative or regulatory protections be passed for employees in this situation?
5. Could TWA have structured the changes differently so that employees did not feel the need to file EEOC charges?

SOURCE

Excerpted from *Finnegan et al. v. Trans World Airlines*, 56 EPD 67,131 (N.D. Ill. 1991).

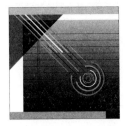

SECTION F
EMPLOYMENT AT WILL

Does an employer have the right to terminate an employee for any reason? Do employees have any guarantees of employment?

2.16 RICHARD WOOLLEY: THE LONG-TERM ENGINEER

Richard Woolley, an engineer, was hired by Hoffman-LaRoche (HL) in its central engineering department in 1969. There was no written employment contract between Woolley and HL. Woolley received his first promotion in 1976 and a second promotion to group leader for civil engineering in 1977. In 1978, he was asked to write a report for his supervisors about piping problems in a building that housed the engineering departments.

Woolley submitted the report a month later and one month after submitting the report was told that the General Manager had lost confidence in him. Woolley was asked to resign by his immediate supervisors, but he refused. A formal letter asking him to resign was then sent, but Woolley again refused to resign. There were no allegations of misconduct; there was only the comment about the "lost confidence." Woolley was fired two months after he was asked for his resignation.

Woolley filed suit for wrongful termination. He cited the language of HL's employment manual and said that there were both express and implied promises in the manual that indicated he could be fired only for cause and not for the unclear reason given.

The court found for Woolley indicating that the procedures for termination noted in the employment manual should have been followed and that the manual does afford protection of contractual rights for employees in the firm.

Discussion Questions

1. Should an employer have the right to dismiss an employee with or without good cause for a loss of confidence?
2. Should employees be entitled to some form of due process requiring warnings and justification before dismissal occurs?
3. Do protections for employees inhibit the employer's ability to make rapid, needed changes for flexibility in operations?
4. In the case, HL argued that allowing employees such protections would bring about a flood of suits by disgruntled employees who were dismissed with good cause. Do you agree?

SOURCE

Woolley v. Hoffman-LaRoche, Inc., 491 A.2d 1257 (N.J. 1985).

2.17   Catherine Wagenseller: The Fired Killjoy

Catherine Wagenseller was hired by Scottsdale Memorial Hospital, in Scottsdale, Arizona, as a staff nurse in March 1975. Wagenseller was recruited for the position by Kay Smith, the manager of Scottsdale's emergency department and Smith served as Wagenseller's manager. Wagenseller was an at-will employee; there was no contract between her and the hospital.

Smith and Wagenseller appeared to have a friendly, professional working relationship. In 1978, Wagenseller was given the position of ambulance charge nurse and one year later was promoted to the position of paramedic coordinator, a management position.

In May 1979, Wagenseller and Smith went with a group of hospital personnel (from other hospitals) for an eight-day raft trip down the Colorado River. During the course of the trip, Wagenseller and Smith experienced strain in their relationship. Wagenseller attributed the strain to Kay Smith's behavior which included public urination, defecation and bathing, heavy drinking and "grouping up" with other rafters. The merry rafters also engaged in a parody of the song "Moon River" which included the finale of the singing group "mooning" the audience. Wagenseller did not participate in any of these activities.

Upon return from the raft trip, Smith's attitude toward Wagenseller changed. Staff members noted the change with Smith using abusive language and embarrassing Wagenseller in front of staff members. Also, Smith and others twice repeated the Moon River skit at the hospital and Wagenseller again declined to participate.

Prior to the raft trip, Wagenseller had been given favorable performance evaluations. Just prior to the river trip, her annual evaluation by Smith rated Wagenseller's performance as "exceed[ing] results expected" which was the second highest rating an employee could receive.

By August, and again in October of 1979, Wagenseller was meeting with Smith and Smith's successor to discuss problems with her performance as paramedic coordinator and her attitude. In November, Wagenseller was asked to resign. When she refused to resign, she was terminated. Wagenseller appealed her dismissals to her supervisor, the hospital's administrative and personnel departments and requested reinstatement. Upon rejection of these appeals, Wagenseller filed suit.

Wagenseller says she was terminated because she refused to bare her buttocks in public, an arguable violation of Arizona's indecent exposure statute. Wagenseller says that being compelled to bare her buttocks under the threat of termination of employment violates public policy. Wagenseller says that her commitment to principles of common decency brought about her termination.

Discussion Questions

1. Isn't the conduct of employees outside the workplace irrelevant for both Wagenseller and the hospital?
2. Was there any harmful activity during the river trip?
3. Should Wagenseller have talked to someone about the raft trip?

4. Would you have supported the termination, given Wagenseller's performance record?
5. Does Wagenseller's termination convey the message that employees must support their supervisors in all forms of conduct outside the workplace?
6. Suppose Smith's rationale for termination was that Wagenseller just didn't fit in. Is the mix of employees critical? On what basis would the fit be determined?

SOURCE

Wagenseller v. Scottsdale Memorial Hospital, 710 P.2d 1025 (1984).

Section G
Whistle Blowing

In a true confrontation between personal values and company policy, employees are often faced with the knowledge that their employer is acting unethically in a way that does or could hurt someone else. How do they react? What should they do? Why do employers often ignore them?

2.18 Beech-Nut and the No-Apple-Juice Apple Juice

Jerome J. LiCari was the director of research and development for Beech-Nut Nutrition Corporation. Beech-Nut, at the time of LiCari's employment (in the late 1970s and early 1980s), was the second-largest baby food manufacturer in the United States. Beech-Nut is a subsidiary of Nestlé, the international food producer based in Switzerland.

In 1977, Beech-Nut entered into an agreement with Interjuice Trading Corporation for apple concentrate. The deal was a lifesaver for Beech-Nut because Interjuice's prices were 20 percent below market and Beech-Nut was heavily in debt, had only 15 percent of the baby food market and was operating out of its eighty-year-old plant in Canajoharie, New York, that was badly maintained.

Beech-Nut had once had a profitable arm with its chewing gum, but its parent, Squibb Corp., sold the chewing gum segment and the Beech-Nut name in 1973. The baby food division had never been a profitable part of Squibb's business, and by 1978, creditors and debts were mounting.

With apple concentrate in 30 percent of its baby food products, the 1977 Interjuice contract was the company's turnaround point. Nestlé was attracted and bought Beech-Nut in 1979. But with its costs for marketing substantially increased, Beech-Nut's cost pressures remained.

Rumors of adulteration (or the presence of bases other than apples) in the apple juice industry were flying at the time of the Beech-Nut/Interjuice contract.

Chemists in LiCari's department were suspicious. At that time, there were no accurate tests for adulteration but LiCari and his chemists found tests to use that revealed fake ingredients in the concentrate — such as corn sugar.

LiCari sent two Beech-Nut employees to Interjuice in Queens, New York, in 1978. Interjuice executives told the Beech-Nut employees the juice was imported from Israel. The Beech-Nut employees were not permitted to see plant processing; they were shown only storage tanks.

By 1981, LiCari was convinced the Interjuice concentrate was adulterated and worked to develop new tests for the juice. LiCari felt Beech-Nut's nutritional image would be greatly harmed by "fake" apple juice. While he developed the tests, LiCari took the circumstantial evidence he had collected on costs, the corn sugar and the Interjuice plant tour and went to head of operations, John F. Lavery, with his concerns. LiCari suggested that Beech-Nut do what Gerber does: require the supplier to prove the concentrate was genuine or switch suppliers. Lavery, calling LiCari "Chicken Little," told LiCari to come up with the proof himself that it wasn't real juice.

In August 1981, LiCari and his chemists felt they had established by tests, that there was no apple juice in the concentrate. LiCari sent a memo to Lavery suggesting that Beech-Nut switch suppliers. Lavery did not respond to the memo and when LiCari went to see him, Lavery said LiCari wasn't a team player and could be fired.

LiCari then took his evidence to Neils Hoyvald, the president and CEO of Beech-Nut. Hoyvald told LiCari he would take up the issue. Several months later, when no action was taken, LiCari resigned. LiCari's performance evaluation for 1981 by John Lavery said LiCari had great technical ability, but his judgment was "colored by naivete and impractical ideals."[1]

After leaving Beech-Nut, LiCari wrote an anonymous letter to the Food and Drug Administration (FDA) disclosing the information on the juice adulteration at Beech-Nut and signed the letter, "Johnny Appleseed."

After LiCari left, the pressure at Beech-Nut to continue with the adulterated product increased because of operating losses. In 1982, a private investigator for the Processed Apples Institute, Inc., went to plant operators at Canajoharie and showed them documents from the Interjuice dumpster and new tests indicating the product was adulterated. Beech-Nut was invited to join the Institute's lawsuit against Interjuice.

Beech-Nut did not join the suit (which eventually closed Interjuice), but did cancel its contracts. However, Beech-Nut continued to sell the juice and juice products on hand until ordered by the FDA to issue a juice recall. Beech-Nut had $3.5 million in apple juice-product inventory, and an FDA investigator observed:

> They played a cat-and-mouse game with us. When FDA would identify a specific apple juice lot as tainted, Beech-Nut would quickly destroy it before the FDA could seize it, an act that would have created negative publicity.[2]

When New York state government tests revealed a batch had little or no apple juice, Beech-Nut had the juice moved during the night using nine tanker trucks.

---

1. Chris Welles, "What Led Beech-Nut Down the Road to Disgrace," *Business Week* (Feb. 22, 1988): 128.

2. *Ibid.*, 128.

Some of the inventory was shipped to the Caribbean. Bogus juice was sold until March 1983.

Both Neils Hoyvald and John Lavery were indicted for consumer fraud. Hoyvald was indicted for 358 violations of the Food, Drug and Cosmetic Act. Lavery was indicted for conspiracy, eighteen counts of mail fraud and 429 violations of federal food and drug laws. Both Hoyvald and Lavery were convicted, but the convictions were later overturned because the trial was held in the wrong jurisdiction. State officials vowed to bring other charges against them. Beech-Nut pleaded guilty to 215 felony counts for violations of federal food and drug laws and agreed to pay a $2 million fine.

LiCari testified at the trials, "I thought apple juice should be made from apples."[3]

Discussion Questions

1. No one was ever ill or harmed by the "fake" apple juice. Was LiCari justified in his concern?
2. Did LiCari follow the lines of authority in his efforts? Is this important for a "whistle-blower"? Why?
3. Did LiCari have just circumstantial evidence at one point? Is this type of evidence sufficient?
4. What pressures contributed to the unwillingness to switch suppliers?
5. When no change was made in the supply contract, could LiCari have stayed with Beech-Nut?
6. Why did LiCari write anonymously to the FDA?
7. Is it troublesome that Hoyvald and Lavery escaped criminal conviction on a technicality? Does this "break" demonstrate that unethical behavior pays?

SOURCE

Haller, Vera. "Baby Juice Scam Nets Executives Fine, Prison Time." *Mesa Tribune* June 17, 1988, A10.

3. *Ibid.*

2.19 NASA AND THE SPACE SHUTTLE BOOSTER ROCKETS

Morton Thiokol, Inc., an aerospace company, manufacturers the solid propellent rocket motors for the Peacekeeper missile and the missiles on Trident nuclear submarines. Thiokol also worked closely with the National Aeronautics and Space Administration (NASA) in the development of NASA's Challenger Space Shuttle, a reusable space vehicle for exploration.

Specifically, Morton Thiokol was the manufacturer of the booster rockets used for launching the Challenger. In January of 1986, a special launch of the Challenger was scheduled. The launch was highly publicized because NASA had conducted a nationwide search for a teacher to send on the flight. On this, NASA's 25th Challenger flight, teacher Christa McAuliffe would be on board.

The scheduled launch day, January 28, 1986, was cloudy and cold at the John F. Kennedy Space Center in Cape Canaveral, Florida. The launch had already been delayed several times, but NASA officials still contacted Thiokol engineers in Utah to discuss whether the shuttle should be launched in such cold weather. Thiokol engineers signed off and approved a launch at 30° F. The contract range for the boosters, as specified by NASA, was 40° F–90° F.

However, the temperature at Cape Canaveral that morning was below 30° F. The launch of the Challenger proceeded. A presidential commission concluded, "Thiokol management reversed its position and recommended the launch of [the Challenger] at the urging of [NASA] and contrary to the views of its engineers in order to accommodate a major customer."[1]

Two Thiokol engineers, Allan McDonald and Roger Boisjoly, later testified that they opposed the launch.

Seventy-four seconds into the Challenger launch, the low temperature caused the seals at the joints of the booster rockets to fail. The Challenger craft was blown up killing all seven astronauts, including Christa McAuliffe, who were aboard the flight.

A subsequent investigation by the presidential commission placed the blame squarely with Thiokol for the faulty rings. Charles S. Locke, Thiokol's CEO, maintains, "I take the position that we never agreed to the launch at the temperature at the time of the launch. The Challenger incident resulted more from human error than mechanical error. The decision to launch should have been referred to headquarters. If we'd been consulted here, we'd never have given clearance, because the temperature was not within the contracted specs."[2]

Both Boisjoly and McDonald testified before the presidential panel regarding their opposition and their managers' (also engineers') decision to override the recommendation. Both Boisjoly and McDonald also testified that following their expressed opposition to the launch and their willingness to come forward, they had been isolated from NASA and consequently demoted. Since then, McDonald has had his original responsibilities restored. Boisjoly has been on medical leave for post-traumatic stress disorder and has left the company, but does receive disability pay from Thiokol.

1. Judith Dobrzynski, "Morton Thiokol: Reflections on the Shuttle Disaster," *Business Week* (Mar. 14, 1988): 82.

2. *Ibid.*

In May 1986, then-CEO Locke stated, in an interview with the *Wall Street Journal,* "This shuttle thing will cost us this year 10¢ a share."[3] Locke later indicated his statement was taken out of context.

NOTE: In 1989, Morton Norwich separated from Thiokol Chemical Corporation. The two companies had previously merged to become Morton Thiokol. Following the separation, Thiokol Chemical became Thiokol Corporation. Morton returned to the salt business. Thiokol remains under contract with NASA through 1999 and has redesigned its motor for the space shuttle rockets to correct the deficiencies.

Discussion Questions

1. Who is morally responsible for the deaths as a result of the 1986 explosion?
2. If you had been in Allan McDonald's or Roger Boisjoly's position on January 28, 1986, what would you have done?
3. Evaluate Locke's comment on the loss of ten cents per share.
4. Should the possibility that the booster rockets might not perform below 30° F have been a factor in the decision to allow the launch to go forward?

SOURCE

"No. 2 Official is Appointed at Thiokol." New York Times June 12, 1992, C3.

3. *Ibid.*

2.20 Dow Corning and the Silicone Implants: Questions of Safety and Disclosure

A. The Development of the Silicone-Filled Breast Implant

In the early 1960s, Dow Corning and other manufacturers began marketing silicone-filled implants for use in breast enlargement procedures. The silicone implants are breast-shaped bags filled with silicone gel. The bag itself is also made of silicone that is like a heavy plastic and is made of the same substances used in sealant and the children's toy, Silly Putty.

The other companies that manufactured the implants include: Heyer-Schulte Corporation to which several Dow Corning scientists and salesmen had migrated along with their silicone gel implant knowledge; and McGhan Medical Corporation, another offspring resulting from the departure of the same original Dow migrants from Heyer-Schulte. Much of the attention regarding the implants has focused on Dow Corning because the Heyer-Schulte and McGhan implants were simply duplications of the Dow Corning product, and the Dow Corning tests were relied upon by these other manufacturers.

The complexity of implant liability is exacerbated by the transfers of ownership of implant firms. That complexity is somewhat simplified in Figure 2–1.

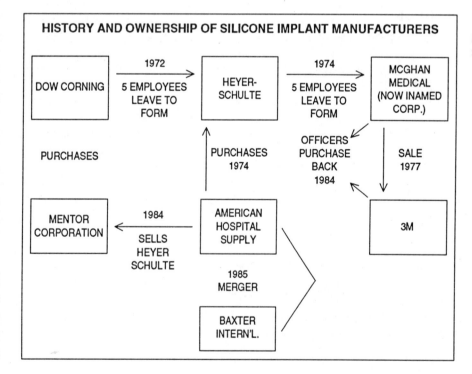

FIGURE 2–1
History and Ownership of
Silicone Implant Manufacturers

Dow Corning conducted animal studies regarding the problems with leakage from the implants. The studies were furnished to the FDA but under a confidentiality procedure that prevented their disclosure under the Freedom of Information Act.

In the course of conducting its research in the mid–1970s, Dow Corning found laboratory animals exposed to silicone gels developed tumors. A panel of research experts examined the Dow Corning studies and concluded that 80 percent of the exposed animals had developed tumors. The figure was so high that the panel deemed the research suspect and labeled the study "inconclusive."

B. Internal Studies and Safety Questions

Thomas D. Talcott, a Dow materials engineer, disputed the findings of the panel and resigned from the firm in 1976 after a dispute with his supervisors over the safety of the implants. Internal documents from Dow Corning, revealed in later ongoing litigation, indicate Mr. Talcott was not a lone dissenter on the safety issue. Also in 1976, the Chairman of the Dow Corning task force working on the new implants wrote, "We are engulfed in unqualified speculation. Nothing to date is truly quantitative. Is there something that migrates out or off the mammary prosthesis? Yes or no? Does it continue for the life of the implant or is it limited or controlled for a period of time? What is it?"[1] A Dow Corning salesman's 1980 characterization of the Dow Corning decision to sell a "questionable lot of mammaries on the market has to rank right up there with the Pinto gas tank."[2] Other internal documents, again revealed in later litigation, verified early company knowledge that the silicone gel could "bleed" and "migrate" into women's bodies.

A Heyer-Schulte chemist has disclosed in a deposition in a case against 3M that, "This phenomenon [gel bleeding] started to become of interest in the mid '70s."[3] He indicated that by placing a breast implant on a blotter, you would see a mark where the implant was, especially if you applied pressure and allowed time to pass.

In 1983, a Dow Corning scientist, Bill Boley, wrote in an internal memo, "I want to emphasize that, to my knowledge, we have no valid long-term implant data to substantiate the safety of gel for long-term implant use."[4]

Mr. Jan Varner, a former Dow Corning employee who is president of McGhan Medical (Inamed) maintains that very few implants leaked and any leakage was "very, very small."[5]

---

1. "Records Show Firm Delayed Breast Implant Safety Study," *Mesa Tribune* (Jan. 13, 1992): A1.

2. "Silicone Blues,"*Time* (Feb. 24, 1992): 65.

3. T. Burton, "Several Firms Face Breast-Implant Woes," *Wall Street Journal* (Jan. 23, 1992): B1.

4. J. Foreman, "Choice on Breast Implants Divides Women," *Arizona Republic* (Jan. 21, 1992): C1.

5. T. Burton, "Several Firms Face Breast-Implant Woes," *Wall Street Journal* (January 23, 1992): B1.

C. Other Companies' Concerns

Outside Dow Corning, other companies were expressing similar concerns. James Rudy, then-president of Heyer-Schulte Corporation, wrote a "Dear Doctor" letter in 1976 to inform physicians about the risk that the implants could rupture. It was in the period between 1976 and 1978 that Congress first gave the FDA the authority to regulate medical "devices" such as these implants. Despite the studies and warnings, the implants continued to be sold with approximately 150,000 women per year receiving the silicone gel device. It was also at this time that a two-year Dow Corning study found malignant tumors in 80 percent of the laboratory animals exposed to silicone gels.

The study concluded:

As you will see, the conclusion of this report is that silicone can cause cancers in rats; there is no direct proof that silicone causes cancer in humans; however, there is considerable reason to suspect that silicone can do so.

In response, the FDA staff noted:

The sponsor, Dow Corning, does not dispute the results of the current blase, i.e., Dow Corning agrees that silicone gel is sarcomagenic. However, this sponsor contends that induction of sarcoma in rats is due to solid-state carcinogenesis (Oppenheimer effect). This is uniquely a rodent phenomenon. Therefore, that it is of no human health consequence as a solid-state cancer in man has not been documented. In support of these contentions, an epidemiological study by Delpco, et. al. [sic], has been cited and shows no increased incidence of cancer in breast implant recipients.[6]

FDA staff members added the following comment in their memo/comment on the studies:

Solid-state tumor has been reported in rats, mice, chickens, rabbits and dogs. It is biologically unconvincing that man is a uniquely resistant species.[7]

At the time of the staff report on the studies, the FDA proposed reclassification of the gel implants as medical devices that required proof of safety of the device before they could be sold. Both surgeons and sellers of the implants objected to the reclassification, but the FDA imposed the stricter classification. The safety data for the implants was not, however, required until April 1991.

D. Problems with the Implants Begin

At the same time the regulatory arena for the implants was changing, product liability suits by women experiencing implant side effects were beginning. Problems experienced by women with the implants included rupture of the silicone sacs which then spilled the silicone gel into the body. The presence of this foreign chemical can cause the body to react with inflammation and accompa-

---

6. Tim Smart, "Breast Implants: What Did the Industry Know, and When?" *Business Week* (June 10, 1991): 94; Tim Smart, "This Man Sounded the Silicone Alarm — in 1976," *Business Week* (Jan. 27, 1992): 34.

7. *Id.*

nying pain. Other autoimmune disorders have appeared in women who experienced leakage or ruptures as their bodies tried to afford protection:

> scleroderma: a disorder which thickens and stiffens the skin and results in the build-up of fibrous tissue in the body's organs;

> lupuserythematosus: a disease characterized by chronic joint pain and rashes; and

> rheumatoid arthritis: a disease of stiffening of the joints.[8]

A landmark case in federal district court in 1984 in which Maria Stern of Nevada was awarded $1.5 million in punitive damages held that Dow Corning had committed fraud in marketing the implants as safe. In ruling on a post-trial motion, U.S. District Judge Marilyn Hall Palel wrote that Dow Corning's own studies "cast considerable doubt on the safety of the product" and those studies were not disclosed to patients including Stern, an act that she labeled "highly reprehensible."[9]

Following the Stern case, Dow's package inserts for the implants (which it began inserting in 1985), mention the possibility of "immune system sensitivity and possible silicone migration following rupture."[10]

A 1987 position statement by Dow Corning did not dispute the possibility of implant leakage but did discount the linkage between those leaks and the immune-system problems. A 1982 medical study cited in the position statement supported Dow Corning's position that there was no connection between implants and breast cancer. Also, the position statement indicated that any leaked silicone is picked up by the lymph system and excreted or stored. The position statement discounted the immune-system problem, maintaining that silicone of lesser purity would cause such problems.

Following Dow Corning's position statement, litigation activity increased as the FDA received twenty-five hundred reports of illnesses or injuries associated with the implants.[11] By the end of 1991, there were nearly one thousand implant lawsuits pending against manufacturers.[12]

In 1991 a sequence of regulatory and legal events led to Dow Corning's withdrawal of its implant product from the market.

Early in the year, a New York jury awarded a verdict of $4.5 million, nearly three times the Stern verdict, to a woman who alleged that her 1983 silicone implant with a polyurethane-foam covering caused her breast cancer.

E. Regulatory Action

While Dow Corning appealed the case, Bristol-Myers withdrew its implant following the FDA's confirmation of a study that linked the foam used to coat the

---

8. A. Purvis, "A Strike Against Silicone," *Time* (Jan. 20, 1992): 40–41.

9. T. Smart, at 98.

10. *Id.*

11. H. Mattern, "New Concerns About Breast Implants," *Arizona Republic* (Jan. 7, 1992): C1 and C4.

12. "Debacle at Dow Corning: How Bad Will It Get?" *Business Week* (Mar. 2, 1992): 36.

implant with a cancer-causing agent known as 2-toluene diamine (TDA). The foam is used primarily in air and auto filters and was banned by the FDA in the 1970s from use in hair dyes because of the risk of birth defects. The FDA's order requiring manufacturers to establish the safety of their implant products or withdraw them from the market became effective in May 1991 and required, after a decade, that the proof be forthcoming from the manufacturers.

At the same time, Ralph Nader's group, the Public Citizen Health Research Group, met in Washington, D.C. with trial lawyers, women who had had the implants and others. The group called for the full release of all safety data to date.

Sybil Goldrich, one of the women leading the movement against implants, was a 1983 implant recipient following her bilateral mastectomy for breast cancer. Nearly a decade of medical problems, including the removal of her ovaries and uterus, resulted, and those problems were attributed by her doctors to the implants. Ms. Goldrich has commented, "There is no way to detoxify from this chemical." Ms. Goldrich's suit is pending in Los Angeles.[13]

In September of 1991, the FDA required implant manufacturers to provide information about risks of the implants to women considering implant surgery. The FDA dictated the information required to be disclosed. The rule was issued as an interim measure while the FDA reviewed data on the safety of the implants. The risks required to be disclosed were:

- hardening of tissue around the implant
- interference with mammography and tumor detection
- questions about leakage and autoimmune diseases and cancer.

The FDA began its hearings on the silicone implants in October 1991. Impassioned testimony was offered on both sides of the issue. Manufacturers had boxes of data claiming their products were harmless. Nearly four hundred women from thirty-seven states traveled to Washington to testify in favor of the implants. Recruited by plastic surgeons, the women testified about the importance of the implants to their physical and mental well-being and their freedom of choice. The women spoke of recapturing their self-esteem and gaining psychological boosts in their battles with breast cancer.[14]

Physicians, professors of pharmacology and toxicology offered testimony to the contrary. Sybil Goldrich, by now the founder of Command Trust Network, a group advocating further study, spoke of the women who testified and asked:

"Do they know that silicone is bleeding into their bodies steadily? Do they know that implants are only good for a limited time and they will have to have surgery again and again?"

Sharon Green, the executive director of Y-ME National Organization for Breast Cancer Information, supported the implant sales and spoke from a different perspective:

"Who are these women and why have so many of them rebuilt their bodies? As can be expected, many of our callers are breast cancer survivors. They have

---

13. T. Smart, at 98.

14. "Women State Case for Breast Implants," *Mesa Tribune* (Oct. 21, 1991): A3.

faced breast loss, a year or two of chemotherapy, and some have had their chests radiated. They face each day hoping that they have overcome cancer. Many no longer want to be reminded every morning and night of the cancer that played havoc with their bodies.

It is estimated that one-third of current breast cancer patients are having reconstruction, most often with silicone implants. Saline implants can be an alternative, but they are not as aesthetically pleasing. An estimated 20% of implants are performed to reconstruct the breast; the rest, for augmentation. Y-ME's most recent survey (October 1991) of its own Hotline counselors — all breast cancer survivors — showed that among the respondents who had implants, the overwhelming majority were satisfied with their implants and 87% believed the devices helped their emotional recovery.

Y-ME's position is clear and simple. If silicone breast implants can be scientifically proved dangerous, then this information should be made available to women. If the data are inconclusive, we demand full disclosure of all information so women can make decisions based on fact and not on unscientific claims and anecdotes. We also understand that no medical device can be guaranteed 100% safe and that some people are willing to take greater risks to improve the quality of their lives. However, it should be a personal choice based on all the medically verified evidence as it is known today.

To ban or severely limit silicone breast implants based on inconclusive data would be one more insult to women by taking away their right to make informed decisions regarding their own bodies. For others to deny the right of a woman to implants because they fundamentally believe implants are unnecessary is arrogance in its ugliest form.[15]

After the hearings, the panel recommended unanimously that implants stay on the market but also concluded that the safety tests of the four largest manufacturers were inadequate and called for continuing tests. The panel cited the following hazards offered during the hearings for specific testing:

Scarring and hardening of breast tissue

Leakage

Reduced effectiveness of mammograms

Autoimmune reactions

Infections

Cancer

F. Impact on Corning

In December 1991, another plaintiff, Mariann Hopkins, was awarded $7.3 million by a San Francisco jury that found Dow Corning knowingly sold her a defective implant.

On December 30, 1991, Dow Corning was sent a warning letter from the FDA regarding the telephone information Dow Corning was giving via a toll-free number carried in ads about the safety of the implants. The FDA stated in the letter that the hotline information was used in a "confusing or misleading context."

---

15. S. Green, "A Woman's Right to Choose Breast Implants," *Wall Street Journal* (Jan. 20, 1992): A12.

On January 6, 1992, the FDA asked the medical device industry to halt the sale of silicone-gel implants until new safety studies could be reviewed. FDA commissioner David Kessler asked all plastic surgeons to discontinue their use of the implants until the FDA could review information from Dow Corning that came to light in two product liability suits against a Dow Corning subsidiary.

With the disclosure of the information in the product liability suits, by mid-January 1992, Corning's stock sank $10 in price to $68.375 while Dow Chemical's stock fell 87.5 cents. The two companies are joint venturers in the breast implant manufacture and sale. Within days of the stock price slip, investor suits were filed against the company with ten suits pending by March.

In February of 1992, the General and Plastic Surgery Devices Panel of the FDA recommended that implants for cosmetic enlargement be restricted but that implants should be made available to women with breast cancer and "anatomical defects."[16]

By March, Dow Corning made the announcement to withdraw from the implant market. Class-action suits are pending against the company by women with immune-system disorders, and Ira Reiner, the Los Angeles County District Attorney, has begun a criminal probe into whether Dow Corning concealed health risks associated with the implants. Reiner is proceeding under California's new so-called "be-a-manager-go-to-jail" law which holds executives criminally liable for product defects that cause harm to employees or customers. Reiner has observed, "There's no deterrent like a clank of a jail cell closing behind you."[17]

In early 1992, two women were hospitalized after using razors to remove their implants themselves because they could not afford surgery for removal. Both were suffering from autoimmune diseases. Both had complications from the attempted self-removals and were treated to complete the implant removals.[18] By the summer of 1992, Dow Corning reported that its second-quarter earnings had dropped 84.4 percent because of a $45 million pretax charge for eliminating its silicone gel breast-implant business. Even without the one-time charge, Dow Corning's earnings were down 19 percent.[19]

G. Ongoing Warnings

The Department of Health and Human Services established a Breast Implant Information Service in mid–1992 and offered information and study enrollment for women with implants. The following is an excerpt:

UPDATE ON SILICONE GEL-FILLED BREAST IMPLANTS

On April 16, 1992, FDA announced that, in keeping with the recommendations of its outside advisory panel, it would allow silicone gel-filled breast implants to be available, but only under special conditions.

---

16. J. Nesmith, "Scientific Panel Suggests Breast Implant Restrictions," *Mesa Tribune* (Feb. 21, 1992): A1 and A12.

17. R. Grover, "The L.A. Lawman Gunning for Dow Corning," *Business Week* (Mar. 2, 1992): 38.

18. "Woman Cuts Breast to Get Implant Aid," *Mesa Tribune* (May 15, 1992): A1; "Woman Claims She Removed Her Own Implants," *Phoenix Gazette* (Apr. 17, 1992): A2.

19. "Dow Corning's Profits Down 84.4% in Quarter," *New York Times* (July 28, 1992): C2.

Since FDA continues to be concerned about the safety of these devices, all patients to receive breast implants must be enrolled in clinical studies. FDA recognizes that there is a public health need for the implants among patients who have lost a breast because of cancer or trauma, or who have a serious malformation of the breast requiring reconstruction. Thus any woman who needs the implant to reconstruct the breast will be permitted access to such studies. Implants for the purpose of augmentation (breast enlargement) will be available only to a very limited number of women who are enrolled in controlled clinical studies approved by FDA and designed to study specific safety questions relevant to the device.

The following should help to answer questions about how FDA's decision will affect women, and what they should know about the implants.

Under what circumstances will the implants be available?

Silicone gel-filled implants will be available for clinical studies in three stages.

Stage 1:

Since FDA's April 16 decision, women with an urgent need for reconstruction with the implants have been allowed access to them. This category includes:

- women with temporary tissue expanders in place for breast reconstruction following mastectomy, who need to complete their reconstruction with gel-filled implants;
- women with silicone gel-filled implants who need replacement for medical reasons, such as rupture, gel leakage or severe contracture; and
- women having mastectomies before the studies are in place and for whom immediate reconstruction at the time of mastectomy is medically and surgically more appropriate than implantation at a later time. For women in this category, physicians must document that saline-filled implants are not a satisfactory alternative.

In order for a woman to get the implants in Stage 1, her doctor must first certify that she falls into one of the above three categories. She will have to sign a special form certifying that she has been told about the risks of the implants, and agree to enroll in a registry so that she can be notified in the future, if necessary, about new information on the implants.

Stage 2:

In this stage, breast implant manufacturers will set up studies which will enroll any woman who needs the gel-filled implants for breast reconstruction. FDA must approve these studies before they can begin.

Eligible women will include those who have had breast cancer surgery, severe injury to the breast, or a medical condition causing a severe breast abnormality. Women who must have an existing implant replaced for medical reasons will also be eligible.

As in Stage 1, all women will have to be told about the risks, provide informed consent, and be enrolled in a registry.

It will probably take until mid-summer until plans are in place for these studies.

Stage 3:

In addition to the Stage 2 studies, FDA will require carefully controlled research studies for each model of silicone implant that manufacturers wish to continue marketing. These Stage 3 studies will include both reconstruction and augmentation patients and will be focused on specific safety questions about the implants, such as how often rupture and hardening of the scar tissue around the implants occur. They will also evaluate the psychological benefits of the implants. The studies will be limited to the number of patients required to answer the safety questions.

As in Stages 1 and 2, women will have to be told about the risks, provide informed consent, and be enrolled in a registry. In addition, women in the Stage 3 studies will be followed more extensively to check for problems related to the implants.

Designing these Stage 3 studies will take time, and so they cannot begin as quickly as the Stage 2 studies.

How can a woman get enrolled in these studies?

She should contact the doctor who would be performing the implant surgery. The doctor can then contact the manufacturer of the implants to find out which hospitals or doctors offices are taking part in the studies in that particular area.

Discussion Questions

1. Who is morally responsible for the harms alleged from the implants?
2. Did Thomas Talcott act ethically in resigning in 1976?
3. If you had been Talcott, what would you have done?
4. Is the freedom of choice issue a moral standard?
5. Did members of the FDA staff have moral responsibilities with respect to the women with implants?
6. Did James Rudy relieve himself of any responsibility through his "Dear Doctor" letter?

2.21 The English Teacher and the Football Players

Candice Robbins is a senior lecturer at State University. Ms. Robbins' Ph.D. is in English, and she is responsible for coordinating instruction in the freshman English classes at State University. Ms. Robbins was awarded a teaching contract on a semester-by-semester basis according to student enrollment demand. Although Ms. Robbins has many graduate students assisting her with grading assignments and teaching break-out sessions, she holds the ultimate responsibility for assigning grades.

As the semester progresses, the students are required to submit more essays and other projects. In the fall semester of 1991, Ms. Robbins was notified by one of her graduate assistants that two of the students in her break-out session were having significant difficulties with the course. Their assignments were tardy if they were turned in at all, and the graduate assistant suspected that the two were "functionally illiterate." The two students are both linebackers on the State University football team. The football team for State is a successful one, having attended a bowl game in each of the past ten years. Last year State went to the Rose Bowl and as Ms. Robbins often says, "We have football fever here."

Ms. Robbins notified her department chair of the problem and her chair suggested that she talk with the students' advisor in the athletic department. Ms. Robbins called the advisor and discussed the problems. The advisor promised that she would "follow up on the problems." For a short time after the phone call, the graduate students reported to Ms. Robbins that there was progress. However, after four weeks, the students practically disappeared from the class. The graduate students were unable to follow up again on the two personally, and the two players missed so many remaining assignments and exams that they failed the course.

As a result of their failure, they were academically disqualified from State and ineligible to play in the Rose Bowl. As luck would have it, State was headed yet again to the Rose Bowl.

The athletic director met with Ms. Robbins and asked her to reconsider, but she told him, "Look, I gave them more of a chance than most students. Your advisor knew and you all dropped the ball!"

Within three days after her meeting with the athletic director, Ms. Robbins' department chair received a notice that due to funding problems, Ms. Robbins' contract for the spring semester would not be renewed. As she listened to her chair describe, in effect, her termination, she wondered if she shouldn't just change the grades.

Discussion Questions

1. If you were Ms. Robbins, what would you do? Would you change the grades?
2. If you were the department chair, would you take any action following the termination notice?
3. Is anyone really harmed if the grades are changed and the students are permitted to participate in the bowl game?
4. Was Ms. Robbins fair to the two students?

2.22 ORDERS OF SHOOT TO KILL

At the time of the existence of the "Iron Curtain", East German border guards who served at the Berlin Wall were given the orders of "shoot to kill" when they were dealing with people trying to escape to West Germany.

During the twenty-eight-year presence of the Berlin Wall, two hundred people were killed and seven hundred injured in their attempts to escape to freedom. Hundreds of border guards were employed during this period. Some of them shot wide, some shot into the ground, and others shot only to apprehend. But some guards, in fact, did follow the orders of "shoot to kill." Records do not permit the identification of all the sharpshooter guards.

However, the new German government has identified Ingo Heinrich and Andreas Kühnpast as East German border guards who shot to kill a twenty-year old waiter in February 1989 as he ran to freedom in West Berlin. Both were tried for manslaughter and convicted. Heinrich was given a three-and-a-half-year prison sentence because Judge Theodor Seidel noted, "Not everything that is legal is right."[1]

Kühnpast was given a suspended sentence because his bullets went wide. Chancellor Helmut Kohl has objected because those giving the orders are not being tried: "While I have no sympathy for people shooting at the borders, it is insufferable that the string pullers are living comfortably and wondering how to get a pension."[2]

Discussion Questions

1. Who is morally responsible for the death of the twenty-year old waiter?
2. Were the border guards unethical in following the laws of their country and not asserting their consciences?
3. Was Kühnpast ethical in choosing to shoot but deliberately miss?
4. Is the trial and conviction justice or vengeance?
5. Was it ethical to become a border guard in East Germany?

---

1. J. Jackson, "The Price of Obedience," *Time* (Feb. 3, 1992): 36.

2. *Ibid.*

2.23 THE CHANGING TIME CARDS

John Michael Gravitt was hired in 1980 at the General Electric jet engine plant as a $9.69 per hour machinist. A Vietnam veteran, Gravitt was pleased to be working at GE's mile-long plant in Cincinnati, Ohio, that employed eighteen thousand people. The plant produced military and commercial aircraft engines. GE was the engine manufacturer for the U.S. military's B-1 bomber.

Within six months of being hired, Gravitt was promoted to foreman. It was when he was promoted to foreman that he was in a position to see workers' time cards. Gravitt discovered that workers' training and idle time were being charged to defense jobs. He also noticed that time cards were altered to be charged to other projects if the projects for which the work was actually done were into overruns.

Gravitt was encouraged to alter the time cards for his workers. Sometimes overruns were charged to projects that weren't even in the plant yet. Karen Kerr, secretary to Gravitt's supervisor, says that she prepared "hot sheets" for the foremans' mailboxes. The "hot sheets" listed the projects that were in cost overruns to help the foreman make the time card changes. Gravitt ignored the "hot sheets" and refused to alter timecards. His supervisor did it for him.

John F. Tepe, Jr., was another foreman who worked with Gravitt. Tepe followed orders and altered 50–60 percent of his workers' daily time cards. Gravitt confronted Tepe and told him he could go to jail for altering the cards. Tepe replied he was "just carrying out orders and there wasn't any chance of getting caught."[1]

By early 1983, Gravitt decided to gather proof of the time card alteration. For two months, on weekend shifts, he went into Ms. Kerr's office and photocopied time cards and "hot sheets." Gravitt wrote an eight-page letter and delivered it along with his documentation on June 29, 1983, to Brian H. Rowe, a senior vice president at the Cincinnati plant. Gravitt was fired that day.

An internal audit by GE showed that 80 percent of Gravitt's allegations had proved true and 20 percent could not be disproved.

Gravitt testified before the Senate Subcommittee on Administrative Practice and Procedure and filed suit against GE under the 1863 False Claims Act which allows private citizens to bring suit against profiteers and recover part of the bounty collected. Fines under the False Claims Act are $5,000–$10,000 per violation with 30 percent going toward those who successfully bring the case. Gravitt hopes for a large amount, "It's the only way people will know they can do something to correct what isn't right."[2] Others argue that the False Claims Act encourages employees not to talk with employers first about problems they spot.[3]

---

1. G. Stricharchuk, "Ex-Foreman May Win Millions for His Tale About Cheating at GE," *Wall Street Journal* (June 23, 1988): 16.

2. *Ibid.*

3. Amal Kumar Naj, "GE's Drive to Purge Fraud Is Hampered by Workers' Mistrust," *Wall Street Journal* (July 22, 1992): A1.

Discussion Questions

1. Was anyone harmed by the altered cards?
2. Did Mr. Gravitt make an ethical choice in reporting the time card alterations?
3. Did Mr. Gravitt have to violate Ms. Kerr's privacy to collect documentation?
4. Is Mr. Tepe correct in saying that he was not responsible because he was just following orders?

SECTION H
EMPLOYEE RIGHTS

Compliance with labor laws. Employment benefit programs. These issues affect employees' attitudes at work and the reputation of the business.

2.24 CHILD LABOR AND BURGERS

Ken Washam was a manager at one of the franchises of Big Bill's Burgers. Big Bill's has approximately 5,500 restaurants throughout the United States. Like many Big Bill outlets, Ken has a number of teenage employees working for him.

Teenagers under sixteen are permitted under the Fair Labor Standards act to work up to three hours per day and eighteen hours per week between the hours of 7:00 A.M. and 7:00 P.M. during school sessions. If school is not in session, teenagers under sixteen can work up to eight hours per day and forty hours per week. Between June 1 and Labor Day, teenagers under sixteen can work until 9:00 P.M.

Also, like many Big Bill outlets, Ken isn't sure that there has been 100 percent compliance with these child labor laws. Ken explains, "It's not like its intentional. But I have so many teenage kids coming and going that I couldn't tell you who is what age and whether they worked too many hours. I don't do the payroll, we have a service that does that. Who knows if they were here at the right time?"

The Labor Department announced in March 1992 that it would be conducting a crackdown on child labor law violations. After the announcement, Ken arrived at his restaurant and found the following message from Big Bill headquarters on his voice mail:

> Please make sure that all the labor manuals that you have in the restaurant are taken out. Make certain that the book in which you keep time or time punches or whatever is out of the restaurant until the labor sweeps blow over.

Ken wants to just leave the books so he can have the labor investigators determine if he has violated the law. But headquarters has issued its mandate.

Discussion Questions

1. If you were Ken, would you leave the books or take them home?
2. Is any real harm done by the teenagers working extra hours?
3. If you were Ken, would you tip off the Labor Department?
4. What conflicts in moral standards does Ken face?

2.25 THE EXTENSION OF BENEFITS TO PARTNERS OF HOMOSEXUAL EMPLOYEES

In 1987, Margie Bleichman, an employee of Lotus Development Corporation, requested the personnel department to provide health insurance benefits for her companion who was another woman. Other employees followed making similar requests, and in 1991, Lotus Corporation announced that it would extend the same benefits to the partners of homosexual employees as offered to the spouses of heterosexual employees.

In spite of the offered coverage, only twelve of an estimated three hundred and ten employees applied for the coverage because "most people don't want to come out." Some firms, such as Ben & Jerry's Homemade, Inc. Ice Cream provide coverage for both homosexual and heterosexual partners. A summary of the private and public sector employers with coverage appears below.[1]

EMPLOYER	DATE INSTITUTED	NUMBER OF EMPLOYEES	HOMO SEXUAL COUPLES	HETERO- SEXUAL COUPLES*
Village Voice	1982	231	Yes	Yes
American Psychological Association	1983	1,500	Yes	Yes
Ben & Jerry's	1989	350	Yes	Yes
Montefiore Medical Center (New York)	1991	9,000	Yes	No
Lotus Development	1991	4,000	Yes	No
Berkeley, CA	1985	1,625	Yes	Yes
SantaCruz, CA	1987	650	Yes	Yes
Seattle	1990	10,000	Yes	Yes
San Francisco	1991	30,000	Yes	Yes

*Unmarried

Upon Lotus's announcement of its new benefits program, employees sent so many messages on the company's electronic bulletin board, that the system crashed. A heterosexual employee commented, "Unless the world follows Lotus, it will almost certainly, over time, make Lotus increasingly gay." Another employee wrote, "I'm insulted that Lotus is going to replace the term 'spouse' with 'spousal equivalent' in all policies. Lotus is taking it upon itself to recognize same-sex couples as married. I find it to be profoundly immoral."

Homosexual employees felt that the availability of the policy was a way to force them to disclose since the coverage was now available. Disclosure of a heterosexual marriage would not have an impact on a career whereas disclosure of a homosexual partnership for purposes of benefits could create a career ceiling for some employees.

---

1. Source: William M. Bulkeley, "Lotus Creates Controversy by Extending Benefits to Partners of Gay Employees," *Wall Street Journal* (Oct. 25, 1991): B1 and B6.

Discussion Questions

1. Is it fair for a policy to cover homosexual couples but not unmarried hetero-sexual couples?
2. Is the disclosure issue a problem of privacy for the employees who could benefit?
3. Evaluate the reactions of Lotus employees to the new policy.
4. Would companies be better served by redefining dependents as opposed to redefining relationships that are covered?

SOURCE

Hammonds, Keith H. "Lotus Opens a Door for Gay Partners." *Business Week* Nov. 4, 1991, 80 and 85.

Section I
Comparable Worth

Women still earn less than men. Are there other pay systems other than equal pay for equal work that would lessen the gap? Are those systems just?

2.26 Seattle's Comparable Worth

The city of Seattle and state of Washington captured the nation's attention with a federal civil lawsuit, *AFSCME v. State of Washington*, 770 F.2d 1401 (9th Cir. 1985). The suit was one brought by approximately 15,500 employees and the American Federation of State, County, and Municipal Employees against the city of Seattle to implement a comparable worth pay scheme for city employees.

AFSCME based its suit on a study conducted by Willis and Associates in 1974 of the state of Washington's compensation practices, with an update in 1976. The so-called Willis studies found discrepancies between the value of the work done by men and women and the pay they received. The Willis study examined sixty-two classifications in which at least 70 percent of the employees were women, and fifty-nine job classifications in which at least 70 percent of the employees were men. The study found a wage disparity of about 20 percent to the disadvantage of employees in jobs held mostly by women.

Title VII of the Civil Rights Act, and more specifically, the Equal Pay Act, prohibit discrimination in levels of pay on the basis of sex (and other factors, but relevantly here, sex). The protections require only equal pay for equal work. The statute does not address pay on the basis of the inherent value of the work.

Job evaluation points were used by Willis and Associates to assign a value to a job. Those points were awarded on the basis of factors such as level of education, knowledge and skills, mental demands, accountability, degree of self-industry in the position, working conditions, levels of responsibility, and so on. For example, a secretary's position that includes shorthand requirements was awarded 197 points and a jail guard was awarded 190 points. A teacher's aide position was awarded 176 points and a truck driver was awarded 97 points. A maximum number of points was allotted to each category: 280 — knowledge; 140 — mental demands; 160 — accountability; 20 — working conditions.

The Ninth Circuit's decision was that the Equal Pay Act did not require a comparable worth system, and the fact that there was a statistical showing of pay disparity between predominantly male and predominantly female positions did not establish discrimination for purposes of Title VII.

Following the Ninth Circuit's determination, the state of Washington went forward with its comparable worth program in an attempt to close the wage gaps between men and women. New pay levels were established for 62,000 employees in the state. The idea was to adjust mostly women's salaries so that they were equal to the salaries of men whose jobs were of comparable difficulty and responsibility. The effect of the new pay system was to close the 20 percent gap to 5 percent.

The result has not been a change in the composition of the workforce for particular types of jobs. The typing pool is still dominated by women, but not low-paid women. Also, the new system has resulted in a "male-drain." The number of men employed in the state system has gone from 50 percent to 47 percent because workers in the male-dominated jobs are being taken by private industry since private industry wages are higher. The state is experiencing shortages in the male-dominated occupational groups. In some of these job groups, male wages have dropped over 30 percent. State personnel officials concede that the biggest problem they face is that the system ignores private industry wages and their work force is being whittled away by the draw of private industry market forces.

Also, cost of living increases have been reduced in order to meet the $400 million cost of all the wage adjustments. Alternatives to comparable worth programs have been suggested including moving women into the traditionally male-dominated work areas. The movement simply does not occur because of women's perceptions about the difficulty of the job, the demands of their external responsibilities, their different career orientation, and the fear of discrimination in entering a male-dominated field or department. Because of these perceived or real obstacles, the movement does not occur, and wage gaps cannot be remedied without comparable worth, according to feminist scholars in the field.

Discussion Questions

1. Would it be prudent for a firm to voluntarily raise wages solely for ethical reasons in order to adopt a comparable worth program, without some corresponding increase in productivity?
2. Does the loss of workers to other firms and industries not under a comparable worth system hurt the enterprise?
3. Would there be an alternative solution? Is the movement of women to male-dominated fields an impossibility?
4. Should disparity in pay in male vs. female-dominated fields be a basis for a discrimination suit?
5. Would you want to work in a firm or agency that used a comparable worth system?
6. Should Washington continue its comparable worth program?

SOURCES

Schiebal, William. "*AFSCME vs. Washington:* The Continued Viability of Title VII Comparable Worth Actions." *Public Personnel Management* Fall 1988, 315–22.

Grider, Doug, and Mike Shurden. "The Gathering Storm of Comparable Worth." *Business Horizons* July-August 1987, 81–86.

Hoffman, Carl C. "Does Comparable Worth Obscure the Real Issues?" *Personnel Journal* January 1987, 82–95.

"Comparable Worth Has Its Price." *Personnel* September 1990, 3–4.

2.27 Unequal Earnings

The following table reflects the wages (for every dollar earned by a man) for women with a college education:

Age	Amount Woman With College Education Earns for Every Dollar Earned by a Man
18–24	92¢
25–34	75¢
35–44	65¢
45–54	59¢
55–64	54¢

As the chart indicates, wages for women drop substantially by age. Karen Nussbaum, executive director of 9 to 5, a national association of working women, asserts that the pay differential exists because companies make more of a profit: "That discrimination pays, otherwise it wouldn't have flourished so long. You can bet people say, 'We can get her for less than we can get him.' You know it goes on."[1]

Data on salaries also shows that women earn less if they work in female-dominated fields such as nursing, social work, clerical jobs and public school teaching.

Carolin Head, the assistant director of the American Association of University Women, says, "The fact of the matter is, many women don't wish to go into nontraditional, male dominated occupations. It is not acceptable in this country to tell nurses and teachers that if they want to make more, they need to choose a different occupation."[2]

Discussion Questions

1. Do the table and the explanation mean that the disparity in wages based on gender is justified?
2. Does it seem that the disparity will continue to exist?
3. Are there other factors that would explain the disparity?
4. Should higher wages be paid in "traditionally female" jobs?

---

1. "Education Doesn't Cut Pay Gap," *Mesa Tribune* (Nov. 14, 1991): A1 and A7.

2. *Ibid.*

UNIT THREE
BUSINESS OPERATIONS

From cash and internal controls to grease payments in foreign operations, businesses face continuing dilemmas about the propriety of funds' use and flow.

Everything a business does from production to shutdown affects its workers, their well-being, the environment and the community. Decisions in these areas require careful balancing of many interests.

Section A
Financial and Cash Management Procedures

Control of funds offers opportunities for misuse of funds. The lack of careful supervision can present tempting opportunities for personal and business gain that later serve to bring about the downfall of the firm. Who's in charge? How much information do they have? Can misuse be controlled? As you review these cases, think of ways better management and ethical codes could have helped the firms.

3.1 BCCI and the Role of Internal Auditors

The Bank of Credit & Commercial International was a $20 billion banking empire that operated in seventy countries. Incorporated in Luxembourg and headquartered in London, BCCI owned First American Bankshare in Washington, D.C. (with Clark Clifford, former Secretary of Defense as chairman), and the National Bank of Georgia.

Clifford had complex roles with First American, beyond that of chairman. He was also the managing partner of Clifford & Warnke, the law firm that represented First American. Clifford & Warnke also defended BCCI against money-laundering charges in 1988. Also, Clifford and his law partner, Robert A. Altman, had borrowed $12 million from BCCI to buy shares in First American Bankshare. BCCI found a buyer for Clifford's shares eighteen months later and Clifford realized an $11 million pretax profit.

BCCI had what regulators referred to as a "Black Network" with fifteen hundred employees who used spy equipment, arms deals, bribery, espionage, extortion and drug trafficking to advance its worldwide presence.[1] BCCI was the

---

1. J. Beaty, and S. C. Gwynne, "The Dirtiest Bank of All," *Time* (July 29, 1991): 42–45.

bank used for the money in the Iran-contra deals. The CIA also had BCCI accounts. Customers of BCCI included Manuel Noriega, Saddam Hussein and Ferdinand Marcos.

BCCI was shut down by regulators in sixty two countries on July 5, 1991. A source for the *Time* magazine story on BCCI told *Time*'s reporter, Jonathan Beaty, of the complexity of BCCI's operations. Beaty reported, "First, he said that as long as I thought of BCCI as just a bank, I wouldn't understand it. It is a nation with its own intelligence service, army, and national bank. It deals in commodities (oil, drugs, grain — even cement, some of which is laced with bricks of heroin) and is one of the largest arms dealers in the world. Banking was important to this nation's success, but it was far from its only field of operations. Second, this was the first time we heard of the 'black network,' the covert-operations arm of BCCI, which was for hire and very capable. This is the first global scandal, made possible by the information revolution with its instant transfers of money and real time, worldwide operations."[2]

After the July 5th shutdown of BCCI, mysteries about its operations unfolded. When Manhattan District Attorney Robert Morgenthau announced that BCCI had been indicted on charges of defrauding investors and stealing more than $30 million, he explained that BCCI's structure was nothing more than a global Ponzi scheme in which money was shifted to maintain a healthy appearance for auditors and regulators while the masterminds kept funds for themselves.[3]

An independent audit undertaken by Price Waterhouse for British authorities, completed and fully released in 1992, concluded that BCCI's board was "taken in" by "dominant and deceitful management."[4] Price Waterhouse also concluded that accounts existed "for the purposes of fraudulently routing funds."[5]

Still facing ongoing investigations by various agencies, BCCI, a hollow shell, pleaded guilty to federal and state charges of racketeering, fraud, and money laundering in December 1991. The fate of the funds of the BCCI depositors remains unknown, but U.S. prosecutors continue to pursue the case. A New York grand jury has indicted Sheik Khalid bin Mahfouz, a top officer of Saudi Arabia's National Commercial Bank, a BCCI subsidiary, to recover a $170 million fine.

At the end of July both Clark Clifford and his law partner, Robert Altman, were indicted for conspiracy and concealing material facts in the BCCI downfall.[6]

---

2. "BCCI: Uncovering A Rogue Empire," *Time Insider* (July 29, 1991): 1–3.

3. E. Kurylo, "Indictment of BCCI Charges 'Largest Bank Fraud in History,'" *Mesa Tribune* (July 30, 1991): A3.

4. T. Petzinger, Jr., and P. Truell, "Biggest Saudi Bank Took Part in Effort to Hide Fraud at BCCI, Auditors Say," *Wall Street Journal* (Feb. 9, 1992): A18.

5. *Ibid.*

6. Steve Lohr, "Indictment Charges Clifford Took Bribes," *New York Times* (July 30, 1992): A1, C5; "An Icon Falls in The BCCI Scandal," *Time* (Aug. 10, 1992): 12–13.

Discussion Questions

1. Would it be possible to sit on the board of BCCI or one of its subsidiary banks and not realize the extent of its activities?
2. Would it be possible for an auditor to issue financial statements that were clean for BCCI?
3. At what point are internal investigations warranted?
4. Suppose you were a member of the BCCI internal audit department and you unraveled the black network. What would you do with the information?
5. Can directors or internal auditors ever detect fraud?
6. Did Clifford and Altman have any conflicts of interest in their various roles?
7. Was BCCI's large, multinational structure a key in avoiding regulatory oversight?

SOURCES

Barrett, P. "Justice Agency, Which Let BCCI Out of Its Grip, Is Now Under Fire From Critics in Both Parties." *Wall Street Journal* Aug. 1, 1991, A14.

Beaty, J., and S. C. Gwynne. "Is That All There Is?" *Time* Dec. 30, 1991, 59.

Kuttner, Robert. "Controlling the Climate That Let BCCI Bloom." *Business Week* July 29, 1991, 16.

"That BCCI Can of Worms." *The Banker* Aug. 19, 1991, 4.

"BCCI: The Never-Ending Story." *The Banker* Jan. 1992, 4.

"The BCCI Trail." *The Economist* July 27, 1991, 13–14.

Dwyer, Paula. "What Clifford and Altman Did Wrong." *Business Week* Sept. 30, 1991, 30.

Prokesch, Steven. "Regulators Agree on Rules to Prevent More BCCI's." *New York Times* July 7, 1992, C1 and C4.

"BCCI Hits Home." *Time* July 20, 1992, 17.

"Long Arm of the Law." *Time* July 13, 1992, 18.

Beaty, Jonathan, and S. C. Gwynne. "The Riyadh Connection." *Time* Aug. 10, 1992, 40–41.

Truell, Peter, and Thomas Petzinger, Jr. "Clifford, Altman Indicted in BCCI Case." *Wall Street Journal* July 30, 1992, A2.

Baquet, Dean. "Tips on BCCI Flowed Freely for Years." *New York Times* Aug. 27, 1992, C1, C4.

"Clark Clifford, Law Partner Indicted in BCCI Fraud." *Mesa Tribune* July 30, 1992, A1.

Demick, Barbara. "Clifford Indicted in Bank Fraud." *Arizona Republic* July 30, 1992, A1, A7.

Frankel, Bruce. "Pair Deny BCCI Charges." *USA Today* July 30, 1992, 2A.

Puente, Maria. "Sen. Hatch Defends his Defense of BCCI." *USA Today* Aug. 27, 1992, 6A.

Baquet, Dean, and Jeff Gerth. "Lawmaker's Defense of BCCI Went Beyond Speech in Senate." *New York Times* Aug. 26, 1992, A1.

3.2 CHECK KITING OR AGGRESSIVE CASH MANAGEMENT AND E. F. HUTTON

E. F. Hutton was, in the 1970s, a highly profitable "retail" securities firm. In 1976, Hutton had a pretax profit margin of 15.5 percent. That year represented the high point in Hutton's earnings. It was in 1977 that Hutton developed a new strategy of full involvement in the capital markets instead of its previously limited focus on its primarily "retail" investors. Becoming a full-fledged investment banker proved to be more difficult than anticipated, and by the 1980s, Hutton's financial condition was growing worse as trading losses mounted.

On April 23, 1982, Perry H. Bacon, an E. F. Hutton branch manager from Alexandria, Virginia, wrote an inter-office memorandum to Steven R. Bralove, a manager of one of E. F. Hutton's offices in Washington, D.C. That memo was in response to Bralove's memo on Hutton's banking activities. Excerpts from the memo include:

> Our banking activities during the last six months have been no different than our banking activities off and on for the last five years. Additionally, *I believe those activities are encouraged by the firm and are in fact identical to what the firm practices on a national basis. Specifically, we will from time to time draw down not only deposits plus anticipated deposits, but also bogus deposits.*
>
> Furthermore, we (as a firm) learned to use the float because it is exactly what the banks do to us (see enclosed article). *I know of at least a dozen managers at E. F. Hutton — managers who along with Bill Sullivan and Tom Morley taught me the system — who do precisely the same thing.*[1]

Just prior to the time of the Bacon memo, a bank clerk in Genesee Country Bank in upstate New York received an $8 million check, something not seen everyday in Genesee. The $8 million check was from a New York branch office of E. F. Hutton. The bank's examiner, John Lounsbury, on that Friday, December 11, 1981, became suspicious. As he checked Hutton's account he found a new deposit of an $8 million check from United Penn Bank in Wilkes-Barre, Pennsylvania.

Lounsbury called United Penn to verify funds coverage. United Penn then discovered that the $8 million check was backed by another uncollected check drawn on another Hutton account in New York City.

Both banks reviewed their records and discovered churning. Both banks bounced both checks and notified the New York State banking authorities and the FDIC. The paperwork on the complaints shuffled around government agencies until May 1982. However, after regulators met with Hutton lawyers in February 1982, an in-house investigation, yielding the Bacon memo, resulted in a shutdown of the system. It was in 1984 that Albert Murray, an assistant U.S. Attorney in Pennsylvania, obtained the indictments against Hutton for what he called "Popeye's Wimpian School of Cash Management" — Hutton was paying on Tuesday for the use of funds today.

---

1. Chris Welles, "Why the E. F. Hutton Scandal May Be Far From Over," *Business Week* (Feb. 24, 1986): 99.

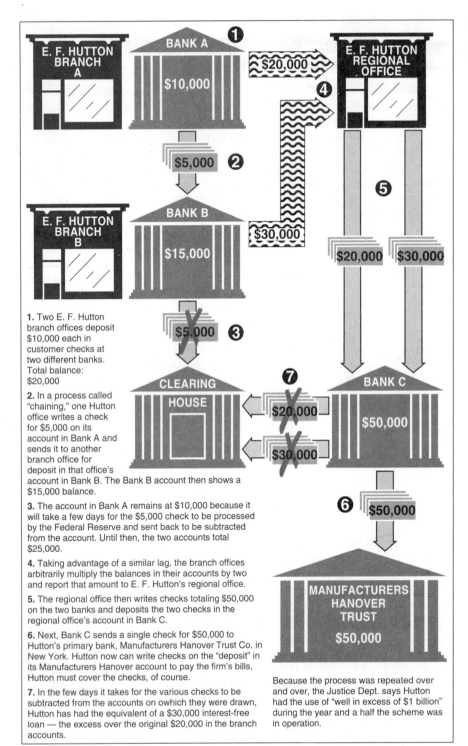

FIGURE 3-1
How E. F. Hutton Created Interest-Free "Loans" [2]

1. Two E. F. Hutton branch offices deposit $10,000 each in customer checks at two different banks. Total balance: $20,000

2. In a process called "chaining," one Hutton office writes a check for $5,000 on its account in Bank A and sends it to another branch office for deposit in that office's account in Bank B. The Bank B account then shows a $15,000 balance.

3. The account in Bank A remains at $10,000 because it will take a few days for the $5,000 check to be processed by the Federal Reserve and sent back to be subtracted from the account. Until then, the two accounts total $25,000.

4. Taking advantage of a similar lag, the branch offices arbitrarily multiply the balances in their accounts by two and report that amount to E. F. Hutton's regional office.

5. The regional office then writes checks totaling $50,000 on the two banks and deposits the two checks in the regional office's account in Bank C.

6. Next, Bank C sends a single check for $50,000 to Hutton's primary bank, Manufacturers Hanover Trust Co. in New York. Hutton now can write checks on the "deposit" in its Manufacturers Hanover account to pay the firm's bills. Hutton must cover the checks, of course.

7. In the few days it takes for the various checks to be subtracted from the accounts on owhich they were drawn, Hutton has had the equivalent of a $30,000 interest-free loan — the excess over the original $20,000 in the branch accounts.

Because the process was repeated over and over, the Justice Dept. says Hutton had the use of "well in excess of $1 billion" during the year and a half the scheme was in operation.

2. Anthony Bianco, et al., "What Did Hutton's Managers Know — And When Did They Know It?" *Business Week* (May 20, 1985): 111. Reprinted with permission.

The Bacon memo became an alleged "smoking gun" for the U.S. Justice Department in its indictment of E. F. Hutton & Co. for two thousand counts of wire and mail fraud. The Banking Authorities of New York and the FDIC discovered a billion-dollar pattern of fund shifting. Hutton pleaded guilty to the charges in 1985 and paid $2.75 million in fines and legal costs to the Justice Department and on May 2, 1985 agreed to make restitution to four hundred banks.

However, Hutton, in the eyes of some experts, simply used a scheme that permitted it access to bank funds of up to $250 million that was not illegal, and certainly not unusual. Hutton's system simply used banks that employ the "float factor." These banks do not use computer analysis for deposits and automatically give customer/depositors one-day availability on all checks.

By zeroing in on these banks, Hutton was able to have excessive overdrafts. Also, Hutton used a process called chaining in which checks that are overdrafts are funneled through the system to various banks so that the float period is an interest-earning period even when there is actually no money passing through the system. Figure 3-1 is a diagram from *Business Week* that illustrates the complexity of the transfers and the ability of Hutton to earn interest on funds that did not really exist for the time interest was earned.

Marshall Sokol, president of MDS Companies of New York evaluated Hutton's activities and felt that Hutton violated business ethics but could have won the case if it had gone to trial:

> All Hutton did was take advantage of the fact that some banks cannot differentiate between ledger and available balances. Hutton was depositing funds that were not immediately available but treating them as if they were. Banks were honoring those checks, and Hutton was covering them.[3]

Professor Bernell K. Stone, professor of banking at the Georgia Institute of Technology notes:

> What Hutton did was probably illegal, but it all depends on how you interpret the vague ambiguous laws. What the case shows is that there is a clear need to clarify the law ... There was no valid business reason for writing those checks (as explained in Figure 3-1). Hutton added them in with other checks it deposited because it was easier to disguise them.[4]

Another comment by Raoul D. Edwards, a banking expert, notes the risk of the Hutton system:

> Was it a crime? Consider one question: What would have happened to the nation's banking system if E. F. Hutton, for any reason, had gone belly up with $250 million drawn from banks without compensation or replacement?[5]

E. F. Hutton hired former Attorney General Griffin Bell to conduct an internal investigation of the check-overdraft scheme. Bell's report concluded that there

---

3. "A Violation of Business Ethics or Outright Fraud," *ABA Banking Journal* (July 1985): 30.

4. *Ibid.*, at 31.

5. Raoul Edwards, "When E. F. Hutton Talks ...," *United States Banker* (July 1985): 4.

was a "relatively loose management structure between 1980 and 1982 with overlapping and often vague reporting responsibilities."[6] Bell concluded the banks involved did not lose money, but there was unethical conduct in the form of "excessive and abusive overdrafts."[7] Bell indicated only 29 percent of the banks Hutton dealt with had filed, or were considering filing, claims. Bell's conclusion: "What we are really dealing with is corporate ethics."[8] An anonymous observer noted, "Hutton pulled a fast one on other players in the game. And it was only able to do that because of its size. Do you think a small bank or manufacturing firm could have gotten away with what Hutton did?"[9]

Discussion Questions

1. What moral standards were violated by the check scheme?
2. Is this a case where the branch managers decided to "cheat the banks out of millions in interest by shady management of accounts with them"?[10]
3. Suppose you were Steve Bralove and you received the Bacon memo. What action would you take? Would it be difficult to take action because most of the branches were doing it?
4. How would you respond if, as Bralove, you raised your concerns and received the response, "Well, that's the way it's always been done"?
5. Would the mounting pressure of financial losses have contributed to the check-kiting?

SOURCES

"Hutton Pleads Guilty to 2,000 Counts of Fraud." *Dun's Business Month* June 1985, 19.

Donnelly, Barbara. "The Man Who Nailed Hutton." *Institutional Investor* Sept. 1985, 80–83.

McMurray, Scott, and A. Pasztor. "Hutton Group Suffers in Series of Reverses in Wake of Overdrafts." *Wall Street Journal* Apr. 9, 1986, 1.

Longs, Perrin H. "What Went Wrong at E. F. Hutton?" *Institutional Investor* Sept. 1989, 35.

Wallace, G. David, and Stan Crock. "The Hutton Investigation: Speaking Softly and Carrying No Stick." *Business Week* Sept. 23, 1985, 34.

Gillespie, Richard J. "Memo in Spotlight at Hearing" *Pensions & Investment Age* Sept. 2, 1985, 13–14.

"E. F. Hutton's Spokesman Idea a "Cos" Celebre." *Advertising Age* April 21, 1986, 1.

---

6. David Cook, and John Yemma, "Bell Probe of E. F. Hutton Check Scam Finds Conduct Unethical," *The Christian Science Monitor* (Sept. 6, 1985): 5.

7. *Ibid.*

8. *Ibid.*

9. "Hutton Aftermath: A Violation of Business Ethics or Outright Fraud?" *ABA Banking Journal* 77 (July 1985): 30–31.

10. Edwards, 4.

3.3 MEDICAL BILLING ERRORS AND PRACTICES

Billie Jean Young is the administrator for Los Lomas, a private hospital located in Palm Springs, California. Los Lomas hospital serves patients who carry insurance in 95 percent of the procedures they have performed. The noninsurance procedures tend to be plastic surgery and all plastic surgery patients pay in advance. The nature of the medical business is largely the result of Los Lomas' location in a retirement/resort area of the upper-middle class.

A recent study shows that 98 percent of all hospital bills have errors. Internal data for Los Lomas shows that complaints of errors are received on approximately 20 percent of the bills.

There is some indication that doctors are "fudging" on insurance claims. For example, coding the removal of a mole as a larger procedure (known as "upcoding") will bring additional funds from an insurer. Breaking down surgeries ("unbundling") into portions such as exploration, removal, and repair of scar tissue will result in substantial increases in claims. Testing can be broken down so that a single blood sample's cost can be tripled ("exploding") by itemizing each test done. These billing strategies are all accomplished by savvy use of the coding process.

Insurers do have computer programs to check for "code creeps" (increased billing by coding), but often such claims are rejected in a report to the patient that explains the charges exceed "usual and customary limits." The patient must then pay personally the amounts considered excessive.

In many cases, miscoding is done to help provide the patients with insurance coverage when coverage might not otherwise be available. For example, routine tests as part of a physical might not be covered. Those same tests, if coded to "rule out cancer," would be covered. Infertility procedures would not be covered but diagnostic surgery to determine the presence of endometriosis would be covered.

Many of these practices result from the inability to collect bills from uninsured patients who are simply unable to pay. Hospitals often use billings for insured patients to cover the costs they must absorb in providing care for uninsured patients. For example, a Florida hospital charged a patient $15 for one ounce of petroleum jelly. However, the five digit CPT coding system is complex, confusing, and fraught with ambiguities. Some errors are the result of these factors.

Medicare recently announced a "bundling" payment policy for heart surgeries. It will pay a package price for coronary by-pass surgeries. The price will include all charges for both hospitals and doctors. Medicare officials maintain "unbundled" bills encourage doctors to do more procedures. Doctors maintain their autonomy in treatment decisions and quality of care will be sacrificed.

Discussion Questions

1. Should Ms. Young commission a study of the billing practices of Los Lomas and implement any changes that would correct the described overbilling?
2. Will Ms. Young be able to have any impact on physician's conduct in coding?

3. Is anyone really harmed by fudging, upcoding, exploding and unbundling? Aren't many patients helped by these practices?
4. If patients are not complaining, is it a wise use of resources to audit bills?

SOURCES

Rundle, Rhonda. "How Doctors Boost Bills by Misrepresenting the Work They Do." *Wall Street Journal* Dec. 6, 1989, A1.

Winslow, Ron. "Medicare Tries to Save With One-Fee Billing for Some Operations." *Wall Street Journal* June 10, 1992, A1 and A5.

Marshall, Steve. "Overcharges Force New Rx in Fla. Hospitals." *USA Today* July 6, 1992, 1A.

3.4 MINISCRIBE AND THE AUDITORS

MiniScribe, founded in 1980, and based in Longmont, Colorado, was a disk drive manufacturer. When MiniScribe hit a slump in the mid–1980s because it lost its largest customer, IBM, the board of directors brought in Q. T. Wiles. Wiles had been called the "Mr. Fix-It" of high technology industries having turned around Adobe Systems, Granger Associates and Silicon General, Inc.

When Wiles took over, he engaged the venture-capital and investment banking firm of Hambrecht & Quist to raise the capital needed for the firm's turnaround. Hambrecht & Quist raised $20 million in 1987 through the sale of debentures. Wiles, was, at that time, the chairman of Hambrecht & Quist. Hambrecht & Quist purchased $7.5 million of the debentures and also purchased a 17 percent interest in MiniScribe.

With the new capital and cost cuts, MiniScribe's sales went from $113.9 million in 1985 to a projected $603 million in 1988. MiniScribe's board asked Wiles in 1987 to stay on for another three years. MiniScribe's stock climbed to $14 per share.

During 1988, the computer industry began another slump and by May, Wiles and other officers were selling stock. Wiles sold 150,000 shares for $11–$12 and seven other officers sold 200,000 shares.

By the time the shares were sold, MiniScribe was in the unenviable position of high inventory and high receivables. Industry sales were down and MiniScribe customers were not paying. In early 1989, MiniScribe announced a $14.6 million loss for the final quarter of 1988. MiniScribe's ratio of inventory to sales was 33 percent (industry average was 24 percent) and its receivables were ninety-four days behind (industry average was seventy). The amount of receivables went from $109 million to $173 million in the last quarter of 1988.

The result of the release of the new financial information was an in-house audit, shareholder lawsuits and an investigation of stock trading by the Securities Exchange Commission. Scrutiny by regulators, outside directors and the SEC revealed that Wiles, through his unrealistic sales goals, had created an environment of high pressure for managers. As managers were interviewed they described "dash meetings" in which Wiles spouted his management philosophies. In one such meeting, Wiles had two controllers stand as he fired them, saying, "That's just to show everyone I'm in control of the company."[1] Wiles' attorney describes him as "fairly autocratic and very demanding of the people who work for him."[2]

The in-house audit uncovered that by late 1986, financial results became the sole criterion for performance evaluations and bonuses at MiniScribe. To be certain the numbers for sales were hit, the investigations revealed that creative accounting maneuvers were used. For example, in one case a customer was shipped two times as many disk drives as had been ordered — at a value of $9 million. Although the extra drives were returned, the sale for all the drives had already been booked.

---

1. Andy Zipser, "Recipe for Sales Led to Cooked Book," *Denver Post* (August 14, 1989): 2B–3B.
2. *Ibid.*

Other details of the investigation revealed that, in some orders, sales were booked at the time of shipment even though title would not pass to the customer until completion of shipment. An examination of the financial records showed that manipulation of reserves was used to offset losses. MiniScribe posted only 1 percent as reserves whereas the industry range was 4–10 percent. In some of the cases uncovered in the audit, shipments sent to MiniScribe warehouses were booked as sales when, in fact, customers were not even invoiced until the drives were shipped from the warehouse.

MiniScribe officers were successful in creating many appearances for the firm's auditors, Coopers & Lybrand. For example, for the 1987 audited financials, company officials packaged and shipped construction bricks (pretend inventory valued at $3.66 million) so that these products would count as retail sales. When bricks were returned, the sales were reversed but inventory increased. Obsolete parts and scraps were rewrapped as products and shipped to warehouses to be counted in inventory.

It was discovered that during the 1986 audit by Coopers & Lybrand, company officials broke into trunks that contained the auditors' work papers and increased the year-end inventory figures.

With the disclosure of the internal audit and the discovery of these creative accounting practices and inventory deceptions, MiniScribe's stock continued to drop, selling for $1.31 per share by September, 1989. By 1990, MiniScribe had filed for bankruptcy and was purchased by Maxtor Corporation.

Lawsuits against Hambrecht & Quist, Wiles, and Coopers & Lybrand were brought by Kempner Capital Management and U.S. National Bank of Galveston and eleven other investors in the debentures sold by Hambrecht & Quist. In February 1992, a jury awarded the investors $28.7 million in compensatory damages and $530 million in punitive damages. Coopers & Lybrand was held responsible for $200 million, Wiles for $250 million, Hambrecht & Quist for $45 million, and Mr. Hambrecht for $35 million.

Discussion Questions

1. What types of pressures led to the "cooked books" by managers at MiniScribe?
2. Were the auditors, Coopers & Lybrand, morally responsible for the investors' losses?
3. Suppose you were a manager who was asked to wrap construction bricks in disk drive packaging. Would you ask, "Why?" Would you be able to continue your employment? Would you be morally responsible for the investors' losses by wrapping the bricks?
4. Would the internal control people (internal auditors) at MiniScribe be morally responsible for the investors' losses?
5. Were the auditors just duped? Should auditors be held responsible for investors' losses when they are tricked?

SOURCES

Sleeth, Peter. "MiniScribe Stock Plunges 36%." *The Denver Post* Sept. 13, 1989, 1D.

Pollack, Andrew. "The $550 Million Verdict." *New York Times* Feb. 9, 1992, C2.

Pollack, Andrew. "Large Award in MiniScribe Fraud Suit." *New York Times* Feb. 5, 1992, C1.

Sleeth, Peter. "Audit to Compound MiniScribe's Troubles." *The Denver Post* Aug. 6, 1989, 1H - 7H.

Schneider, Michelle. "MiniScribe Execs Rigged Huge Fraud, Audit Says." *Rocky Mountain News* Sept. 12, 1989, 1B - 2B.

Sleeth, Peter. "MiniScribe Details 'Massive Fraud.'" *The Denver Post* Sept. 12, 1989, 1C and 4C.

"ITT Qume Chief Named President at MiniScribe." *Electronic News* Nov. 5, 1984, 20–21.

Zipper, Stuart. "MiniScribe Seeks Chapter 11 Sale of Firm for $160M." *Electronic News* Jan. 8, 1990, 1 and 54.

"Internal Probe Underway by Directors at MiniScribe." *Electronic News* May 29, 1989, 19.

Zipper, Stuart. "Filings Reveal MiniScribe Struggle." *Electronic News* Jan. 15, 1990, 38 and 40.

3.5 THE MANAGER'S TURN AT THE CASH REGISTER

Jay Hunt was the night manager at an Alphacom Super Store, a nine-store grocery chain in Wyoming. Hunt managed the Laramie store. At least once each night, Hunt took over the cash register for Paula Simpson, a student and young mother who worked the night shift while her husband watched their eighteen-month old son and studied. Her husband, Tom, was in his second year of law school at the University of Wyoming School of Law. Paula was generally the only cashier on duty with Hunt, although others were available on call as needed.

When Hunt came to take over the cash register, he would tell Paula, "Go take a break, Paula. Put your feet up for a few minutes. I can handle things for awhile. Go in the back room where the phone is and if things get busy, I'll buzz for help."

Paula was always grateful for the break that Hunt gave her in addition to her other shift breaks and used the time to study for her classes. Paula was six credit hours away from her degree in speech pathology. Paula felt Jay Hunt was the most compassionate boss she had ever had.

One night Paula returned from the back room after twenty minutes. She usually took a thirty-minute "rest." She noticed that Hunt's girlfriend was at the checkout and had purchased a substantial order. Hunt was just finishing the order on the cash register, and Paula helped bag the groceries.

The next week the regional manager for Alphacom was in the store during Paula's shift. She overheard him use the term "sweethearting" and complain that the store had shortages. When the manager left, Paula asked Hunt, "What is sweethearting?" Hunt replied, "Oh, that's when you only ring up part of someone's merchandise or you don't ring it up at all. You haven't been doing that, have you, Paula? Because we've got a real shortage problem here at the store." Paula assured Hunt that she would never cheat the store because her job was too important to her and her family.

That night Paula had her usual extra break from Hunt. Instead of heading to the backroom, she waited near the deli section where she could hear but not be seen. Hunt's girlfriend came in and shopped for her usual large grocery order. When Hunt checked out the order, Paula heard him say, "The regional manager is on to something. You better pay for this one tonight until this blows over. I can't risk ringing up only half of this stuff right now."

Paula sank into the backroom and wondered if she should tell anyone. She needed the job but she was likely to get blamed for shortages since she was the only night cashier. If she reported Hunt, she would lose her job for sure especially since she had no direct proof. She had only overheard a conversation. She could tell Tom but he would only make her report it. The regional manager was staying at the Holiday Inn and would be leaving in the morning.

Discussion Questions

1. If you were Paula, would you talk to the regional manager?
2. Is Hunt's conduct Paula's responsibility?
3. Is Hunt stealing?
4. Is Paula helping in the commission of a crime?

5. What if Hunt told Paula he would back her up 100 percent — that there was no way she was doing any sweethearting because Hunt watched her all the time?

Section B

Conflicts Between the Corporation's Ethical Code and Accepted Business Practices in Foreign Countries

Although we have a global market, we do not have global safety laws, ethical standards or cultural customs. Businesses face many dilemmas as they decide whether to conform to varying standards of various nations or attempt to operate with universal (global) standards.

3.6 UNION CARBIDE AND BHOPAL

Bhopal is a city in central India with a population of 800,000. Home to the largest mosque in India, Bhopal is a major railway junction. Its main industries consist of manufacturing heavy electrical equipment, weaving and printing cotton cloth and flour milling.

The construction of a Union Carbide plant in Bhopal in 1969 along with the creation of Union Carbide India, Ltd., a 51 percent-owned subsidiary of American Union Carbide Corporation, based in Danbury, Connecticut, were welcomed by the Indian government for several reasons. First, the plant would produce pesticides — a needed aid for India's agricultural productivity. Second, the plant would provide an economic boost for Bhopal and India by creating jobs. Finally, the plant would provide management training for local employees because the day-to-day management of the plant was to be left to Indian managers.

The Bhopal plant was attractive to Union Carbide because of low labor costs, very low taxes, and safety standards far less stringent than those imposed by OSHA and EPA on U.S. chemical plants.

The match of Union Carbide with Bhopal was not a perfect one. By 1980, the Bhopal plant was consistently posting annual losses. American Union Carbide considered closing the plant but was persuaded by government officials to let the plant remain open because of its contributions to the Bhopal and Indian economies.

The plant at Bhopal manufactured pesticides and used methyl isocyanate (MIC) gas in the process. MIC is a highly toxic chemical that reacts strongly with any other agent — even nontoxic substances such as water.

In the early morning hours of December 3, 1984, the MIC in a tank at the Bhopal plant was contaminated with water or some other substance and the reaction was an explosive boiling in the tank. Back-up safety systems, including cooling units, did not function properly.

Workers began to feel at first only burning eyes, but slowly, as the gas from the mixture leaked, they began choking. Eventually, the pressure from the MIC interaction in the tank caused the tank's safety valves to explode and a white cloud of noxious fumes escaped through a pipestack and out to the city of Bhopal.

Near the Bhopal plant were the shanty towns comprised of huts and tents filled with Bhopal's poorest. The white cloud of toxins drifted over these makeshift residences. By the time the toxicity dissolved, thirty-five hundred city residents were left dead and two hundred thousand others were blinded, burned, or left with lesions in their respiratory systems.

The long-term damage to health continued long after the night of the accident. One-fourth of the women who were in the first trimester of pregnancy at the time of the leak miscarried or had children born prematurely or with birth defects. Children in Bhopal have chronic breathing problems. Smaller children died after months of vomiting following the accident. Many children suffer from large boils that will not heal. For those victims from the shanty towns, their tuberculosis was aggravated by the use of steroids to help their breathing problems.

Within the first year following the accident, the Indian government spent $40 million for food and medical care for Bhopal victims. Union Carbide's then-chairman, Warren M. Anderson, in initial press accounts, said the company would get quick relief to the victims and that he would devote the remainder of his career to solving problems resulting from the accident. Within a year, Anderson responded, "I overreacted. Maybe they, early on, thought we'd give the store away. [Now] we're in a litigation mode. I'm not going to roll over and play dead."[1]

Carbide's stock fell sixteen points following the accident and it became a takeover target. GAF Corporation, a small chemical company, made a takeover offer during the depressed stock price period with financing from junk bonds. Union Carbide bought 56 percent of its stock, incurring $3.3 billion in debt. The company remained on the self-described "defensive" through 1992 as it coped with Bhopal, the debt from the thwarted takeover and the fast changing chemical industry.[2]

By December 7, 1984, just four days after the accident, more than one hundred lawsuits were brought in federal district court by American lawyers on behalf of Bhopal victims. The Indian government, determined to recover U.S. levels of compensation for its victims, sued on behalf of the victims in the U.S. in 1985. Eventually the cases were moved to India as a more appropriate forum.

The Indian Supreme Court upheld a $465 million settlement agreement reached between Union Carbide and the Indian government on February 14, 1988.

There were 592,635 claims filed with the Indian government by Bhopal victims seeking compensation for physical and psychological injuries. The government accepted 200,000 of those claims. Government officials expected the number to reach 400,000. The victims would thus receive about $1,000 each. Ordinarily, when a government bus or train runs over an Indian, the payment to the victim or the victim's family would be $130 to $700.

In spite of the settlement of the civil case, the Indian government continued with criminal proceedings. Warren Anderson, although retired in 1986, has been ordered by a magistrate in Bhopal to answer for charges of culpable homicide. Lawyers for Anderson say the court has no jurisdiction.

In May 1992, the same magistrate seized all of Union Carbide's assets in India at the request of the Indian government. The reason for the requested seizure was Union Carbide's announcement that it would be selling its 50 percent stake in Union Carbide India, Ltd. As part of that announcement, Carbide indicated it would use about $17 million from the sale proceeds to build a hospital in Bhopal to treat victims of the accident, following a suggestion by India's Supreme Court.

The plant no longer makes pesticides, but dry-cell batteries.

---

1. Leslie Helm, et al., "Bhopal, A Year Later: Union Carbide Takes a Tougher Line," *Business Week* (Nov. 25, 1985): 96–101.

2. Scott McMurray, "Union Carbide Offers Some Sober Lessons in Crisis Management," *Wall Street Journal* (Jan. 28, 1992): A1.

Discussion Questions

1. Should the Bhopal plant have been operated using U.S. safety and environmental standards?
2. Would Union Carbide's settlement figure have been higher if the accident had occurred in the U.S.?
3. What were the costs to Union Carbide of the Bhopal accident?
4. Who is morally responsible for the deaths and injuries at Bhopal?
5. Was the seizure of Union Carbide's Indian assets appropriate action for the Indian government to take?

SOURCES

Spaeth, Anthony. "Court Settlement Stuns Bhopal Survivors." *Wall Street Journal* Feb. 22, 1989, A12.

Dockser, Amy. "U.S. Lawyers Seek Share of Money in Settlement of Bhopal Litigation." *Wall Street Journal* Feb. 16, 1989, B8.

Adler, Stephen, and Stephen Wermiel. "India's Justices Approve Settlement." *Wall Street Journal* Jan. 2, 1990, B4.

Adler, Stephen. "Bhopal Ruling Tests Novel Legal Theory." *Wall Street Journal* May 18, 1988, 33.

"Under a Noxious Cloud of Fear." *Time* Aug. 26, 1985, 13.

Harris, Marilyn, and Resa Kinin. "The Threat That's Stirring Carbide's Survival Instincts." *Business Week* Sep. 16, 1985, 25.

Glaberson, William, et al. "India's Bhopal Suit Could Change All the Rules." *Business Week* Apr. 22, 1985, 38.

Koenig, Richard, and S. Adler. "Experts Doubt India's Ability to Push Carbide." *Wall Street Journal,* Jan. 23, 1990, B8.

McMurray, Scott, and Christi Harian. "Carbide's Assets in India Ordered Seized." *Wall Street Journal* May 1, 1992, B5.

3.7 PRODUCT DUMPING

Once the Consumer Product Safety Commission prohibits the sale of a particular product in the United States, a manufacturer can no longer sell the product to wholesalers or retailers in the United States. However, the product can be sold in other countries that have not prohibited its sale. The same is true of other countries' sales to the United States. For example, the sale of the prescription sleeping pill, Halcion, was outlawed in Great Britain, but sales continue in the United States. The conclusion of the medical community in Great Britain regarding the pill's safety was different from the conclusion reached by the medical community and the Food and Drug Administration here. Studies on the drug differed, and some researchers simply concluded that stronger warning labels were needed.

The Consumer Product Safety Commission outlawed the sale of three-wheel all terrain cycles in the United States in 1988. While some manufacturers had already turned to a four-wheel model, other manufacturers still had inventories of the three-wheel cycle. Testimony on the cycles covered a wide range: the vehicles themselves were inherently dangerous, or the vehicles were safe but the drivers too young, too inexperienced and more inclined to take risks (i.e., "hot dog"). However, the three-wheel, outlawed vehicles can still be sold outside the United States.

For many companies, chaos follows a product recall because inventory of the recalled product may be at high levels. Often the firms are faced with the decision of "dumping" the product in other countries or taking a large write-off that negatively affects earnings, stock price and employment stability.

Discussion Questions

1. If you were a manufacturer holding a substantial inventory of a product that had been outlawed in the United States, would you have any ethical concerns about selling the product in countries outside the United States where there were no prohibitions?

2. Suppose the inventory write-down that you will be forced to take because of the regulatory obsolescence is material — nearly a 20 percent reduction in income will result. If you can sell the inventory in a foreign market, legally, there will be no write-down and no income reduction. An income reduction of that magnitude will have a substantial impact on share market price. The impact on price will cause your large, institutional shareholders to demand explanations and possibly seek changes in the board of directors. In short, the write-down will set off a wave of events that will change the structure and stability of the firm. Would you feel justified in selling the product legally in another country?

3. In selling the product in another country, is it simply a matter of believing one aspect of the evidence — that the product is safe?

4. Would you include any warnings with the product?

SOURCES

"Outlawing a Three-Wheeler." *Time* Jan. 11, 1988, 59.
"The Price of a Good Night's Sleep." *New York Times* Jan. 26, 1992, E9.

3.8 THE TABOO OF WOMEN IN MANAGEMENT

Burns & McCallister is an international management consulting firm. Burns & McCallister is listed by *Working Mother* magazine as one of the top fifty firms in the United States for employment of working mothers and listed as one of the top ten firms for women by *Working Woman* magazine. Burns & McCallister has earned this reputation because of several factors. First, nearly 50 percent of its partners are women. Second, it has a menu of employee benefits including such things as flex hours, sabbaticals, family leave, home-based work and part-time partner-track positions.

However, Burns & McCallister has recently been the subject of a series of reports by both the *Los Angeles Times* and the *New York Times* because its policy on female executives in certain nations has become public. Burns & McCallister has learned, through its fifty years of consulting, that there are certain countries in which they negotiate for contracts where women cannot be used in the negotiation process. The cultures of many of these countries is such that women are not permitted to speak in a meeting of men. Burns & McCallister has thus implemented a policy prohibiting women partners from being assigned these potential account negotiations and later the accounts themselves. Clerical help in the offices can be female, but any contact with the client can be only through a male partner or account executive.

For example, Japan still has a two-track hiring system with only 3 percent of professional positions open to women. The remainder of the women in the workforce become office ladies who file, wear uniforms and serve tea. Dentsu, Inc., a large Japanese ad firm, had a picture of the typical Dentsu "Working Girl" in its recruiting brochure. Surrounding the photo are comments primarily about her physical appearance: (1) Her breasts are "pretty large." (2) Her bottom is "rather soft."

Burns & McCallister is being criticized for its posture. The head of Burns & McCallister's New York office has explained:

> "Look, we're about as progressive a firm as you'll find. But the reality of international business is that if we try to use women, we don't get the job. It's not a policy on all foreign accounts. We've just identified certain cultures in which women will not be able to successfully land or work on accounts. This restriction does not interfere with their career track. It does not apply in all countries."

The National Organization for Women (NOW) would like Burns & McCallister to take the position that its standards in the United States apply to all its operations. No restrictions are placed on women here, and other cultures should adapt to our standards; we should not change our standards to adapt to their culture. NOW maintains that without such a posture, change can never come about.

Discussion Questions

1. Do you agree with Burns & McCallister's policy for certain cultures with regard to women partners?

2. Is Burns & McCallister doing anything that violates federal employment discrimination laws?
3. Given Burns & McCallister's record with regard to women, is the issue really relevant to women's advancement in the firm?
4. What if the cultures in which the prohibition of women applied traditionally bring in the highest dollar accounts? Would your opinion regarding the posture be different?
5. Do you agree with the position that change can never come about if Burns & McCallister does not take a stand?
6. Would Burns & McCallister be sacrificing revenues in changing its policies? Is this an appropriate sacrifice?

SOURCE

Holden, Ted, and Jennifer Wiener. "Revenge of the 'Office Ladies.'" *Business Week* July 13, 1992, 42–43.

3.9 TOSHIBA AND THE SOVIETS

Toshiba Machine Company is a subsidiary of Toshiba Corporation of Japan. Toshiba Machine sold steel pipe, drilling equipment, bulldozers and dump trucks for construction and mining to the Soviet Union.

Kazuo Kumagai was a trade representative for Wako Koeki Company, a Japanese trading company that handled Toshiba's and other company's exports. Regulations prohibited the Japanese from exporting to the Soviet Union items such as scientific testing equipment, high-tech composite fibers and armored vehicles. However, these equipment requests were often part of large orders placed by the Soviets for routine items like construction cranes and squid catchers. As a result, Kumagai and his supervisors did not always catch the illegal items.

In 1980, Kumagai arranged, along with a Norwegian firm, for the sale of eight robotized milling machines that were sophisticated enough to produce propellers for large ships. It was later discovered that the machines were used to make propellers for Soviet submarines that were quieter and more difficult to detect in military operations.

Five years after the transaction, Kumagai left Wako Koeki and informed government officials about the transaction and others he witnessed during his twenty-two years of work on Soviet trade for the Japanese. His documentation was limited, but he observed that Japan was pursuing deals regardless of the impact on international and national security:

> It was as if they dangled a delicious fruit in front of a hungry man. My company demanded results. I have a conscience, but I also have a family on my shoulder. Other companies were under the same pressures. Others were doing that too. Toshiba is only the tip of the iceberg.[1]

Shortly after Kumagai's revelation, Congress banned Toshiba goods in military stores and U.S. consumers began boycotts. Demonstrations against Toshiba were held on Capitol Hill.

A two-month investigation by lawyers and Price Waterhouse found that Toshiba executives did not know of the sales because of their hands-off management style. Also, the investigation revealed that a French machine toolmaker may have sold the same type of machines to the Soviets as early as 1974. As a result of the investigation, Toshiba agreed to set up a control division to scrutinize exports to the Soviets.

The Chief Executive Officer and Chairman of the Board of Toshiba, Shoichi Saba, resigned following the investigation. *Forbes* magazine described the resignation as follows:

> In a U.S. company the chief executive might have fired some subordinates and announced he had cleaned house of the malefactors, but in Japan it is different. The person on top bears full responsibility for what his subordinates do.[2]

---

1. Damon Darlin, "Japanese Firms' Push to Sell to Soviets Led to Security Breaches," *Wall Street Journal* (Aug. 4, 1987): 1.

2. Andrew Tanzer, "The Man Toshiba Hung Out to Dry," *Forbes* (Sept. 7, 1987): 94.

Eventually, a Trade Bill was passed that imposed sanctions on Toshiba. The Pentagon awarded a $104 million lap-top computer contract to Zenith instead of Toshiba.

Discussion Questions

1. Was the milling equipment legal without the military use?
2. Why did Kumagai remain silent for five years?
3. Would records have helped Kumagai with his disclosures?
4. Was anyone really harmed by the shipment, or by the quieter submarines?
5. Suppose history had taken a different turn and there was a loss of lives because of the Japanese equipment shipments. Who would be morally responsible for those deaths?
6. Evaluate the ethics of Toshiba's resigned chairman and Chief Executive Officer, Shoichi Saba.

SOURCES

"Toshiba Products Ordered Out of Military Stores as Punishment." *Arizona Business Gazette* Aug. 3, 1987, B8.

Armstrong, Larry, et al. "The Toshiba Scandal Has Exporters Running for Cover." *Business Week* July 20, 1987, 86–87.

Honigsbaum, Mark. "Toshiba Urges U.S. to Rethink Sanctions After Export-Case Probe." *Electronic News* Sept. 14, 1987, 8.

Smart, Tim, and J. Weber. "Why Congress is Letting Toshiba Off the Hook." *Business Week* Apr. 4, 1988, 34–35.

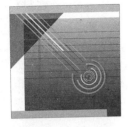

SECTION C
UNAUTHORIZED PAYMENTS TO FOREIGN OFFICIALS

What we would call a bribe and illegal in the United States may be culturally acceptable and necessary in another country. Could you participate?

3.10 THE ADOPTION AGENCY AND SENIOR JOSE'S FEES

Ninos and Ninas, Inc., is an adoption agency located in El Paso, Texas, that focuses on international adoptions. Most of the infants Ninos and Ninas places are from South American countries.

Couples, primarily from the United States, work with the Ninos and Ninas agency to adopt children. The fee for Ninos and Ninas' work ranges from $15,000–$20,000. Couples pay the fee willingly because of the agency's twenty-year history of excellent work and its extensive knowledge of requirements for adoption of the infants in South American countries.

Joan and David Ryan have applied with Ninos and Ninas for the adoption of a child. Their U.S. certification is complete and they have submitted their application along with a $10,000 deposit to Ninos and Ninas.

After their application is processed, the Ryans receive a notice from Esther Tomkin, Ninos and Ninas' director of adoption services, that a baby girl is now available. Ms. Tomkin instructs them that she will need an additional $5,000 as well as $5,000 in cash in unmarked bills in an envelope to be placed in a postal box located in El Paso. Ms. Tomkins' letter explains:

> You should bring the $5,000 with you when you come to El Paso to pick up your new daughter. Once you have paid the $5,000 to Ninos and Ninas and deposited the $5,000 in cash, you will have your little girl within 24 hours. You should be prepared to come to El Paso on April 10. The envelope with the cash should be marked for "Senior Jose."

130

Joan is concerned about the odd cash payment and phones Ms. Tomkin to discuss it. Ms. Tomkin assures Joan that "the payment is just the way adoption works in these countries. It is not a bribe; it is not a violation of the Foreign Corrupt Practices Act; it is simply a requirement to get the adoption paper work through. Your adoption just can't get through the system without it. This is the way we've been doing business for 20 years." Joan asks, "Who is Senior Jose?" Ms. Tomkin responds, "He is just an official in the social agency that handles adoptions. He isn't even the judge that approves the adoption. Without this money, your little girl ends up a street child or malnourished in an orphanage."

Discussion Questions

1. Would the payment to Senior Jose violate U.S. laws? Does the international nature of the adoption agency's operations affect its operational standards?
2. Is the payment a bribe or a grease payment? Is there a difference? Does the fact that the payment is legal control in the determination of whether it is ethical?
3. Does the benefit for the infant girl counteract the method for accomplishing that benefit?
4. Would you go forward with the adoption?
5. Would you feel comfortable working for Ninos and Ninas?

SECTION D
WORKPLACE SAFETY

Some issues of safety evolve. There are no current regulations, but eventually workers will experience harm. How much responsibility does an employer have? Is an employer required to be proactive?

3.11 JOHNS-MANVILLE AND THE ASBESTOS EXPOSURE

A. Early History of Asbestos

Asbestos is a gray-white mineral that is heat-resistant and possesses great strength. It was mined in Canada and South Africa and processed at plants throughout the world. The largest processors were Johns-Manville, Raybestos-Manhattan, Pittsburgh- Corning, Owens-Corning, GAF, UNR, AMATEX, Owens-Illinois, Nicolet, Celotex, Eagle-Picher, Keene, Fibreboard, Standard Asbestos and Armstrong Cork. By the end of the asbestos drama, UNR, AMATEX and Manville would all declare Chapter 11 bankruptcy. The qualities of asbestos made it seem unique and irreplaceable. At the height of its use in the United States, it could be found in everything from hair dryers to potholders to brake drums.

While much of the public knowledge regarding the dangers of asbestos was gained after the litigation against asbestos manufacturers began, that body of knowledge had been building for some time. A retracing of the historical, scientific, medical, legislative and litigation events that led to the bankruptcy of Johns-Manville offers insight into the steady progression of this business crisis.

As early as 1 A.D., Strabo and Pliny the Elder mentioned a sickness of the lungs in slaves who had jobs weaving asbestos into cloth. Hippocrates (460–377 B.C.) described silicosis in a metal digger and noted that the man "breathes with great difficulty." Marco Polo even learned of the "mineral in the mountain" that contained threads like those of wool. Autopsies performed on stonecutters in 1672 by Ijsbrand van Diemerbroech, a professor of medicine at the University of

Utrecht, found that the vesicles of their lungs were so clogged with fine dust that it was like cutting through sand. In 1700, Bernardino Ramazzini, a professor of medicine at the University of Padua, suggested that stonecutters do their work with their backs to the wind.

It was in the late eighteenth century that the properties of asbestos were discovered by the Western World. The material came to be used as an insulator for boilers, steampipes, turbines, ovens, kilns, and any other high-temperature equipment. In 1819 in England, the workers who were grinding dry stones had such a high rate of silicosis (called "grinders asthma") that a proposal was made that criminals should be used for the task.

B. The Connection Between Industrial Dust and Lung Disease

The problem of lung-dust infestation came to light in the United States in 1887 when an autopsy was performed on a stove-foundry worker from Poughkeepsie, New York. The lungs showed the presence of silicosis. In 1898, Henry Ward Johns, the founder of H. W. Johns Manufacturing (forerunner of Johns-Manville) died in Yonkers with his death certificate listing the cause of death as "dust phthisis pneumonia," or what appeared to be a description of asbestosis.

Dr. Montague Murray established a "presumptive connection" between a man's occupation as an asbestos-textile factory worker and severe pulmonary fibrosis. The disease killed a thirty-three-year-old man and Dr. Murray found spicules of asbestos in the man's lungs during the course of an autopsy in 1900.

After Dr. Murray's finding, other physicians reported finding a connection between asbestos workers' occupations and their deaths by lung disease. By 1918, the U.S. Government became involved in the health issues surrounding asbestos workers, and the Bureau of Labor Statistics published a report by statistician Frederick L. Hoffman that established that asbestos workers were experiencing unusually early deaths and that many American and Canadian insurance companies were no longer issuing policies to asbestos workers because of the assumed "health-injurious conditions" existing in the asbestos industry.

The first asbestosis death in medical literature was described in the *British Medical Journal* in 1924 by Dr. W. E. Cooke who gave the disease the name of asbestosis. Shortly after, state governments began to note worker's compensation claims being filed by asbestos workers. As early as 1928, Johns-Manville sponsored studies by Dr. Leroy U. Gardner who was able to produce asbestosis in test animals by allowing them to inhale asbestos fibers. These studies were not released and only uncovered through litigation in the *Borel* case in 1971.

The Medical Inspector of Factories for the British Home Office conducted an epidemiological study of asbestos workers in 1928 that showed, among other things, that workers who had been in the industry twenty years or more had an 81 percent rate of fibrosis. Based on the study findings, Parliament enacted legislation in 1931 designed to provide protection for asbestos workers. Subsequently, a study by Dr. Anthony Lanza for Metropolitan Life Insurance showed that 106 of 126 asbestos workers who were x-rayed had already developed asbestosis.

During this period of medical discovery in the asbestos industry, the so-called "silicosis suits" began to appear around the country. These workers, who alleged harmful exposure to silica dust and their resulting lung problems, brought suits that totaled $300 million by 1934. Motivated by increasing numbers of suits, several insurance companies made the recommendation that silicosis and other pulmonary dust diseases be taken out of the courts and covered under workers' compensation.

C. Johns-Manville's Initial Approach to Liability

It was also during this period of medical discovery and silicosis litigation that Johns-Manville experienced its first asbestos litigation. In 1933, the Board of Directors of Johns-Manville directed the CEO and president to settle eleven asbestosis lawsuits that had been brought in New Jersey courts against Johns-Manville by Samuel Greenstone, an attorney for the eleven workers involved. A $30,000 settlement payment was made in exchange for Greenstone's promise that he would not "directly or indirectly participate in the bringing of new actions against the Corporation."[1] The settlement terms were documented in the Board's minutes and were not revealed until discovery during litigation some forty-five years later. The minutes of the meeting were as follows:

> The President advised the meeting that Messrs. Hobart & Minard of Newark had been approached by the attorney for the plaintiffs in the eleven pending "asbestosis" cases with an offer to settle all the cases upon a much lower bases than had ever been previously discussed. He further stated that our general counsel, Messrs. Davis Polk Wardell Gardiner & Reed, as well as Messrs Hobart & Minard, had recommended that we settle for approximately $30,000 provided written assurances were obtained from the attorney for the various plaintiffs that he would not directly or indirectly participate in the bringing of new actions against the corporation.[2]

Johns-Manville was the largest producer of asbestos fiber in the United States. The fiber was then sold to other companies, as noted above, for its insulation qualities. Manville thus had the greatest exposure liability.

When Dr. Lanza was to submit his x-ray study results to the U.S. Public Health Service and was asked by one of Johns-Manville's attorneys, George S. Hobart and Vandiver Brown, a corporate attorney for Johns-Manville, to soften his description of his asbestosis studies in the report, Hobart remarked:

> It is only within a comparatively recent time that asbestosis has been recognized by the medical and scientific professions as a disease. One of our principal defenses in actions against the company on the common law theory of negligence has been that the scientific and medical knowledge has been insufficient until a very recent period to place upon the owners of plants or factories the burden of taking special precautions against the possible onset of the disease to their employees.[3]

Brown added the following in forwarding along Hobart's remarks:

---

1. Paul Brodeur, "The Asbestos Industry on Trial," *The New Yorker* (June 10, 1985): 64.

2. *Ibid.*

3. *Ibid.*, at 63.

I am sure that you understand fully that no one in our organization is suggesting for a moment that you alter by one jot or tittle any scientific facts or inevitable conclusions revealed or justified by your preliminary survey. All we ask is that all of the favorable aspects of the survey be included and that none of the unfavorable be unintentionally pictured in darker tones than the circumstances justify. I feel confident we can depend upon you ... to give us the 'break' and mine and Mr. Hobart's suggestions are presented in this spirit.[4]

By 1935, asbestosis was widely discussed at medical meetings and ongoing research was conducted. During that year, Vandiver Brown wrote to Sumner Simpson, the president of Raybestos-Manhattan. Through a series of letters, both agreed that asbestosis should not appear in any industry trade journals. However, Raybestos-Manhattan did join with other asbestos product manufacturers in sponsoring long-range research programs on the biological effects of asbestos. On October 1, 1935, Sumner Simpson sent a letter to Miss A. S. Rossiter, the editor of *ASBESTOS,* a trade magazine, that included the following language:

As I see it personally, we would be just as well off to say nothing about it until our survey is complete. I think the less said about asbestos, the better off we are, but at the same time, we cannot lose track of the fact that there have been a number of articles on asbestos dust control and asbestosis in the British trade magazines. The magazine ASBESTOS is in business to publish articles affecting the trade and they have been very decent about not re-printing the English articles.[5]

Vandiver Brown responded to the Simpson letter by writing directly and stated:

I quite agree with you that our interests are best served by having asbestosis receive a minimum of publicity.[6]

D. Widespread Medical Evidence of Asbestosis and Asbestos as a Carcinogen

As medical research progressed, it was discovered that there were two diseases that can result from exposure to asbestos dust. The first, the focus of the research, was asbestosis, which is a scarring of the lung tissue. Asbestosis does not appear immediately and may not manifest itself for ten to thirty years after initial exposure. During this time period, the worker or inhalant will appear healthy and normal and will experience no signs of asbestosis. However, inhaled asbestos fibers remain in the lungs. These fibers cause a tissue reaction in the lungs that continues to progress and is, apparently, irreversible. The result is a slow build-up of problems such as breathing difficulties severe enough to make any physical exertion impossible. The second disease, mesothelioma, is a malignant cancer of the chest lining and is extremely painful. This cancer has only

---

4. *Ibid.*

5. *Ibid.*

6. *Ibid.*

been associated with asbestos exposure and is generally fatal within one year after the symptoms appear. Like asbestosis, this malignant cancer may not appear for twenty years after initial exposure. For example, the mother of an asbestos worker, whose only exposure to asbestos came through washing his factory clothes in the 1960s, died of mesothelioma in 1983.

In 1936, Vandiver Brown and Sumner Simpson informed Dr. Leroy Gardner of their willingness to fund his asbestosis research, but a condition of the funding was a "bargain of silence." Gardner would be unable to publish the results of his work. In 1977, attorney Karl Asch discovered the agreement and the results of Gardner's work which indicated a connection between exposure to asbestos and pulmonary dust disease. Called the "Sumner Simpson papers," they were used by Asch as a "smoking gun" to show that Raybestos-Manhattan not only knew of the disease dangers but attempted to suppress the information.

The U.S. Public Health Service recommended in 1938 an average dust level of five million particles per cubic foot to be the acceptable level of exposure for American asbestos workers. However, research into asbestosis continued producing hundreds of medical journal articles on the disease. There were conflicting theories of what constituted an appropriate level of exposure with some research suggesting no level was appropriate.

In 1948, Dr. Kenneth Smith, the medical director for Canadian Johns-Manville, conducted an industrial hygiene survey of 708 men working at an asbestos plant in Quebec and discovered that only 4 of the men had x-rays that showed normal, healthy lungs. The findings were not published and were not revealed to the workers. The study results were not public until 1976 when litigation discovery revealed the study and the results.

Because of the mounting research findings, some workers began wearing respirators due to concerns about inhalation of asbestos dust. Finally, in the early 1950s, the information on asbestosis and asbestosis research made its way into the popular press. In 1952, the January issue of *Search*, a monthly journal of the California Tuberculosis Association, had a picture of Johns-Manville's Lompac, California plant and a caption that read, "Death by Dust." The articles in the journal described poor working conditions at the plant. In that same year, a week-long symposium was held on the subject of asbestos-related lung cancer but the results of the symposium were never published, and again, were discovered only during later litigation.

By 1955, unions for asbestos workers and miners began raising the issue of asbestosis. Also at this time, the general counsel for the Quebec Asbestos Mining Association (Johns-Manville was a leading member of the trade group) warned the members that asbestos exposure posed a serious health problem for the industry.

Shortly thereafter, Johns-Manville experienced an unprecedented third-party lawsuit for negligence and breach of warranty brought by Frederick LeGrand, a New Jersey asbestos insulator who had developed asbestosis. A similar suit was filed by another New Jersey insulator in 1961, and these two suits represented the beginning of a landslide of third-party liability suits Manville would experience over the next thirty years.

From 1961 to 1963, Dr. Silikoff conducted studies of asbestos workers. His work was presented at an international conference on the "Biological Effects of

Asbestos" where he concluded that asbestos workers were dying of lung disease at an epidemic rate.

E. The Beginning of the End — Manville's Litigation Crisis

In 1966, attorney Ward Stephenson filed suit against eleven asbestos manufacturers on behalf of his client, Claude Tomplait, an insulator who had developed asbestosis. This was Stephenson's first third-party liability case, but would not be his last. Stephenson also handled Clarence Borel's case, another insulator who sued several asbestos manufacturers. The trial court found for Borel, but, more significantly, the trial court verdict was upheld by the Fifth Circuit Court of Appeals. The appellate decision triggered 25,000 third-party asbestos lawsuits that would be brought against the asbestos manufacturers over the next decade. The 1973 *Borel*[7] decision marked the beginning of the end for the asbestos industry. The dramatic increase in asbestos litigation from 1974–1988 was tenfold.

By this time, OSHA had just been created by Congress and numerous recommendations were made to change the exposure levels for asbestos workers. Raybestos-Manhattan shut down its New Jersey plant in 1973 and Pittsburgh-Corning, faced with multimillion dollar claims against it, shut down its Tyler, Texas asbestos plant in 1974.

The 1974 annual report for Raybestos-Manhattan included the following language:

> For many years it has been known that prolonged inhalation of asbestos dust by factory workers could lead to disease. As early as 1930, Raybestos-Manhattan commissioned the Metropolitan Life Insurance Company to survey all of its factories and to make recommendations for the elimination of conditions which might present health hazards. Following presentations of the reports and recommendations, extensive long-range engineering programs were instituted at all plants to develop effective dust control systems.
>
> In addition to pioneering in the design of engineering controls, Raybestos-Manhattan joined with other asbestos products manufacturers in the mid–1930's in funding long-range research programs on the biological effects of asbestos.
>
> Because of the long latent period of asbestos-related disease, the disease being found today among some industry employees is a result of conditions existing decades ago when little was known about the health effects of asbestos or proper means of control.[8]

By 1976, 159 cases were filed against Johns-Manville; in 1978 there were 792 claims; and by 1982, the suits were being filed at a rate of 6,000 per year. Manville was settling the suits for an average of $21,000 until 1982 when the settlement amount doubled.

---

7. *Borel* v. *Fibreboard Paper Products Corp.*, 493 F.2d 1076 (5th Cir. 1973).

8. Paul Brodeur, *The New Yorker* (June 17, 1985): 69.

F. Attempted Legislative Remedies for the Asbestos Litigation Crisis

The first federal legislation designed to aid the beleaguered asbestos manufacturers was introduced in 1977 by Representative Milicent Fenwick, a New Jersey Republican, whose district included the town of Manville. Called the Asbestos Health Hazards Compensation Act, it would have prohibited workers from bringing third-party negligence or product liability suits against the asbestos industry, the tobacco industry or the federal government. Victims, instead, would be compensated through a federally administered central fund. Claims accruing before 1980 would be paid by the federal government, and claims after that time would be paid from mandatory contributions from the asbestos and tobacco industries and the federal government. Under the plan, the maximum payment for a totally disabled asbestosis victim would be $500 per month ($1000 if he had a wife and two children). The bill met with anger and criticism in the House and was easily shelved.

The second bill was introduced in 1980 by Senator Gary Hart of Colorado. Johns-Manville had moved its headquarters from New York to Denver in 1972. It was later revealed in testimony by John McKinney, Manville's CEO and chairman, that the Manville PAC had contributed to Senator Hart's campaigns. Hart's bill was also called the Asbestos Health Hazards Compensation Act, and it too eliminated tort claims by victims but left compensation solely to the state worker compensation systems. The bill also would have required claimants to prove their claims in contested proceedings with insurers and employers. The bill, labeled a "Manville bail-out," was easily rejected by Congress in that session as well as in later sessions when it was reintroduced.

G. Manville's Chapter 11 Resolution

With the Congressional bail-out beyond the realm of possibilities, the asbestos manufacturers faced the mounting litigation. Ultimately, it was an accounting rule, FASB-5, that led Manville into Chapter 11. Coopers & Lybrand had been the auditor for eight successive SEC filings and was required under FASB-5 to provide an estimate for the disposition costs of future asbestos lawsuits. Coopers & Lybrand had stated under FASB-5 that the amounts could not be reliably estimated. However, a special group of consultants to Manville, called the Litigation Analysis Group (LAG), estimated the cost of disposition of all future suits to be one billion nine hundred million dollars. Coopers & Lybrand could thus no longer be used, and Price Waterhouse & Company was hired to do the audited financials. The partner from Price Waterhouse, Robert O. F. Bixby, confirmed the LAG's report. With the inability to issue financials, Manville filed for Chapter 11 protection on August 26, 1982. The effect of the filing was protection from all lawsuits.

After the bankruptcy filing, the Committee of Asbestos-Related Litigants was formed and took an active role in the Manville bankruptcy. The Committee filed a motion to dismiss the bankruptcy in November of 1982 on the grounds that Manville had filed the Chapter 11 proceedings in bad faith. The Committee also had the Senate Judiciary Committee convene a hearing on November 10, 1982 to investigate whether it was proper for a solvent company to file for reorganization under the federal Bankruptcy Code. Although there was significant testimony during the hearing, the Committee declined to get involved in making any changes to the Bankruptcy Code.

The big problem facing Judge Lifland in the Chapter 11 proceedings was the disposition of all the suits and pending suits against Manville. The issue involved dealing with Manville, its insurers, and the lawyers for the litigants. The bankruptcy proceedings continued through 1989 when Manville and others agreed to the Manville Personal Injury Settlement Trust. Under the agreement, Manville was required to give $2.5 billion in assets (mostly stock) to the trust. Manville was also required, beginning in 1991, to pay $75 million to the trust annually as well as 20 percent of its annual net income each year. So far, 152,000 claims have been filed and 3,000 more are expected. The average settlement has been $42,000, but the claims will not be paid until 2004 because of cash shortages with the trust.

In 1976, 31 percent of Manville's business ($1.6 billion) was asbestos sales. Today, Manville has 42 percent of its sales ($2.2 billion) in fiberglass insulation. However, Manville admits to lost customers and a stock price that seems to keep dropping.

Some unknowns remain in the asbestos saga. For example, clean-up of asbestos in the Chicago school districts has an estimated cost of $500 million, and the Illinois Supreme Court has ruled that the school districts can proceed to recover the property damages from the asbestos manufacturers. The EPA has begun issuing complaints against school districts that do not move quickly enough in the replacement programs and the possibility of a $25,000 fine for failure to clean up represents additional costs of the asbestos problem.

Today the asbestos liability continues for other manufacturers. In mid–1992, after a two-year jury trial, six other companies were found negligent in installing, manufacturing or supplying asbestos. The case involved 8,555 plaintiffs and damages will be determined in separate proceedings. Punitive damages have been awarded in some cases. 90,000 pending claims remain.

Discussion Questions

1. Suppose that you had been attorney Samuel Greenstone. Would you agree to no further lawsuits in exchange for the Manville settlement?
2. Suppose that you had been Dr. Anthony Lanza. Would you take any action with respect to the actions of George Hobart and Vandiver Brown?
3. Is Sumner Simpson morally responsible for the deaths of asbestos workers?
4. If you were Dr. Leroy Gardner, would you accept Manville's funding under the conditions required?
5. Should Dr. Kenneth Smith have disclosed his findings in his x-ray study to the involved workers?
6. Could Johns-Manville have taken alternative steps?
7. Was asbestos a needed commodity?
8. Did Johns-Manville get rewarded by ignoring the problem for so long?
9. Should Manville (as it exists today) be required to liquidate its assets to pay all the claims?

SOURCES

Whitaker, Leslie. "Monster in the Closet." *Time* Feb. 6, 1989, 53.

Wingo v. Celotex Corp., 834 F.2d 375 (4th Cir. 1987).

Feder, Barnaby. "Asbestos: The Saga Drags On." *New York Times* Apr. 2, 1989, 1 and 11.

Lambert, Wade, and E. J. Pollock. "Owen-Illinois's Insurers Receive Setback in Asbestos Case Ruling." *Wall Street Journal* Apr. 10, 1990, B11.

Lambert, Wade, and E. J. Pollock. "Manville to Add Funds to Asbestos Trust." *Wall Street Journal* Sept. 10, 1990, B111.

Charlier, Marj. "Manville Trust, Victims' Lawyers Plan Payment Pact." *Wall Street Journal* Nov. 19, 1990, B5.

Sanchez, Sandra. "Asbestos Firms Ruled Negligent." *USA Today* July 14, 1992, 1A.

"Asbestos Defendants Must Pay Punitive Damages." *Wall Street Journal* July 31, 1992, B6.

"A Big Win for Asbestos Workers." *Time* July 27, 1992, 17.

3.12 ELECTROMAGNETIC FIELDS (EMF): EXPOSURE FOR WORKERS AND CUSTOMERS

A. EMF Is Discovered

Technology has brought to us the phenomenon of the electromagnetic field (EMF) — magnetic fields that result from electrical current. These fields can be found around transmission lines, appliances in the home and video display terminals for computers. Wherever there is electric power, there are electric and magnetic fields. These fields result from the electric charges in the electric power system. Electric fields are the result of the amount of the charge, and magnetic fields result from the motion of the electric charge. Together these two types of fields are often called electromagnetic fields (EMF)[1]. Much has been written recently about the health hazards of electromagnetic fields, but the controversy has been developing over a forty-year period.

In 1950, the first study of electromagnetic fields appeared when the U.S. Public Health Service issued a report stating that workers who were exposed to alternating electromagnetic fields developed cancer at a significantly higher rate than the population as a whole. Following this first study public, concerns about EMF arose as utilities turned more and more to extra-high voltage (EHV) transmission lines to handle large increases in electricity demand. The public first noticed EHV lines as nuisances; their TVs and radios had interference.

During the 1960s, Dr. Robert O. Becker conducted experiments with salamanders that demonstrated their regenerative process was initiated by electric current associated with their nervous systems. Later Dr. Becker, while working with Dr. Howard Friedman, discovered that exposing human volunteers to pulsed magnetic fields of similar frequency and considerably greater strength than those associated with magnetic storms found that doing so significantly reduced the volunteers' ability to react to the appearance of light.

While the research on EMF continued, U.S. military projects brought the first public involvement in the EMF issue. The Navy and GTE Sylvania's joint project for an extra-low-frequency (ELF) test facility in Wisconsin (called Project Sanguine) met powerful objections in 1968 from environmental groups. Residents along the Navy's Clam Lake facility reported that they were receiving electrical shocks when they turned on water faucets.[2] Environmentalists claimed that alternating magnetic fields generated by the ELF antennas could produce dangerously high voltages in power and telephone lines.[3] The Navy responded to the objections in an environmental impact statement by demonstrating that household appliances give off stronger magnetic fields than the ELF facility.

---

1. "Biological Effects of Power Frequency Electric and Magnetic Fields," Congressional Background Paper, Office of Technology Assessment (1989).

2. P. Brodeur, "Annals of Radiation: The Hazards of Electromagnetic Fields," *The New Yorker* (June 12, 1989): 51–58, 62.

3. *Ibid.*

Reactions to EMF were initially minimal, first because there is no transfer of energy as in x-rays where chemical bonds are broken or microwaves where there is tissue heating. Also, scientists were aware that all cells in the body have natural electric fields and those fields are at least one hundred times more intense than any fields induced by exposure to common power-frequency fields.[4]

Dr. Becker strongly urged the Summer 1972 meeting of the Institute of Electrical and Electronic Engineers to begin an early program for the study of human exposure to electromagnetic fields. Shortly thereafter, in 1973, Becker was asked to serve on the Navy's Bureau of Medicine and Surgery to review the Navy's research program on the biological and ecological effects of ELF radiation. Becker and other members of the advisory committee recommended that the Navy make further studies of the effects of Project Sanguine on human beings and animals. The Navy distributed the findings of the advisory committee only to committee members and proceeded with Project Sanguine. The warnings of Becker and others were never made public.[5]

B. Power Line Placement Becomes an Issue

During the time of the initial EMF research and the military controversies, the siting of power lines became an issue as the public became more aware of EMF. In 1973, the Power Authority of the State of New York (PASNY) was considering the construction and placement of a 765-kilovolt power line in upstate New York. Becker wrote to PASNY and urged them to delay their decision on the line placement until the Project Sanguine experiments were completed. The Public Service Commission of New York (PSC) began hearings on the 765-k line in 1973.

The hearings on the 765-k line were long and complicated with utility experts testifying there was no biological hazard to citizens with regard to the line placement. Andrew Marino, a colleague of Becker, testified about his work with exposure of rats to sixty-hertz (ELF) electric fields. The rats gained less weight, drank less water and showed altered levels of blood proteins and enzymes. After Marino testified that ELF radiation could cause biological effects in humans, the PSC hearings were postponed for a year at the request of the utilities involved. The hearings resumed in late 1975, and after pressure from Governor Hugh Carey, the PSC authorized construction of the line in 1976 but left open the issue of the required right of way width.

Both Becker and Marino were heavily attacked following the testimony at the PSC hearing. The chair of the National Academy of Sciences' Committee told *The Saturday Review*:

> The judges threw out the case with prejudice. They ruled that Marino's not a believable witness, that he's evasive and deceitful. Here we were, being attacked by people who ultimately were thrown out of a court of justice in that way. They've all been thrown out. These guys are all a bunch of quacks.[6]

---

4. "Biological Effects of Power Frequency," 1.

5. Brodeur, 67.

6. Brodeur, 76.

Simultaneously, politically based environmental opposition drove Project Sanguine from Wisconsin. Eventually, the Navy's advisory committee report with Becker's recommendation to study the effects of Project Sanguine on residents near Clam lake, was made public when Senator Gaylord Nelson of Wisconsin received a copy of the report. In a press release, Senator Nelson accused the Navy of suppressing evidence and failure to follow through on the effects of radiation.[7]

C. The Werthemeier Seminal Study on EMF

In the spring of 1975, epidemiologist Nancy Werthemeier, began her study of children who had died from leukemia in the greater Denver area. Her studies suggested a connection between the proximity of their homes to transmission lines and the leukemia rate. The studies, published in *The American Journal of Epidemiology* in 1979, concluded that the cancer rate of children from homes located near high-current configurations (HCC) was two to three times the normal rate of cancer. That is, if one child in a thousand gets cancer in the general population, two to three children living near HCCs would be expected to get it.[8] HCC homes included:

1. Homes less than 40 meters from large-gauge primary wires or arrays of six or more thin primary wires;
2. Homes less than 20 meters from an array of 3–5 thin primary wires or high-tension (50–230 KV) wires; and
3. Homes less than 15 meters from 240 volt wires.[9]

D. Cape Cod's PAVE PAWS

In 1976, the Air Force proposed the installation of the PAVE PAWS radar facility at Cape Cod, Massachusetts. No environmental impact statement was prepared and installation of the radar facility began with public input. PAVE PAWS is an acronym for Precision Acquisition of Vehicle Entry Phased Array Warning System. PAVE PAWS differs from regular radar in that there is no rotating antenna — only solid-state components, radiating elements, controlled by computer and steered electronically. PAVE PAWS was used to detect sea-launched ballistic missiles.[10] Dr. W. Ross Adey found in his studies that weak ELF fields could alter the flow of calcium from membrane surfaces of the brain cells and change the chemistry of the brain. Adey's experiments used chick-brain tissue and observed behavioral effects on live monkeys and cats. In both 1976 and 1979, Carl F. Blackman of the EPA duplicated Adey's experiments and reached the same conclusions.[11]

---

7. Brodeur, 63.

8. N. Werthemier, and E. Leeper, "Electrical Wiring Configuration and Childhood Cancer," *American Journal of Epidemiology* 109(3):283.

9. *Ibid.*, at 277.

10. *Ibid.*

11. P. Brodeur, "Annals of Radiation: The Hazards of Electromagnetic Fields," *The New Yorker* (June 19, 1989): 47.

The Air Force did issue a 250-page environmental assessment that mentioned PAVE PAWS might affect cardiac pace makers by making them skip a beat or two.

While PAVE PAWS was being constructed, the PSC issued its final decision on the 765-k line. Although the opinion found that ELF fields would have effects on humans, the right of way was authorized so long as it was widened to 350 feet.

As construction began on Cape Cod for the PAVE PAWS project, alarmed residents requested assistance from their representative, Gerry E. Studds. Representative Studds asked the Air Force for the research to document its conclusion that PAVE PAWS represented no long-term danger to human health. At a town meeting, an Air Force official told concerned residents that he could not guarantee that the residents would be safe from the effects of PAVE PAWS radiation.[12]

Following these public meetings, the Cape Cod Environmental Coalition (CCEC) filed suit against the Air Force for its violation of the National Environmental Policy Act in not issuing an environmental impact statement prior to the construction of PAVE PAWS. As a result of the suit, the Air Force agreed to do an EIS and studied the radiation from towers, but the measures were diluted through the Air Force methodology of averaging figures over time.

In January of 1980, Adey appeared at a symposium and denounced the Air Force for its unwillingness to study PAVE PAWS and its effects on residents prior to construction of the towers. Reports of Adey's denunciation appeared in newspapers across the country.

E. Corroboration of Werthemeier's Work

Studies continued to verify initial findings about EMF exposure. In June of 1982, a preliminary report by Dr. Lennart Tomenius corroborated Werthemeier's results through a childhood leukemia study in Sweden. Also in 1982, Werthemeier and Leeper published the results of their adult cancer study which indicated a correlation between transmission lines and adult incidences of cancer. At nearly the same time, Dr. Samuel Milham's study correlating leukemia to occupational exposure to electric and magnetic fields was published in the *New England Journal of Medicine*. Later that year studies from USC's school of medicine confirmed Milham's studies.[13]

Late in 1982, the *Cape Cod Times* published an article about the possible health effects of PAVE PAWS revealing that Arthur Guy was conducting a study for the Air Force of the long-term effects of low-level microwave radiation. The article entitled, "PAVE PAWS: Where Has the Controversy Gone?" discussed the studies to date and questioned the acceptance of Air Force figures.

In 1983, Adey and Daniel B. Lyle published the results of their further studies in *Bioelectromagnetics*. They concluded that a PAVE PAWS carrier frequency could significantly suppress the ability of cultured T-lymphocyte cells in mice to kill cultured cancer cells. At this same time, the first studies of electrical workers

---

12. *Ibid.*, at 48.

13. *Ibid.*

appeared when Michael McDowell released the results of his studies which showed an increased risk of leukemia among all electrical occupations. A 1984 study was released showing a significantly higher than expected number of white males in Maryland who had died of brain tumors had been employed in electrical occupations. The Electromagnetic Energy Policy Alliance was formed in 1984 by leading electronics and communications firms to downplay the hazards of radiation. That same year, the Illinois Institute of Technology Research prepared a report for the Navy that showed that magnetic fields from household appliances dropped off so quickly that the devices could not be considered major sources of indoor magnetic field exposure.

In 1985, Dr. Guy released his study showing that there were higher incidences of cancer in rats exposed to microwave radiation. A study of Polish military personnel done by Dr. Stanislaw Szmigielski and published that same year indicated that servicemen who worked with or near radiation-emitting devices were more than three times as likely to develop cancer as unexposed personnel.

F. Houston Light's Case and Public Knowledge of EMF

The first court case involving power lines was brought by Houston Lighting & Power Company in 1985 against the Klein Independent School District for the district's refusal to grant right-of-way access for the construction of power lines. The jury found for the school district and awarded compensatory and punitive damages. An appellate court later reversed the punitive damages but upheld the right of the school district to refuse the right-of-way on the grounds that there were potential health hazards caused by the electromagnetic fields resulting from the wires.

Following the Houston case, a nearly continuous stream of studies on EMF and health hazards were conducted and reported. In 1986, Werthemeier and Leeper released yet another study that demonstrated a direct connection between fetal development and the use of electric blankets and water beds. The electromagnetic fields from the water bed heaters and the blankets sent pulses that damaged the developing fetuses at a significantly higher rate than unexposed fetuses. Also in 1986, the Electric Power Research Institute (EPRI), an organization funded by electric utilities, released results of its "swine" study which indicated lower birth weights and a significant increase in the number of birth defects among swine exposed to electromagnetic radiation.

As these study results were being released, the impact of previous projects was assessable based on epidemiological studies. In March of 1986, the Massachusetts Department of Health released its study showing that women living near PAVE PAWS experienced a significantly higher rate of cancer than the general population.

By 1987, landowners were beginning to question power line placement and request government intervention. Residents of Washington protested the installation of a 230-kilovolt line in the state and produced studies showing that magnetic fields strengths were high and that the cancer risk could not be dismissed. That same year, Congress took action when the House Subcommittee on Water and Power Resources held hearings on the health hazards associated with transmission lines.

The first lawsuits alleging declines in property value because of power line location and public fear began in 1988, when New York landowners filed suit against the New York Power Authority alleging that the 345-k line, the subject of the landmark hearings in the 1970s, created a cancer corridor and had destroyed the market value of their properties.

The most recent study to be released involved Texas Utility workers who were shown to have a cancer rate thirteen times greater than that of workers who were not exposed to electromagnetic fields. The research compared 202 men who died from brain tumors in Texas between 1969 and 1978. A later study by USC established that electrical workers with ten years on the job had a higher risk for certain forms of brain tumors than those with five years on the job. By 1990, many counties had approved measures limiting construction of power lines. School boards, following the Texas case lead, were closing off buildings near power lines to afford protection for their children.[14]

In a report issued by the Congressional Office of Technology Assessment, the following conclusion regarding EMF was reached, "The emerging evidence no longer allows one to categorically assert that there are no risks."[15] The Department of Energy's researchers conclude, "There is clearly cause for concern but not for alarm."[16] Dr. David Carpenter, dean of the school of public health at SUNY, Albany observes, "This is really harming people. In my judgment the present state of affairs is like the correlation between smoking and lung cancer 30 years ago."[17]

Public utilities, through EPRI, have quadrupled spending on EMF research since 1986. But public concern continues to build. Some environmental consultants predict that EMF will become the biggest environmental challenge utilities must face.

Cyrus Noe, the editor of "Clearing Up," a utility newsletter, comments that electricity is a necessity of modern life, and "no one is going to say that we have to turn off the lights. But utilities cannot simply gin up a plan, award a bunch of contracts and spend the EMF dilemma away. We just don't know the answers."[18]

Discussion Questions

1. Is there a clear causal connection between EMF and cancer?
2. What companies should be concerned about liability?
3. What regulation do you foresee?
4. What problems do you see for landowners located near existing lines?
5. If you were a human resources officer in an electric utility, would you take any action?
6. If you were a manufacturer or seller of electric blankets or water beds, would you include warnings in your products?

---

14. D. Kirkpatrick, "Can Power Lines Give you Cancer?" *Fortune* (Dec. 31, 1990): 80–85.

15. *Ibid.*

16. *Ibid.*

17. *Ibid.*

18. K. Schneider, "Electricity and Cancer? The Mystery Increases," *The New York Times* (Feb. 3, 1991): E3.

3.13 VIDEO DISPLAY TERMINALS AND THE MISCARRIAGE AND CATARACT CLUSTER STUDIES

A. Initial Findings on VDTs

It has been known since the 1960s that different electrical devices give off different magnetic fields. Certain household appliances such as hair dryers and electric mixers actually have stronger electromagnetic fields than the Navy's ELF projects. However, the strength of the magnetic fields from these appliances fall off with distance. Few consumers are aware of the dangers and yet millions are users of an appliance with strong fields — video display terminals (VDTs). It is estimated that there are 30 million VDTs in homes, schools and offices. When a VDT is running, it gives off ultraviolet, visible-light, infrared, microwave, ELF and static electric fields.

In 1975, Swedish scientists reported than an unusually high number of VDT operators complained of eye difficulties and a 1977 Swedish National Board of Occupational Safety Health Study found that 85 percent of all Scandinavian Airlines System employees who worked with VDTs experienced blurred vision or temporary nearsightedness.

B. The Newspaper VDT Studies

Ironically, the first evidence of EMF field-strength from VDTs came from studies of VDTs in newspaper offices around the country where the VDT was pioneered and quickly used. In 1976, two *New York Times* copy editors (ages twenty-nine and thirty-five) who had worked with VDTs for 16 months were discovered to have developed opacities in the lenses of both eyes (opacities generally precede cataracts). Dr. Milton M. Zaret, of NYU, had studied servicemen who worked in radar and found the same opacification. Dr. Zaret examined the copy editors and found they were suffering from identical problems.

The Newspaper Guild of New York charged that the VDTs posed a safety and health threat and demanded a study which was conducted by the National Institute for Occupational Safety and Health (NIOSH). The study concluded that the radio-frequency emissions on the VDTs at the Times were well below the 1966 level standards set by the United States of America Standards Institute and could not have caused the precataract conditions. Studies over the next four years at other newspapers, including the Oakland Tribune, the *San Francisco Chronicle* and the *Examiner* confirmed the findings that the frequencies could not cause biological injury.

Between 1978 and 1981 researchers at Bell Telephone Laboratories in Murray Hill, New Jersey, conducted tests that demonstrated that the low frequency radiation from VDTs could have detrimental health effects on workers. The results of the work were published in the *American Industrial Hygiene Association Journal* in 1979 and presented at a national health conference in 1981.

C. Pregnancy Cluster Studies of VDT Workers

In 1980, it was revealed that four of seven pregnant VDT operators in the classified-advertising department of the Toronto *Star* had given birth to infants with defects. The defects included a clubfoot; a cleft palate; an underdeveloped eye; and multiple head abnormalities. The women were between the ages of twenty and thirty, did not smoke and had taken no drugs during pregnancy.

The Ontario Ministry of Labor conducted a study and inquired of IBM, the VDT manufacturer for the *Star* terminals, whether any data was available. After an extensive study, the minister of health issued the following statement:

> We left no stone unturned to find a case where a single machine emitted a dangerous level of radiation ... there is not a single scrap of evidence to indicate any danger from VDT radiation.[1]

Over the next two years, seven additional clusters of birth defects among VDT workers were reported in the United States and Canada:

- Seven of 13 pregnant women who worked part time at Air Canada's check-in counter at Montreal's Dorval airport miscarried.
- In 1980 six of ten pregnant VDT operators at Sears, Roebuck's Southwest Regional Office in Dallas miscarried. A seventh operator gave birth to a premature baby who then died. The women all worked in Department 168 of the Sears offices which contained 25 VDTs. The Center for Disease Control issued the following statement:

> "Even though we found a definite association between working in Department 168 and having an adverse reproductive outcome, we consider VDTs an unlikely cause."

- In 1980 three cases of congenital malformation and seven cases of first trimester miscarriages were reported among VDT workers at the Department of Defense's logistics agency in Marietta, Georgia. The Army's Environmental Hygiene Agency investigated and concluded it was "an unusual statistical event for which no explanation could be found."
- In 1982 it was revealed that of seven pregnancies among clerks in the accounts departments of Surrey Memorial Hospital in Vancouver, British Columbia, there were the following results:

  - 3 miscarriages
  - 1 premature birth
  - one infant with a club foot
  - one infant in need of eye surgery
  - one infant with bronchitis at birth

- In 1982 of seven pregnancies in the Solicitor General's Office among VDT operators the following occurred:

  - 4 miscarriages
  - 1 premature birth
  - 2 infants with respiratory problems

---

1. P. Brodeur, "Annals of Radiation: The Hazards of Electromagnetic Fields — Power Lines," *The New Yorker* (June 26, 1989): 43.

■ In 1982 five VDT operator pregnancies at Pacific Northwest Bell in Renton, Washington resulted in three miscarriages, one stillborn baby and one baby with spina bifida.

Concerned about the cluster study results, the House Committee on Science and Technology opened hearings on VDTs in 1982, but no action was taken other than to recommend that exposure standards be set by the Bureau of Radiological Health.

Studies involving VDT workers continued during the next five years both in the United States and abroad. In 1983 the Canadian Centre for Occupational Health and Safety published reports of Czechoslovakian studies that indicated radiation measurements taken near operators (and not directly by the screen) indicated higher levels of radiation. The Centre recommended that pregnant workers be relieved of VDT work and noted that lead aprons were ineffective for deflecting or absorbing VDT radiation.

In 1984, the *Columbia Journalism Review* published several articles on the dangers of VDT and noted the conflict journalists had in reporting VDT health hazards when their industry was so dependent on VDTs. Also, in 1984, several additional birth defect clusters appeared: Twenty-four out of forty-eight pregnancies among VDT operators at United Airlines' reservation center in San Francisco resulted in miscarriages, birth defects, neonatal deaths and premature births.

It was reported that seventeen out of thirty-two pregnancies among VDT operators at the Alma, Michigan office of General Telephone Company ended in miscarriages, birth defects or other abnormal results. However, both NIOSH and the College of Obstetricians and Gynecologists issued statements indicating VDTs did not cause the clusters of defects.

The Coalition for Workplace Technology was formed and lobbied against legislation for protection of VDT workers. The Coalition was a trade group formed in 1984 and supported by IBM and other VDT manufacturers.

D. Scientific Debate on the Safety of VDTs

Professor Arthur Guy of Bioelectromagnetics Research Lab at the University of Washington released his 1984 results on VDT radiation which demonstrated their significant effect on chicken embryos. The results remained unpublished until 1985 when the *Wall Street Journal* ran an article on VDTs and reported Guy's conclusion that older VDTs needed to be shielded. The April 1985 issue of *VDT News* carried a similar report which prompted Robert J. Siegel, IBM's director of information, to write the following:

> Your recent ... story misinterprets a report prepared for IBM by Dr. A. W. Guy. Your story is inaccurate and grossly misleading.
>
> This is especially distressing since IBM provided you in advance with additional clarifying information. You also had Dr. Guy's report summary which states there is "no valid evidence that would indicate any health hazards associated with ... persons operating VDTs."
>
> Dr. Guy since has added a preface to his full report which states "VDTs are safe to use." He adds that the emissions from "both older and new model VDTs are well below the levels shown to cause harmful biological effects."

Here, again, are the facts:

- No place in the report or summary does Dr. Guy recommend refitting older VDTs with shielding because of possible health problems. Dr. Guy reconfirms this in his preface by saying: "I do not feel ... that unshielded VDT emission levels represent a potential health hazard."
- IBM has not kept Dr. Guy's findings confidential. In accordance with standard scientific practices, Dr. Guy has been reporting his findings at appropriate scientific forums and he will continue to do so. Also, Dr. Guy's summary has been available since September and the full report is available now.
- Dr. Guy's basic conclusion is that VDTs are safe and present no health hazards to users.

I have enclosed Dr. Guy's full report, including the preface.

Because we believe that the public is best served by a discussion of VDT safety based on the facts, I would appreciate your printing this letter in its entirety in your next issue.[2]

However, the editor included the following with Siegel's letter:

We strongly dispute IBM's contention that our story is inaccurate and misleading. We offered no judgment on the question of VDT safety. We simply reported what we consider to be a clear recommendation by Guy for shielding VDTs which do not meet the 1983 electromagnetic interference (EMI) rules set by the Federal Communications Commission.

Referring to older model VDTs in a section entitled "Recommendation" on page 56 of his report to IBM, Guy states: "The localized E-fields at the surface of an unshielded cover of a VDT nearest the flyback transformer can reach extremely high values as a result of the associated high voltage and close proximity of the transformer to the cover. Since these fields have a capability of inducing much greater currents in an exposed user of the device than the relatively low magnetic field emissions, it certainly is desirable to shield the cover of the VDT". We regret that IBM does not address this recommendation in its letter.

Indeed, to avoid any possibility of misrepresenting Guy's advice to IBM, *Microwave News* reprinted the full text of his recommendations. We refer interested readers to page 11 of our April issue.

On receiving IBM's letter, we contacted Guy at the University of Washington in Seattle, but he refused to comment on either our story or Siegel's letter.

Guy's new preface, cited by IBM, is dated April 18; the original report is dated December 2. (By April 18, our April issue was already on its way to our subscribers.) While the preface may help everyone better understand Dr. Guy's position, in no way does it alter the contents of the report itself.

Last fall, when *Microwave News* first learned that Dr. Guy was preparing a report for IBM, we repeatedly asked for a copy. We were told that it was for internal use only. Later, IBM released a six-page report summary that did not include Guy's recommendations. Only after we published our story did IBM finally release the full report.

We stand by our story.[3]

---

2. Brodeur, 57.

3. Brodeur, 57.

In 1986, scientific studies of VDT radiation increased dramatically and reports were run on evening national news. NIOSH also proposed an exhaustive study of VDT workers and industry representatives voiced strong objections to then-President Reagan.

In 1987, McGill University released results of a study of Canadian women which demonstrated that the spontaneous abortion rate was significantly higher for VDT operators. Also in 1987, the Swedish National Board of Occupational Safety and Health reported results of higher genetic defects among VDT operator pregnancies. By 1988, IBM was marketing shielded VDTs in the Scandinavian countries.

E. New Studies and Legislation

IBM announced the availability of low-radiation VDTs in 1989 but received little response. Firms such as American Airlines indicated its employees had not expressed concern. Bell Atlantic indicated its VDT employees complained about repetitive-motion problems but not VDT radiation.[4]

A study released in March of 1991 and appearing in the *New England Journal of Medicine* concluded that long hours of work with a VDT do not increase the risk of miscarriage. The study, conducted by NIOSH, focused on 730 directory assistance operators at two telephone companies in eight states. Between 1983 and 1986, the operators had a miscarriage rate of 15 percent in the first three months of pregnancy with the normal miscarriage rate being 11–20 percent for women with no known risk factors.[5] Louis Slesin, editor of *VDT News,* commented that the study did not correlate particular machines with pregnancy outcomes, and radiation levels can vary by as much as a factor of fifteen depending on the machine.

San Francisco passed an ordinance in 1991 that imposes requirements on employers for the comfort and safety of employees who use a VDT four or more hours per day. Among other requirements, employees must be given a fifteen-minute break from the computer every two hours. Ergonomical requirements in the ordinance include adequate legroom, swivel chairs and arm rests.

A 1992 Finnish study found that pregnant women working at older VDTs were three times as likely to miscarry.[6]

Discussion Questions

1. You are a manager in a major travel agency in Phoenix. Approximately 80 percent of your agents are women and 60 percent of them are of childbearing age. One agent, who is eight weeks pregnant, has come to you expressing concern about her work with a VDT eight hours per day. Corporate headquarters responds to your query with a simple statement: "Legal indicates there are no prohibitions." Would you make any changes in your operations?
2. Would you purchase low-radiation VDTs?

---

4. "Low-Radiation VDTs," *Wall Street Journal* (Dec. 19, 1989): A1.

5. "VDTs 'R' OK?" *Vegetarian Times* (June, 1991): 24.

6. Julia Lawlor, "Study Cites High Risk of Older VDTs," *USA Today* (Sept. 9, 1992): 1B.

3. Would you discuss the VDT studies with your employees?
4. Would you consider implementing the San Francisco requirements?

SOURCES

Okie, S. "VDTs Safe During Pregnancy, Study Says." *Arizona Republic* Mar. 14, 1991, A3.

Waldholz, M. "VDTs Are Said Not to Increase Miscarriage Risk." *Wall Street Journal* Mar. 14, 1991, B1.

Brodeur, Paul. "Annals of Radiation: The Hazards of Electromagnetic Fields —Video-Display Terminals." *The New Yorker* June 26, 1989, 39–68.

Ingley, K. "Laying Down Arms." *Arizona Republic* May 12, 1991, F1.

"San Francisco Firms Confront Computer Law." *Wall Street Journal* July 16, 1991, B2.

3.14 AIRLINE WORKERS AND RADIATION

In 1985, some scientists began expressing concerns about the radiation from the sun and the stars for flight crews and passengers. In March 1986, the Federal Aviation Administration reviewed the evidence and decided not to classify members of cabin crews as radiation workers. The FAA, at that time, stated that the crews were receiving higher doses of radiation than the amount that Federal standards say the public should be exposed to. Scientific studies continued during this period (with an FAA study released in 1988 — inconclusive), and in December 1989, the Department of Transportation released a study showing that pilots and flight attendants on many airline routes are exposed to more radiation than most workers in nuclear power plants. Currently, the Nuclear Regulatory Commission imposes extensive safety requirements, including education, monitoring, and procedures to minimize exposure for nuclear power plant workers. Currently, there are no similar safety requirements for cabin crews.

The study results indicate that the higher a plane flies and the closer the plane's route to the poles, the greater the radiation exposure for crews. For example, a plane flying at an altitude of 40,000 feet near the equator is exposed to .4 millirems per hour. A plane flying at 40,000 feet over the North Pole is exposed to 1.4 millirems per hour.

In the study, the exposure of flight crews who flew twenty years for 960 hours per year on east-west routes would result in fifty-nine to sixty-one premature cancer deaths per hundred thousand crew members. For a hundred thousand passengers flying 480 hours per year on east-west routes (nine hours/week), there would be an additional twenty-nine to thirty premature cancer deaths.

One recommendation of the study was to caution pregnant passengers and crew members. Dr. Michael E. Ginevan of Geomet Technologies, Inc., who did the cancer death computations, noted:

> If I were a woman in the critical period of pregnancy for retardation, I would tend to avoid flights to Europe.[1]

A physician with the FAA noted:

> We think it would be appropriate to educate people, particularly pregnant crew members who may be flying. It might be appropriate for some to consider alternate routes or leaves of absence.[2]

It is possible to detect periods of extensive solar activity, and pilots could be warned of those periods and fly at lower altitudes. Intense solar outbursts are monitored by the National Oceanographic and Atmospheric Administration and their reports are passed along to the FAA. However, neither the FAA nor the pilots have known that the value of the information is in knowing when to fly lower. Speed and fuel efficiency are reduced if planes fly at lower altitudes.

---

1. M. Wald, "Radiation Exposure Is Termed a Big Risk for Airplane Crews," *The New York Times* (Feb. 14, 1990): A1 and A18.

2. *Id.*

Currently, there are airline regulations on the length of time pregnant crew members can work, but those standards do not deal with radiation and apply well past the first trimester of pregnancy when radiation exposure is critical for the vulnerable fetus.

The Airline Pilots Association has responded to the study results by emphasizing that the FAA has far more critical problems of concern to crews, such as aircraft maintenance and air traffic control.

Federal standards for radiation exposure are 500 millirems per person per year in the non-nuclear fields. The standard for the public is 100 millirems per year. The FAA has computed that crew members on airlines flying an Athens-New York route would reach an exposure level of 910 millirems per year. Federal standards for exposure of pregnant women is 50 millirems per month.

Discussion Questions

1. Assume that you are a vice president for human resources for Atlantic Airways, an airline that flies from New York to several continental destinations including London, Rome, Athens, Stockholm, Paris and Dublin. After receiving a copy of the Department of Transportation's report, would you make any changes in flight paths or altitudes?
2. Would you make any changes in crew monitoring for millirem exposure levels?
3. Could you make any changes in your policies with respect to pregnant flight attendants?
4. Is the risk of exposure too small to justify the additional costs in fuel and lost time?
5. Would you make the report available to your flight crews?
6. Would you make the report available to passengers?

Section E
Plant Closures and Downsizing

Economic downturns, intense competition, and cost reductions often force employers to close facilities and lay off workers. What obligations do the businesses owe to their employees? To the communities where their facilities are located? The dilemma of employer loyalty and shareholder profit is a difficult one to resolve.

3.15 Chrysler and its Cost of Closing

Lee Iacocca, Chairman and CEO of Chrysler, announced on January 27, 1988, that it would be virtually closing its plant at Kenosha, Wisconsin. Iacocca and his board were under significant pressure from shareholders because of continuing poor financial performance of Chrysler. The Kenosha, Wisconsin plant had been acquired as part of American Motors when Chrysler purchased that auto manufacturer in 1987. In his announcement, Iacocca faulted national trade policy for Chrysler's declining sales and resultant earnings problems.

The Kenosha plant was responsible for manufacturing the Dodge Omni and the Plymouth Horizon. The announced plans were to lay off 5,500 of the 6,500 workers at the plant. Omni and Horizon production would be moved to a Detroit plant.

The announcement of the closing came at a critical time for Chrysler. It was involved in renewal negotiations with the United Auto Workers (UAW). Also, the Kenosha plant carried a history of union financial assistance. The UAW had loaned American Motors Corporation over $60 million to keep the Kenosha plant running. Chrysler had assumed the loan obligations as part of the acquisition. Also, the state of Wisconsin paid $5 million for job training at the Kenosha plant in 1987 based upon a Chrysler promise that the plant would build Omnis and Horizons for at least five more years.

Peter Pfaff, a member of the United Auto Workers Union Local 72 of Kenosha and an employee at the Kenosha plant since 1972, said, "I was there. We've got it on tape and in writing. They said they'd stay ... Greenwald (Chrysler Motors Chairman) keeps saying Chrysler never said that, but I was there when he said it."[1]

The UAW local in Kenosha threatened a national delay in negotiations on renewal for the 64,000 workers. After the threat, Iacocca announced that Chrysler would establish a $20 million trust fund to aid the 5,500 workers. Assistance in the form of housing payments and educational funding would be offered. Iacocca indicated Chrysler was not setting a precedent, but recognizing a "moral obligation" to Kenosha and stated the fund would be for assistance to workers in addition to their severance pay, extended unemployment benefits and repayment of the loans.

The state of Wisconsin threatened a suit against Chrysler on the $5 million job training program but agreed to delay in exchange for Iacocca's promise to extend production at the plant for several months into the fall of 1988.

Iacocca stated that Chrysler was "guilty as hell of being cockeyed optimists. Blame us for being dumb managers, for spending $200 million to put two old cars (Chrysler Fifth Avenue and Dodge Diplomat) in an eighty-six-year-old plant, but please don't call me a liar when I've got to close it sooner than I thought."[2] Iacocca travelled to Washington to gain Congressional support for turning the Kenosha plant to defense work by Chrysler.

The UAW renegotiated its contract which included provisions for additional unemployment benefits for the 5,500 laid off workers and more job security for the 1,000 workers who would go elsewhere. Ultimately, the plant closing resulted in 3,700 jobless workers.

By mid–1990, Kenosha, a city of 77,000 on the shores of Lake Michigan, was enjoying unprecedented economic growth. At a July 1990 ceremony in which engineers detonated explosives to destroy the 250-foot smokestack of the Chrysler plant, both dignitaries and former workers cheered. Resident T. R. Garcia said at the blasting, "I think it's about time they got rid of it. What we need to do is develop the lake front, and this thing is the last to leave."[3] City planner Ray Forgianni, Jr., said, "The community's image is probably the best it's been in 100 years. The closing was almost like a catalyst. The handwriting was on the wall — the economy needed to diversity."[4]

Discussion Questions

1. Did Chrysler have a moral obligation to the Kenosha workers and Wisconsin, or was it just responding to pressure?

---

1. David C. Smith, "Chrysler's Kenosha Caper: When Is a Lie a Lie?" *Ward's Auto World* (March 1988): 9.

2. Geoff Sundstrom, and Mary Connelly, "Iacocca Sees Hope of Defense Work for Kenosha Plant," *Automotive News* (Feb. 22, 1988): 3.

3. Anthony Shaded, "Blasted: Kenosha Marks Revival by Burying Remains of Ex-Chrysler Plant," *Automotive News* (July 30, 1990): 45.

4. *Ibid.*

2. Do these types of arrangements interfere with the ability to make business decisions? Review Iacocca's quote on the business mistakes as you evaluate the issue.

3. Were the shareholders required to pay twice for the closing? Once for severance and again for extended benefits?

4. Was Chrysler simply putting its duty to shareholders above its duty to Wisconsin, Kenosha and UAW workers? Is this proper? Is it ethical?

5. Was Chrysler's action just a catalyst for needed economic development?

SOURCES

Clunk, Laura. "State Money Sought for AMC Kenosha." *Automotive News* Jan. 19, 1987, 53.

127 *Labor Law Reporter* (1988), 178–179, 275–276, 285.

128 *Labor Law Reporter* (1988), 50–51.

Kertesz, Louise. "Chrysler, UAW at Odds on Kenosha Engine Pact." *Automotive News* Mar. 28, 1988, 6.

3.16 THE CLOSURE OF THE STROH'S PLANT UPON MERGER

Stroh's Brewery of Detroit acquired Schlitz Brewing Company in 1982. Five breweries were acquired. Stroh's brewery in Detroit had been operating for over seventy years and was not as modern as the newly acquired plant. In 1985, the decision was made to close the Detroit plant with its eleven hundred jobs, sixty of which were managerial. Eighty-five percent of the hourly employees and 22 percent of the salaried employees had worked at the Detroit plant for more than twenty years. The president of Stroh's, Peter Stroh, was keenly aware of the impact the closure would have.

At that time, unemployment in Detroit was 9 percent. Normal unemployment rates are 4–6 percent. To lessen the impact on employees and the sagging Detroit economy, the announcement of the closure was made four months early.[1]

Peter Stroh worked with other CEOs in the Detroit area to find jobs for the displaced employees. Stroh's and the union established an outplacement program that helped employees in the areas of counseling, job skill analyses, resumé preparation and interview tips.

Stroh's spent $1.5 million on the outplacement program. State and local governments contributed $600,000 to the program. Ron Cupp, manager of corporate personnel at Stroh's stated, "The people who had come to work here came to stay. It was very tough to have to let them go. We wanted to develop an aggressive program that would assist these people in a new beginning — be that a new career, their own business, retirement, or whatever their goal might be. In short, we wanted every employee to feel that Stroh's was a good place to work while it was open and a good company to have been associated with after it closed."[2]

The outplacement program had the following components:

- Orientation sessions to explain the overall concept and give employees ample opportunity to ask questions;
- Individual skills testing and assessment;
- Development of an individualized job-search strategy;
- A job-development effort and a computerized job bank;
- Individual job-search counseling;
- Job-search skills workshops;
- Counseling sessions on financial planning, retirement planning, relocation, and starting a new business;
- Available psychological counseling;
- A research library, free phones, and secretarial facilities; and
- Extended health and severance benefits.[3]

---

1. Under the Worker Adjustment and Retraining Notification Act, passed in 1988, Stroh's would have been required to give 180 days notice of closure. The law applies to employers of 100 or more employees.

2. Joseph Jannotta, "Stroh's Outplacement Success," *Management Review* (Jan. 1987): 52–53.

3. *Ibid.*

In just slightly over a year, all of Stroh's 125 salaried employees and 98 percent of the total 655 union (hourly) employees had found other employment. The cost including Stroh's and government contributions, was $2,000 per employee.

Discussion Questions

1. Was the outplacement program an appropriate expenditure for the Stroh's?
2. Would the announcement of the closure four months early have an impact on morale at the plant?
3. Would the announcement of the closure four months early affect Stroh's cost of capital in the market place? Its share value?
4. Suppose Detroit represented a significant sales market for Stroh's. Could the outplacement program be viewed as goodwill?

3.17 GM Plant Closings and Efforts at Outplacement

Bleeding from losses of $4.45 billion for 1991, General Motors Corporation (GMC) announced on February 24, 1992, that it would close twenty-one plants over the next few years and named twelve plants to be closed in 1992 affecting over 16,300 workers.

GM is the nation's largest manufacturer, and the $4.45 billion loss was the largest ever in American corporate history. Robert C. Stempel, GM's chairman, said the U.S. was in an unusually deep automotive slump, "The rate of change during the past year was unprecedented. And no one was immune to the extraordinary events which affected our lives and the way in which we do business."[1]

More than 3,400 workers at GM's North Tarrytown, New York plant will be laid off by 1995. The Tarrytown plant manufactured GM's mini-vans: the Chevrolet Lumina, the Pontiac Trans Sports and Oldsmobile Silhouettes. The mini-van, originally designed in the U.S., was executed by GM with a wide stance and a sloping, futuristic nose. Projections were that 150,000–200,000 of the vans would be sold annually. Instead sales reached only 100,000 per year which represented one-half of the Tarrytown plant's capacity. Dealers maintained the shape of the van was too avant-garde for significant sales. "It looks like a Dustbuster," noted a GM manager anonymously.[2]

GM executives acknowledged that building one model per plant was a sloppy and expensive way to do business.

Tarrytown UAW had negotiated with GM in 1987 to get the mini-van plant. The union members voted for innovative and cooperative work rules to replace expensive union practices. Also, state and local governments contributed job training funds, gave tax breaks, and began reconstruction of railroad bridges to win the mini-van production plant.

"The workers did all the right things to get the mini-van but GM was just too optimistic about how many it could sell."[3]

In his speech, Stempel said, "We are asking you to help remake the world's largest automobile company. We can't wait."[4]

Discussion Questions

1. When unions (workers) and governments make payments in exchange for promises from a manufacturer to locate a plant in a particular area, should the plant owner have an obligation to continue operations?
2. Did GM just make a business decision to stop losses?
3. Should workers and governments absorb business risks such as a poor-selling mini-van?

---

1. Doran P. Levin, "GM Picks 12 Plants to Be Shut as It Reports a Record U.S. Loss," *New York Times* (Feb. 25, 1992): A1.

2. Doran P. Levin, "Vehicle's Design Doomed Van Plant," *New York Times* (Feb. 26, 1992): C4.

3. *Ibid.*

4. William McWhirter, "Major Overhaul," *Time* (Dec. 30, 1991): 56.

3.18 EFS, THE UNION AND ITS CREDITORS AND SUITORS

Erico Fastening System is a company engaged in the manufacture and sale of stud welding fasteners and equipment. EFS has its primary facility located in Moorestown, New Jersey (151 employees) with a smaller manufacturing plant in Houston, Texas and warehouse facilities in Boston, Chicago, San Francisco and Los Angeles.

EFS has a collective bargaining agreement with its employees through Local 397 of the International Union of Electrical, Salaried, Machine and Furniture Workers, AFL-CIO. The agreement was three years in length with an effective date of July 1, 1989.

During 1987, EFS experienced book losses of $5 million. For 1988, EFS broke even but the earlier losses caused its financial situation to remain precarious. In 1989, EFS experienced yet another loss of $3.1 million and EFS's parent, Erico International Corporation, provided a $1.9 million loan to EFS.

AmeriTrust Company National Association was a secured creditor of EFS, holding a security interest in all of EFS's assets except real property. AmeriTrust had security in EFS of $6 million to secure its line of credit. In 1989 AmeriTrust demanded that Erico "do something about EFS." Erico funneled $2 million into EFS through intercompany loans during 1990, but AmeriTrust continued its threats to withhold advances or increase its rate of interest.

By the spring of 1990, AmeriTrust refused to extend credit to EFS, and talks with other lenders including Citicorp, Manufacturers Hanover, National City Bank, and Prudential failed to produce an alternative line of credit for the ailing firm.

Simultaneously, EFS began efforts to find a purchaser, contacting five different firms, ESAB, Nelson Stud Welding, Betterman, Cromp Arc and Rostra. Nelson, ESAB and Rostra had ongoing discussions with EFS, but by August 24, 1990, all three had notified EFS that no purchase would occur. That same day, the Board of Directors of Erico decided to close EFS. Also that day, the general manager of the Moorestown facility was told of the closure.

EFS's Moorestown facility was closed on August 27, 1990 with all employees terminated immediately. Neither the employees nor Local 397 had been given any prior notice of closure. Plant manager, Jeffrey Church, told the employees that the closing of the plant and their termination was due to the "financial situation" at the company. At the time of closure, EFS owed four hundred creditors, both secured and unsecured, nearly $1.7 billion. EFS proceeded with liquidation of its assets.

Local 397 filed suit claiming the layoff and closure violated the Worker Adjustment and Retraining Notification (WARN) Act of 1988, a federal law that requires six months advance notice to covered employers (one hundred or more employees) of a plant closing or layoff. The court found that WARN did apply and that EFS should have given notice. However, the court refused to place the employees' damage claims under WARN in a priority position ahead of EFS's other creditors.

Discussion Questions

1. Did the Moorestown workers have the right to know about the creditor and suitor discussions?
2. Would EFS jeopardize its chances for credit or sale if it disclosed its status to employees?
3. Whose rights should have priority as a company works through a financial crisis? The employees? The shareholders? The creditors?
4. Should the employees be compensated beyond statutory unemployment benefits?

SOURCE

IUE, Local 397, AFL-CIO v. Midwest Fasteners, Incorporated dba Erico Fasteners Systems, 763 F.Supp. 78 (D.N.J. 1990).

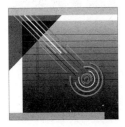

SECTION F
ENVIRONMENTAL ISSUES

The quality of the environment has become a personal issue. Many consumers base their buying decisions on the commitment of manufacturers and other businesses to environmental protections and precautions. The environment has become a stakeholder in business operations.

3.19 HERMAN MILLER AND ITS RAIN FOREST CHAIRS

In March 1990, Bill Foley, the research manager for Herman Miller, Inc., began a routine evaluation of new woods to use in Miller's signature piece — the $2,277 Eames chair. The Eames chair is a distinctive office chair with a rosewood exterior finish and leather seat.

At that time, the chair was made of two species of trees: rosewood and Honduran mahogany. Foley realized that Miller's use of the tropical hardwoods was helping destroy rain forests. Foley banned the use of the woods in the chairs once existing supplies were exhausted. The Eames chair would no longer have its traditional rosewood finish.

Foley's decision prompted the following reaction from CEO, Richard H. Ruch, "That's going to kill that [chair]."[1] Effects on sales could not be quantified.

Herman Miller, based in Zeeland, Michigan, was founded in 1923 by D. J. DePree, a devout Baptist. In addition to the Eames chair, Miller manufactures other office furniture, partitions and systems. The corporation follows a participatory-management tradition and the vice president of the Michigan Audubon Society has noted that Miller has cut the trash it hauls to landfills by 90 percent since 1982. He has also stated, "Herman Miller has been doing a super job."[2]

---

1. D. Woodruff, "Herman Miller: How Green Is My Factory?" *Business Week* (Sept. 16, 1991): 54–55.

2. *Ibid.*

Herman Miller has built an $11 million waste-to-energy heating and cooling plant. The plant saves $750,000 per year in fuel and landfill costs. Last year the company found a buyer for the 800,000 pounds of scrap fabric it has been dumping in land fills. A North Carolina firm buys it, shreds it and sells it as insulation for car-roof linings and dashboards. This sale of scrap fabric saves Miller $50,000 per year in dumping fees.

Prior to last year, Miller employees used 800,000 styrofoam cups. But last year 5,000 mugs were distributed to employees and styrofoam banished. The mugs carry the following admonition: "On spaceship earth there are no passengers … only crew." Styrofoam was also reduced 70 percent in packaging for a cost savings of $1.4 million.

Miller just spent $800,000 for two incinerators that burn 98 percent of the toxic solvents that escape from booths where wood is stained and varnished. These furnaces exceed the requirements of the 1990 Clean Air Act requirements.

It is likely that the incinerators will be obsolete in three years when new, nontoxic finishing products become available for staining and finishing wood. Under questioning from the board of directors, CEO Ruch responded that having the machines was "ethically correct."[3]

Miller keeps pursuing environmentally safe processes including finding a use for its sawdust byproduct. However, for the fiscal year ended May 31, 1991, Miller's net profit had fallen 70 percent from 1990 to $14 million on total sales of $878 million.

Discussion Questions

1. Evaluate Foley's decision with respect to changes in the chair woods. Consider the moral standards at issue for various stakeholders.
2. Is it troublesome that Miller's profits were off when Foley made the decision?
3. Is Miller bluffing with "green marketing"? Would Albert Carr support Miller's actions for different reasons?
4. Why would Herman Miller decide to exceed the 1990 Clean Air Act standards when the equipment won't be needed in three years?
5. Would you be less comfortable with Herman Miller's environmental decisions if they advertised them?

---

3. *Ibid.*

3.20 GREEN MARKETING AS A BUSINESS BLUFF

Henry Taylor, the British statesman said, "Falsehood ceases to be falsehood when it is understood on all sides that the truth is not expected to be spoken." Examples would include human interaction in situations that involve diplomacy or poker. Albert Carr maintains that Taylor's idea also applies to business. All action business takes would be with the understanding that it is done to help the business and not necessarily for some noble cause. Thus, even though a business may tout a decision as ethical or socially responsible, its decision is still based on the bottom line profits, either for the short term or over the long run.

One example that is cited as a form of business bluffing is the attention given to environmental concerns. Some critics maintain that businesses are not really interested in the environment but only taking environmentally sound positions because it will sell more products for them or give them an edge in the market because of consumers' commitments to the environment. In other words, the businesses may be doing the right things, but not for a noble reason.

Star-Kist offers its tuna as "dolphin free." No nets are used in the catch that would also bring in and kill dolphins. Detergents, pre-wash stain removers and other soap products focus on their biodegradable qualities. Known as "green marketing," a company's focus in its ads on environmental issues often raises doubts about the sincerity of the company's efforts. In many cases, the "environmental qualities" of the product do increase sales.

Currently, the FTC is examining the issue of "green advertising" to determine whether there should be standards set before a company can claim that its product is "good for the environment."

Discussion Questions

1. Is it unethical to do the right thing for the wrong reason?
2. Is it unethical to increase sales and profits because of a focus on a social cause?
3. Are companies being dishonest when they profess their commitment to the environment?
4. Does the motive for introducing the environmental qualities matter?

3.21 EXXON AND ALASKA

On March 24, 1989, the Exxon tanker, Valdez, ran aground on Bligh Reef, south of Valdez, Alaska, and spilled nearly 10.8 million gallons of oil into Prince William Sound. The captain of the tanker was Joseph Hazelwood.

Hazelwood had a history of drinking problems. He had lost his New York driver's license after two drunken-driving convictions. In 1985, with the knowledge of Exxon officials, Hazelwood joined a twenty-eight-day alcohol rehabilitation program. Almost a week after the Prince William Sound accident, Exxon revealed that Hazelwood's blood-alcohol reading was 0.061 in a test taken 10½ hours after the spill occurred. When announcing the test results, Exxon also announced Hazelwood's termination.

The magnitude of the spill seemed almost incomprehensible. U.S. Interior Secretary, Manual Lujan, called the spill the oil industry's "Three Mile Island." After ten days, the spill covered 1,000 square miles and leaked out of Prince William Sound onto beaches along the Gulf of Alaska and Cook Inlet. A clean-up army of 12,000 was sent in with hot water and oil-eating microbes. The workers found more than 1,000 dead otters. The otter population in the area is 15,000 to 22,000. The workers found 34,400 dead sea birds and 151 bald eagles who died from eating the oil-infested remains of the sea birds.

By September 15, Exxon pulled out of the clean-up efforts. At the time of the pull-out, Exxon had spent $2 billion, but had recovered only 5–9 percent of the oil spilled. Alaskan officials said about 20–40 percent of the oil evaporated. These figures meant that 50–75 percent of the oil was either on the ocean floor or on the beaches.

Joseph Hazelwood was indicted by the state of Alaska on several charges including criminal mischief, operating a watercraft while intoxicated, reckless endangerment and negligent discharge of oil. He was found innocent of all charges except the negligent discharge of oil, was fined $50,000 and was required to spend 1,000 hours helping in the clean-up of the Alaskan beaches.

When the Valdez was being repaired, shipworkers commented that Hazelwood and his crew kept the tanker from sinking because they acted quickly to seal off the hatches to the ship's tank, thus making a bubble that helped stabilize the ship. Citing incredible seamanship, the workers noted that an eleven-million-gallon spill was preferable to a sixty-million-gallon one.

Following the spill, critics of Exxon maintained that the company's huge personnel cutbacks during the 1980s affected the safety and maintenance levels abroad the tankers. Later hearings revealed that the crew of the Valdez was overburdened with demands of speed and efficiency. The crew was working ten- to twelve-hour days and often had interrupted sleep. Also, lookouts were often not properly posted and junior officers were permitted to control the bridge without the required supervision. Robert LeResche, oil-spill coordinator for the state of Alaska said, "It wasn't Captain Ahab on the bridge. It was Larry and Curly in the Exxon boardroom."[1] In response to critics, then-CEO of Exxon, Lawrence Rawl stated, "And we say, 'We're sorry, and we're doing all we can.' There were 30

---

1. Jay Mathews, "Problems Preceded Oil Spill," *Washington Post* (May 18, 1989): A1 and A18.

million birds that went through the sound last summer, and only 30,000 carcasses have been recovered. Just look at how many ducks were killed in the Mississippi Delta in one hunting day in December! People have come up to me and said, 'This is worse than Bhopal.' I say, 'Hell, Bhopal killed more than 3,000 people and injured 200,000 others!' Then they say, 'Well, if you leave the people out, it was worse than Bhopal.'"

On January 1, 1990, Exxon experienced a second oil spill when an oil pipeline running under the Arthur Kill waterway between Staten Island and New Jersey burst and spilled 567,000 gallons of heating oil. New York and New Jersey officials criticized Exxon, citing shoddy equipment and poor maintenance. It was six hours after an alarm from the pipeline safety system went off before Exxon workers shut down the pipeline. Albert Appleton, New York City's Commissioner on the environment said, "Exxon has a corporate philosophy that the environment is some kind of nuisance problem and a distraction from the real business of moving oil around."[2]

Late in February 1990, Exxon was indicted by an Anchorage grand jury on felony charges of violations of maritime safety and antipollution laws. The charges were federal and were brought after negotiations with Exxon and the Justice Department were terminated. Also, both the state of Alaska and the Justice Department brought civil suits against Exxon for the clean-up costs associated with the spill. In addition, there were approximately 150 other civil suits filed by fisherman and tour boat operators whose incomes were eliminated because of the spill. At the time of the indictment, Exxon had paid out $180 million to 13,000 fisherman and other claimants.

By May 1990, Exxon had returned to its clean-up efforts with targeted sites and 110 employees. Twice during 1991, Exxon reached a plea agreement with the federal government and the state of Alaska on the criminal charges both had brought against the company. In the second agreement, negotiated after a dissatisfied state of Alaska refused to agree to the terms of the first, Exxon consented to plead guilty to three misdemeanors and pay a $1.15 billion fine. The civil litigation was settled with an agreement by Exxon to pay $900 million to both Alaska and the federal government over a ten-year period.

The plea agreement with the government agencies did not address the civil suits pending against Exxon. At the end of 1991, an Alaska jury awarded sixteen fishermen more than $2.5 million in damages and established a pay-out formula for similar plaintiffs in future litigation against Exxon. There remained eight hundred other civil cases pending at the time of the verdict.

Discussion Questions

1. Evaluate Exxon's "attitude" with regard to the spill.
2. What was the company's purpose in cutting back on staff and maintenance expenditures?
3. Was Hazelwood morally responsible for the spill?
4. Was Exxon management morally responsible for the spill?
5. What changes in Exxon's ethical environment would you make?

---

2. Barbara Rudolph, "Exxon's Attitude Problem," *Time* (Jan. 22, 1990): 51.

Sources

McCoy, Charles. "Exxon Reaches $1.15 Billion Spill Pact That Resembles Earlier Failed Accord." *Wall Street Journal* Oct. 1, 1991, A3.

Hayes, Arthur S., and Milo Geyelin. "Oil Spill Trial Yields $2.5 Million." *Wall Street Journal* Sept. 11, 1991, B2.

"Exxon Stops the Flow." *Time* Mar. 25, 1992, 51.

"Exxon to Pay $1.1 Billion in Spill." *Arizona Republic* Mar. 13, 1991, A3.

Satchell, Michael, and Betsy Carpenter. "A Disaster that Wasn't." *U.S. News & World Report* Sept. 18, 1989, 60–69.

Galen, Michele, and Vicky Cahan. "Getting Ready for Exxon vs. Practically Everybody." *Business Week* Sept. 25, 1989, 190–92.

Welles, Chris. "Exxon's Future: What Has Larry Rawl Wrought?" *Business Week* Apr. 2, 1990, 72–76.

"Like 'Punch in Gut': Exxon Skipper Talks." *Arizona Republic* Mar. 25, 1990, A1 and A12.

Dietrich, Bill. "Is Oil-Spill Skipper a Fall Guy?" *Arizona Republic* Jan. 28, 1990, A2.

"Exxon Labeled No. 1 in Bungling a Crisis." *Arizona Republic* Mar. 24, 1990, A8.

Sullivan, Allanna, and Arthur S. Hayes. "Exxon's Plea Bargaining." *Wall Street Journal* Feb. 21, 1990, B8.

Galen, Michele, and Vicky Cahan. "The Legal Reef Ahead for Exxon." *Business Week* Mar. 12, 1990, 39.

Rubin, Julia. "Exxon Submits Final Oil-Spill Cleanup Plan." *Burlington Vermont Free Press* Apr. 28, 1990, 2A.

"Nice Work, Joe." *Time* Dec. 4, 1989, 48.

Rempel, William C. "Exxon Captain Acquitted." *Arizona Republic* Mar. 23, 1990, A1.

Foster, David. "Oily Legacy." *Mesa Tribune* Mar. 18, 1990, D1.

3.22 THE DISPOSABLE DIAPER DILEMMA

Currently, you are the administrator of a large private hospital that uses disposable diapers in its nursery and for pediatric patients. You have been reading about the environmental concerns raised by the need to dispose of the diapers in municipal landfills and that landfill space is scarce and becoming more so. The average child uses 7800 diapers in the first 130 weeks of life.

The debate on disposable diapers is a complex one. Disposable diapers account for just 2 percent of municipal solid waste. The average time required for plastic to break down is two to five hundred years. Eighteen billion disposable diapers go into landfills each year. An Arthur D. Little study comparing environmental impact of cloth vs. disposable diapers over the products' lifetimes finds cloth consumes more energy and water than disposable. The Little study also finds cloth costs more (even before adding in the diaper-service cost) and that there is greater air and water pollution with cloth diapers because of washing requirements. As critics point out, the study was commissioned by Procter & Gamble, the largest maker of disposable diapers, holding 50 percent of the market.

Four of five American parents prefer disposables, and technology on disposal of the disposables is improving. Procter & Gamble has developed industrial composting of solid-waste and is spending $20 million in research to develop diapers that break into humus.

However, environmentalists have been quite successful in obtaining regulation of disposables. Twenty states have considered taxes or complete bans on disposables. Nebraska has a ban on nondegradable disposables to take effect in 1993. Maine has a law requiring day care centers to accept children in cloth diapers. New York has considered imposing informational requirements for new mothers (brochures explaining the environmental threat of disposables). Wisconsin defeated a bill on taxing disposables in 1990.

Alternatives to disposables are being developed. Currently, R Med International distributes Tender Care - a biodegradable diaper that degrades in two to five years because of an outlining made of cornstarch. However, Tender Care's price is substantially higher than disposables.

Unlike acid rain, rain forests and other environmental issues, people seem to relate to the disposable diaper as an issue because their actions can be so direct. Your hospital staff (nursery and pediatrics) favors disposable use though, privately, many use cloth diapers. It would cost about 2.5 percent more to switch to cloth diapers. Currently, there are no municipal or state regulations applicable to your hospital.

Discussion Questions

1. Does Arthur D. Little have a conflict of interest with Procter & Gamble's sponsorship of its work?
2. What long-term regulatory possibilities exist?
3. Is it a breach of duty to the hospital patients and shareholders to adopt a position (i.e., cloth diapers) that increases costs?
4. Is there an alternative solution to the dilemma?

SOURCES

Schiller, Zachary. "Turning Pampers into Plant Food?" *Business Week* Oct. 22, 1990, 38.

Deveny, Kathleen. "States Mull Rash of Diaper Regulations." *Wall Street Journal* June 15, 1990, B1.

Deard, Betty. "Disposable Diapers Are Challenged." *Arizona Republic* May 29, 1989, A1.

3.23 THE UNCLEAR AND UNRESEARCHED CANCER CONNECTION

Oak Ridge, Tennessee, is home to a federal complex built forty-nine years ago to manufacture nuclear bombs. The Oak Ridge complex, like many of the nation's other nuclear weapons plants, has produced byproducts of its manufacture, both radioactive materials and hazardous wastes. Clean-up efforts are under way at all of the plants, but byproducts such as asbestos, mercury and uranium have infiltrated the surrounding land, water and wildlife.

Deer and frogs have caused geiger counters to go off, and there are both "No Fishing" and "No Water Contact" signs near the Oak Ridge Creek. Open-air ponds near the complex which contained volatile and nuclear wastes have seeped into nearby streams. Barrels with waste stacked on the complex site take up more space than the buildings of the complex (2.7 million gallons total).

The complex, in spite of defense cutbacks, still remains the largest employer in the area. In 1983, the Department of Energy reported that 2.4 million pounds of mercury had been accidentally lost through the smokestacks of the complex and its nearby streams. Mercury has been found in Oak Ridge's two high schools and in the blood of the complex employees.

Dr. William Reid, a physician who came to the Methodist Medical Center in Oak Ridge in 1991, says that his treatment of patients with kidney cancer and immune system problems represented high clusters for a small population area. Reid called Martin Marietta Corporation, now the manager of the complex, to determine what chemicals the patients should be tested for. Methodist Medical began a disciplinary process against Reid three weeks after his inquiry.

Dr. Reid's story has appeared in local newspapers but residents appear unconcerned. Cancer deaths in Oak Ridge are 142 per 100,000; the rate for the state is 145 per 100,000. Employees of the complex are 20 percent less likely to die of cancer than all other Americans because of insurance and excellent medical care.

No studies of cases of cancer (no deaths), immune system disorders or birth defects have been done. Physicist Chester Richmond maintains, "People here just don't accept the arguments that this material is going to give you cancer."[1] Dr. Reid says, "They are worried they're going to have a Bhopal on their hands."[2]

Discussion Questions

1. Are the complex workers and Oak Ridge residents more concerned about their livelihoods?
2. If you were an officer of the Martin Marietta complex, would you take any action?
3. If you were Dr. Reid, to whom would you turn now?
4. Is it possible the Oak Ridge residents and complex workers just accept cancer and other illnesses as a price to be paid for economical survival?
5. Does this acceptance exonerate the complex from any responsibility?

---

1. Dick Thompson, "Living Happily Near a Nuclear Trash Heap," *Time* (May 11, 1992): 53.
2. *Ibid.*

Unit Four
Business and Its
Competition

Business's relations with its competitors is evidenced in its advertising, product similarity and pricing. The heat of the market place often creates difficult dilemmas on what to say in ads or how similar to make a product.

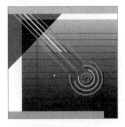

Section A
Advertising Content

Ads sell products. But how much can the truth be stretched? Are ads ever irresponsible in encouraging harmful behavior?

4.1 Joe Camel — The Cartoon Character Who Sells Cigarettes

Old Joe Camel, originally a member of a circus that passed through Winston-Salem, N.C., each year, was adopted by R. J. Reynolds' (RJR) marketers in 1913 as the symbol for a brand being changed from "Red Kamel" to "Camel." In the late 1980s, RJR revived Old Joe with a new look in the form of a cartoon. He became the camel with a "Top Gun" flier jacket, sunglasses, a smirk and a lot of appeal to young people.

In December 1991, the *Journal of the American Medical Association* published three surveys that found that the cartoon character, Joe Camel, was very effective in reaching children. Children between the ages of three and six were surveyed and 51.1 percent of them recognized old Joe Camel as being associated with Camel cigarettes.[1] The children in the study who were six-years old were as familiar with Joe Camel as they were with the Mickey Mouse logo for the Disney Channel. The surveys also established that 97.7 percent of students between the ages of twelve and nineteen have seen Old Joe and 58 percent of them think the ads are cool. Camel is identified by 33 percent of the students who smoke as their favorite brand.[2]

---

1. K. Deveny, "Joe Camel Ads Reach Children, Research Finds," *Wall Street Journal* (Dec. 11, 1991): B1.

2. W. Konrad, "I'd Toddle a Mile for a Camel," *Business Week* (Dec. 23, 1991): 34.

Before the studies appeared in the *AMA Journal*, the American Cancer Society, the American Heart Association and the American Lung Association had petitioned the FTC to ban the ads as "one of the most egregious examples in recent history of tobacco advertising that targets children."[3]

In 1990, Camel shipments rose 11.3 percent. Joe Camel has helped RJR take its Camel cigarettes from 2.7 percent to 3.1 percent of the market.[4] Michael Pertschuk, former head of the Federal Trade Commission and co-director of the Advocacy Institute, an antismoking group, has said, "These are the first studies to give us hard evidence, proving what everybody already knows is true: These ads target kids. I think this will add impetus to the movement to further limit tobacco advertising."[5] Joe Tye, founder of Stop Teenage Addictions to Tobacco, has stated, "There is a growing body of evidence that teen smoking is increasing. And it's 100 percent related to Camel."[6]

One researcher who worked on the study, Dr. Joseph R. DiFranza, stated, "We're hoping this information leads to a complete ban of cigarette advertising."[7] Dr. John Richards summarized the study as follows, "The fact is that the ad is reaching kids, and it is changing their behavior."[8]

RJR spokesman David Fishel responds to the allegations with sales evidence, "We can track 98 percent of Camel sales; and they're not going to youngsters. It's simply not in our best interest for young people to smoke, because that opens the door for the government to interfere with our product."[9] At the time of the AMA study announcement, RJR along with other manufacturers and the Tobacco Institute began a multimillion dollar campaign with billboards and bumper stickers to discourage children from smoking but announced it had no intention of abandoning Joe Camel. The Tobacco Institute publishes a popular pamphlet called, "Tobacco: Helping Youth Say No," which it distributes free of charge.

U.S. Surgeon General Antonia Novello has been very vocal in her desire to change alcohol and cigarette advertising. By March of 1992, she was calling for the withdrawal of the Joe Camel ad campaign: "In years past, R. J. Reynolds would have us walk a mile for a Camel. Today it's time that we invite old Joe Camel himself to take a hike."[10] The AMA's executive vice president, Dr. James S. Todd concurred:

> "This is an industry that kills 400,000 per year, and they have got to pick up new customers. We believe the company is directing its ads to the children who are 3, 6 and 9 years old."[11]

Cigarette sales are in fact declining 3 percent per year in the United States.

---

3. K. Deveny, B1.

4. Konrad, 34.

5. Deveny, B6.

6. Laura Bird, "Joe Smooth for President," *Adweek's Marketing Week* (May 20, 1991): 21.

7. W. Konrad, 34.

8. "Camels for Kids," *Time* (Dec. 23, 1991): 52.

9. *Ibid.*

10. W. Chesire, "Don't Shoot: It's Only Joe Camel," *Arizona Republic* (Mar. 15, 1992): C1.

11. *Ibid.*

An RJR spokeswoman responds that the average Camel smoker is thirty-five and, "Just because children can identify our logo doesn't mean they will use our product."[12]

The Center for Disease Control reported in March 1992 that smokers between the ages of twelve and eighteen prefer Marlboro, Newport or Camel cigarettes, the three brands with the most extensive advertising.[13]

Joe Camel t-shirts are appearing on teenagers throughout the country. Brown & Williamson, the producer of Kool cigarettes began testing a cartoon character for its ads. The character is a penguin in sunglasses and Day-Glo sneakers. Joseph Helewicz, spokesman for Brown & Williamson stated that the ads are geared to smokers in the twenty-one to thirty-five age group. Helewicz added that cartoon advertisements for adults are not new — the Pillsbury Doughboy and the Pink Panther are effective adult cartoons used in advertising.

In mid–1992, Surgeon General Antonia Novella, along with the American Medical Association, began a campaign called "Dump the Hump" to pressure the tobacco industry into stopping ad campaigns that teach kids to smoke.

Discussion Questions

1. Is it ethical for R. J. Reynolds to continue with its Joe Camel ads?
2. Suppose you were the executive in charge of the R. J. Reynolds account at your advertising agency. The account represents nearly 20 percent of your firm's business. Would you recommend an alternative to the Joe Camel character? What if RJR threatened to withdraw its account if you did not continue with Joe Camel?
3. Suppose you work with a pension fund that holds a large investment in RJR. Would you consider selling your RJR holdings?
4. Do you agree with the statement that identification of the logo does not equate with smoking or smoking Camels?

SOURCES

Dagnoli, Judann. "RJR Aims New Ads at Young Smokers." *Advertising Age* July 11, 1988, 2–3.

Rausch, Gary. "Tobacco Firms Unite to Curb Teen Smoking." *Mesa Tribune* June 24, 1991, B1 and B6.

Lippert, Barbara. "Camel's Old Joe Poses the Question: What is Sexy?" *Adweek's Marketing Week* Oct. 3, 1988, 55.

"March Against Smoking Joe." *The Arizona Republic* June 22, 1992, A3.

---

12. W. Konrad, 34.

13. "Selling Death," *Mesa Tribune* (Mar. 16, 1992): A8.

4.2 THE SEXIST BEER ADS

It came from Tustin, California — a new beer called Nude Beer. The label on the bottle included a photo of a bare-breasted blonde and the advertising campaign included plans for a new bare-breasted model each month for the bottle labels. Entrepreneur William H. Boam, formerly a commercial photographer, was in the process of applying for approval for his new beer's label and was running into opposition from the California Department of Alcohol Beverage Control and the U.S. Bureau of Alcohol, Tobacco & Firearms.

The California regulators referred to the label as "blatant and obnoxious" and "contrary to public welfare and morals." Mr. Boam responded, "They can try to stop me, but they are not going to win. This is a fun product. It's not obscene. It's like having a six-pack of *Playboy*."[1]

The BATF has a regulation that provides packaging for malt beverages "shall not contain any statement, design, device or representation which is obscene." The U.S. Brewers Association's advertising guidelines provide that beer advertising "should not include risque material, suggestive double entendres, 'cheesecake', or any other material that might be considered even slightly lewd or obscene."

Mr. Boam says that, "It's just a good-looking gal on a good-tasting beer. Society should not be so uptight about nudity. It's not filthy." Mr. Boam is planning other marketing tools including Nude Beer Nuts with a model on the label wearing only a cowboy hat and boots. He is considering nude males "for the girls."

Molson Canadian, a Canadian beer, ran a series of advertisements in its "Canadian Wildlife" campaign featuring a scantily-clad woman called, "The Rare Long-Haired Fox." Canadian women complained to Ontario's Consumer and Commercial Relations Minister, Peter Kormos. Kormos announced that the ads were sexist and inappropriate and that his administration would enact strict regulations. Kormos was forced to resign the day after his announcement of regulations because he appeared in a beefcake pose in the newspaper. However, the Canadian government moved forward with regulation of the beer advertisements focusing on content guidelines for sex, race and class.

Discussion Questions

1. Don't all ads with attractive women in them have a sexist overtone?
2. Is it possible to regulate sexism in ads?
3. Is nudity in alcohol advertising appropriate?
4. Won't every ad be objectionable to someone?
5. Should First Amendment protections exclude regulation of ad content (other than misrepresentation)?

---

1. Ruth Stroud, "Brown Bag Needed for Nude Beer?" *Advertising Age* (Oct. 18, 1982): 38.

SOURCE

Koeppel, Dan. "Molson and Labatt's Ignite a Backlash." *Adweek's Marketing Week* Apr. 8, 1991, 6.

4.3 ALCOHOL ADVERTISING: THE COLLEGE FOCUS

The mix is unquestionably there. Alcohol ads mix youth, fun and enticing activities like scuba diving and skiing. There is Spuds McKenzie, the "Party Animal" dog of Anheuser-Busch Companies' Bud Light ads. There is Stroh's Swedish Bikini Team. There are large promotions for beer on the beaches during spring break.[1]

U.S. Attorney General Antonia Novello has asked the industry for a voluntary ban on ads that attract minors. Novello has stated, "I must call for industry's voluntary elimination of the types of alcohol advertising that appeal to youth on the bases of certain life style appeals, sexual appeals, sports appeal, or risky activities, as well as advertising with the more blatant youth appeals of cartoon characters and youth slang."[2] A 1991 survey revealed that 10.6 million of the 20.7 million students in grades seven through twelve have had at least one drink in the last year.[3] Of this group that drinks, 8 million drink weekly, 5.4 million have drinking binges and one-half million have five or more drinks in a row at least once a week.[4]

Industry officials have responded that they are very active and very generous with programs for alcohol-use education. The officials point to their support for groups such as Mothers Against Drunk Driving (MADD).

Anheuser-Busch spends $20 million of its $260 million ad budget on a campaign that features the slogan, "Know when to say when." Miller Brewing Company runs a thirty-second ad with the slogan: "Think When You Drink." Miller spends $8 million per year on ads promoting responsible drinking.

During spring breaks in 1991 and 1992, Miller and Anheuser-Busch did not use their multi-story inflatable beer cans on the beaches of spring break meccas in Florida, Texas and Mexico. In Daytona Beach, Florida, Miller put billboards along the highways with the slogan: "Good beer is properly aged. You should be too." Miller's manager for alcohol and consumer issues, John Shafer, explains, "It's just good business sense to make sure we're on the right side of these issues."[5]

Patricia Taylor, a director at the Center for Science in the Public Interest responds to the efforts as follows: "The beer companies are spending hundreds of millions every year to present a very positive image of drinking. That overwhelms all attempts to talk about the other side of the issue."[6]

Novello has ordered new studies of the link between alcohol advertising and underage drinking. She has urged the industry to drop advertising meant to

1. The industry has scaled back in its spring break promotions for 1991 and 1992. Jeffrey Zbar, "Spring Break: Inflatable Beer Bottles Gone But Other Marketers Move In," *Advertising Age* (Apr. 1, 1991): 16.

2. Hilary Stout, "Surgeon General Wants to Age Alcohol Ads," *Wall Street Journal* (Nov. 5, 1991): B1.

3. J. Siler, "It Isn't Miller Time Yet, and This Bud's Not for You," *Business Week* (June 24, 1991): 52.

4. *Ibid.*

5. *Ibid.*

6. *Ibid.*

appeal to young people.[7] Anheuser-Busch has just created an ad campaign for retailers with ads in trade magazines and posters for stores to remind retailers not to sell beer to underage buyers. Novello responds, "These ads may be a stronger influence on students than they realize."[8]

Discussion Questions

1. Suppose that you were an officer in a brewery whose advertising campaign focused on youthful beach activities and your company's beer. Would you change your campaign?
2. Won't your ads be appealing to various groups regardless of their focus?
3. Would it be censorship for the government to control your ad content?
4. Are campaigns on responsible drinking sufficient?
5. Do the company's ads attempt to encourage underage people to drink?

SOURCES

Buck, R. "Ode to Miller Beer." *Adweek's Marketing Week* May 27, 1991, 16.
Colford, S. "FTC May Crash Beer Promos' Campus Party." *Advertising Age* Mar. 25, 1991, 3-4.

7. S. Elliott, "A Rising Tide of Rhetoric Over Warnings on Alcohol," *New York Times* (Apr. 2, 1992): C18.

8. *Ibid.*

4.4 THE OBLIGATION TO SCREEN? THE OBLIGATION TO REJECT?, *SOLDIER OF FORTUNE* CLASSIFIEDS

Soldier of Fortune (SOF) magazine, started in 1975, is a national magazine with a focus on guns and military clothing. Its stated audience is "professional adventurers." It has a very large classified advertising section. The ads are placed by individuals and companies for gun sales, other gun-related products, gun and equipment repairs, and employment for collectors and users.

Some of the classified ads printed between 1975 and 1984 offered services with language such as "Mercenary for Hire," "bounty hunter," "high risk contracts," "dirty work," "mechanic," and "do anything, anywhere at the right price." During the 1975 to 1984 period, SOF ran two thousand classified ads and about three dozen involved titles such as these.

Stories from various media sources including the Associated Press, United Press International, *The Rocky Mountain News, The Denver Post, Time* and *Newsweek* reported links between SOF classified ads and crimes or criminal plots. These links were reported on five SOF ads and alleged on four more ads. Law enforcement officials have contacted SOF staffers during investigations of two crimes linked to SOF personal service classifieds.

A. Nature of SOF Ads

Dr. Park Dietz, a forensic psychiatrist, has studied the SOF ads and concluded that the average SOF subscriber — a male who owns camouflage clothing and more than one gun — would understand some phrases in SOF's classified ads as solicitations for illegal activity given the "context" of those ads. SOF contained (at that time) display ads for semiautomatic rifles, books with titles such as "How to Kill," and articles including "Harassing the Bear, New Afghan Tactics Stall Soviet Victory," "Pipestone Canyon, Summertime in 'Nam and the Dyin' was Easy," and "Night Raiders on Russia's Border."

Dr. Dietz suggested that the SOF personal service ads carry the connotations of domestic crimes because of the nature of the magazine. He noted that the same ads would not carry that connotation if they appeared in *Esquire* or *Vanity Fair.*

B. The Hearn Ad

In September, October and November of 1984, SOF ran the following ad:

EX-MARINES — 67-69 'Nam Vets, Ex-DI, weapons specialist — jungle warfare, pilot, M.E., high risk assignments, U.S. or overseas. (404) 991-2684

"Ex-DI" means ex-drill instructor; "M.E." means multi-engine planes; and "high risk assignments" means work as a body guard or security specialist.

The ad was placed by John Wayne Hearn who said he placed it to recruit Vietnam veterans for work as bodyguards and security men for executives. Hearn's partner said they also hoped to train troops for South America. Hearn said he did not place the ad with an intent to solicit criminal employment but that 90 percent of the calls in response to the ad sought his participation in illegal activities such as beatings, kidnappings, jailbreaks, bombings, and murders. His only lawful inquiry was from a Lebanese oil conglomerate seeking bodyguards, and Hearn received a commission to place seven men with them.

Robert Black contacted Hearn through the *SOF* ad. Between 1982 and 1984, Black had asked at least four friends or co-workers from Bryan, Texas, to kill his wife, Sandra Black, or help him in killing her. Initially, Black discussed body-guard work with Hearn and their conversations focused on Black's gun collection. In October 1984, Hearn traveled to Texas from his Atlanta home to see Black's gun collection. While viewing the gun collection, Black discussed his plans for murdering his wife with Hearn. Hearn returned to Atlanta and Black called repeatedly. Black offered Hearn $10,000 if Hearn would kill Black's wife. The offer was made to Debbie Bannister, Hearn's girlfriend, and she communi-cated it to Hearn.

Hearn had no previous criminal record but on January 6, 1985, he killed Bannister's sister. On February 2, 1985, he killed Bannister's husband and on February 21, 1985, he killed Sandra Black. He was sentenced to concurrent life sentences for the murders.

C. The Victims' Suit Against SOF

Sandra Black's mother, Marjorie Eimann, and her son, Gary Wayne Black, brought suit against *SOF* for the negligent publication of Hearn's ad. The trial court awarded Eimann and Black $9.4 million in damages.

The decision was reversed on appeal. The court held that *SOF* was not liable and noted:

> Given the pervasiveness of advertising in our society and the important role it plays, we decline to impose on publishers the obligation to reject all ambiguous advertisements for products or services that might pose a threat of harm. The burden on a publisher to avoid liability from suits of this type is too great.

In a previously placed ad, litigation against SOF resulted when Douglas Norwood was ambushed, assaulted, shot, and became the victim of a car bomb late in 1985, each time by men hired through the following *SOF* ads:

> GUN FOR HIRE: 37-year-old — professional mercenary desires jobs. Vietnam Veteran. Discreet and very private. Bodyguard, courier, and other special skills. All jobs considered. [Phone number].
> GUN FOR HIRE: Nam sniper instructor. SWAT. Pistol, rifle, security specialist, bodyguard, courier plus. All jobs considered. Privacy guaranteed. Mike [Phone number].

This case was settled out of court in 1987.

Assume that you are the new director of advertising (both classified and commercial) for *SOF*. *SOF* was relieved of any liability for Sandra Black's death, so *SOF* does not have the obligation to check and/or reject ads.

The finding of legality does not ease your conscience as you review ads with language such as "high risk assignment" and "bounty hunter." As you think about the Sandra Black case, you rationalize that John Wayne Hearn was on a murder spree and Sandra Black was simply a victim of Hearn's sudden violence. On the other hand, Hearn would never have known Sandra Black if his classified ad had not facilitated his connection with Robert Black. Further, only five to ten ads of over a total of two thousand classifieds have resulted in crimes or criminal plots. Over lunch, you discuss the ad dilemma with your senior staff member who responds: "Yes, but we could have prevented those crimes by not running the ads."

Screening the ads will take time, private detectives, and an assumption of liability the law does not require you to make. Will you change *SOF's* ad policy? Will you conduct ad background checks?

Discussion Questions

1. Are there conflicting moral standards?
2. To whom do you owe your loyalty in making the decisions?
3. Should *SOF* feel morally responsible for Sandra Black's death?
4. Is the court's decision not to impose liability on *SOF* an application of utilitarianism?
5. Should the advertising policy decision be different after the Sandra Black murder than it was before?
6. Prosser, a legal scholar, has stated that, "Nearly all human acts ... carry some recognizable possibility of harm to another." Why do we allow recovery for some of those harmful acts and not others?

SOURCES

Eimann v. Soldier of Fortune Magazine, Inc., 880 F.2d 830 (5th Cir. 1989).

Adapted from Jennings, M. *Legal Environment of Business.* 2d ed. (1991), 229–31.

Tomlinson, Don. "Choosing Social Responsibility Over Law: The *Soldier of Fortune* Classified Advertising Cases." *Business & Professional Ethics Journal 9,* (1990) 79–96.

Norwood v. Soldier of Fortune Magazine, Inc., 651 F.Supp. 1397 (W.D. Ark. 1987).

4.5 BLACK DEATH: THE VODKA WITH A TWIST

Black Death is a beet-based vodka imported from a distillery in Belgium. The recipe for Black Death is Icelandic and "Black Death" is a term used by Iceland Drinkers for all strong alcoholic drinks. The label on the Black Death bottle features a skull in a top hat. Also, the vodka bottle is packaged in a black coffin.

The marketer in the U.S. for Black Death, Black Death U.S.A., announced an endorsement contract with Slash (Saul Hudson), the guitarist for Guns 'N Roses. U.S. Surgeon General Antonia Novello criticized the use of the rock group idol, "We realize that adolescents, when targeted by people that they believe are heroes in their culture, will go ahead and buy it."[1] Black Death U.S.A. will run ads with Slash and his tattoos in *Rolling Stone*, *Spin* and *L.A. Style*.

Saul Hudson (Slash) is probably best remembered for his performance on the live MTV awards show some years ago in which he used vulgar language. He explained that he drank wine before the show and has published interviews in which he discusses drug use and rehabilitation. The rock group Guns 'N Roses is well-known itself for its partying excesses, drug addiction and its controversial lyrics that have been criticized as racist and sexist.[2]

Thomas Lines, CEO for Black Death U.S.A., maintains that Slash has "great credibility as a musician" and that he was not chosen "because he has a hell-raising image."[3]

Although the U.S. Bureau of Alcohol, Tobacco and Firearms approved the Black Death label in 1989, it recently took action to block sales on the grounds of misleading advertising. The enforcement action alleges the skull logo creates the impression of bubonic plague and poison.[4]

Mr. Lines calls the enforcement action a "witch hunt"[5] and maintains that preventing young people from drinking is a matter of education and enforcement. Lines was required to market the vodka under the name "Black Hat" pending the outcome of ATF's enforcement action.

In mid–1992, a federal judge ruled that Lines could reinstate use of the label "Black Death." Lines had argued in the proceedings, "No one believes that 'Apple' computers are made of apples … no one believes that 'Moosehead' beer contains moose heads."[6] George Wickhardt, Cabo's attorney, praised the judge's decision, "This was an example of bureaucracy run amok. We were saved by the bell today from the extinction of the client's business."[7]

---

1. L. Bird, "New Vodka Sold as Black Death Riles Regulators," *Wall Street Journal* (Apr. 3, 1992): B1.

2. *Ibid.*

3. *Ibid.*

4. *Ibid.*

5. *Ibid.*

6. "Black Death Vodka Given OK to Keep Name, Logo," *Tribune Newspapers* (July 11, 1992): H1.

7. *Ibid.*

Discussion Questions

1. If you were Thomas Lines, would you continue your Black Death campaign as planned?
2. Do you think the decision to use Slash in ads is an ethical one? Is the use of Slash a good marketing decision?
3. Doesn't advertising provide information for making buying decisions? Is there a way to control the influence of ads on particular groups?
4. Do advertisers have some First Amendment protection for their ads? Will it be difficult to draw lines for which ads will be approved and which will not?
5. Does Slash (Saul Hudson) have a responsibility to his fans when he makes endorsement decisions?

4.6 MALT LIQUOR ADS: CRACK, GANGS AND GHETTOS

Malt Liquor, a high-alcohol content beer, is manufactured by G. Heileman Brewing Company, Pabst Brewing Company, McKenzie River Corporation, and Stroh/Schlitz Brewing Company. Sales for the malt liquor are highest in ghetto areas and ads are focused on inner cities.

These ads have recently come under scrutiny by the Bureau of Alcohol, Tobacco and Firearms. Makani Themba of the Marin Institute, a California organization dedicated to alcohol and drug abuse prevention observes:

> What the government has done through its lack of regulation, has been to close its eyes to some of the most obscene and heinous advertising ever produced. This crackdown wouldn't have happened without community outcry.[1]

The ads for the various brewing companies are described in the chart below:

Company	Brand Name	Ad
Pabst	Olde English 800	Inner-city billboard and point-of-sale materials with slogan, "It's the Power"; use of "Eight Ball" in ads; street slang for an eight ounce of crack or cocaine[2]
Heileman	Colt 45 PowerMaster	Lightning Bolt — "It's got more."
Stroh/ Schlitz	Red Bull	"The Real Power"
McKenzie River	St. Ides (has 5.9% alcohol)	"No. 1 strongest malt"[3] Radio spot by Rapper Ice Cube[4] In some posters, Ice Cube makes a gang sign.

At the time of its introduction of PowerMaster, Heileman was in Chapter 11 bankruptcy. When the ads for PowerMaster began, Surgeon General Antonia Novello asked both the Bureau of Alcohol, Tobacco and Firearms (BATF) and the Federal Trade Commission (FTC) to take regulatory and enforcement action.

Two clergymen from Chicago, the Revs. George Clements and Mike Pfleger, traveled to La Crosse, Wisconsin, to meet with Heileman's CEO and refused to leave before they saw him. The clergymen were arrested for trespassing.

Rev. Clements and Dewitt Helm, the president of the Association of National Advertisers (ANA), appeared on "Nightline" to discuss the issue. Clements said,

1. A. Freedman, "Malt Advertising that Touts Firepower Comes Under Attack by U.S. Officials," *Wall Street Journal* (July 1, 1991): B1.

2. A Harlem drug dealer commented on the "8 Ball" poster, "What Olde English is trying to put over is that this is a cheaper high than drugs." *Ibid.*

3. BATF regulations prohibit references in ads to strength or alcohol content.

4. The Washington State Liquor Control Board banned the Ice Cube ads when blacks complained about the crudeness of the rap lyrics.

"I don't see how this man Helm can say that advertising has no role in the consumption of beer."[5] Helm responded:

> "I am an elder in the Presbyterian Church, and I take my religious conviction seriously, but that doesn't give a Catholic priest or a holy roller or anyone else the right to impose their will on the majority."
>
> "We trust these people [black Americans] to vote, we trust them to make decisions in their lives, but suddenly, if someone doesn't like a brand coming into their neighborhood, a plantation mentality sets in and we have to prevent them from buying it."[6]

Heileman withdrew its PowerMaster within ten days. By the end of 1991, Pabst was issued an BATF order to withdraw the "It's the Power" ads by December 31, 1991. In May 1992, Heileman introduced a new malt called Colt 45 Premium. Still in Chapter 11, Heileman's ad campaign is "Be a Premium Player." In gang terminology, members refer to themselves as "players." The Marin Institute, dedicated to the prevention of drug and alcohol abuse, calls the ad campaign one designed to exploit racial and ethnic communities.[7]

Discussion Questions

1. Is the reference to eight ball ethical?
2. Is the ghetto thrust of all the campaigns ethical?
3. If you were the marketing director for McKenzie River, would you continue the Ice Cube campaign? The campaign has been very successful in increasing sales.

SOURCES

Warner, Fara. "Feds Censure Pabst for Olde English Ads." *Adweek's Marketing Week* Nov. 4, 1991, 5.

Bird, Laura. "An 'Uptown' Remake Called PowerMaster." *Adweek's Marketing Week* July 1, 1991, 7.

---

5. R. Buck, "PowerMaster Trips ANA's Dewitt Helm," *Adweek's Marketing Week* (July 8, 1991): 12.

6. *Ibid.*

7. A. Freedman, "Heileman Tries a New Name for a Strong Malt," *Wall Street Journal* (May 11, 1992): B1 and B6.

4.7 TELEMARKETING TRIPS: THE GREAT HYPE

Martha Burham received the postcard in the mail. The postcard said she had won a luxury vacation in Hawaii. She would have five glorious days in Hawaii for $320 in administrative costs. In addition to the Hawaii trip, Martha's postcard said she would receive two round-trip tickets to the Bahamas. Martha could not resist. She called the "800" number on her postcard to claim her trip.

The telemarketer on the other end of the phone was about as pleasant as Martha could imagine. "Sheila" was full of hearty congratulations for Martha. When Martha inquired, "What's the catch?" Sheila replied, "There's no catch, Martha. We are a new nationwide travel agency called Itinerary. We are large and can get the price discounts. We selected a few discriminating individuals for our prize package so that we could rely on them for word-of-mouth advertising about our quality trips at low, low prices."

Martha was partially flattered and partially perplexed. Sheila asked for Martha's credit card number so that the administrative costs could be charged and the trip materials and tickets forwarded to Martha. Sheila explained that Martha's prize could only be collected within twenty-four hours after she received the postcard.

Martha thought that a five-day Hawaii trip for only $320 was well worth the money even if she had to sleep on the beach. Martha gave Sheila her credit card number and the trip materials arrived in the mail three days later.

Martha opened the materials with great anticipation but discovered that her "free" trip had some conditions. She had agreed to use Itinerary to book fourteen nights of lodging over the course of the next year. The lodging had to be booked only at hotels Itinerary listed as "qualifying". Rates in the hotels for Itinerary customers were at a "reduced" fee of $195.00 per night.

Martha called the Itinerary "800" number and asked for Sheila. Martha told Sheila, "I am so angry that you can probably see fumes coming from my ears!" Sheila proceeded to explain that Itinerary had a "no refund" policy and that the credit card charges had already been processed. Martha hung up to call her credit card company.

Sheila looked at her co-worker, Blair and said, "That's the tenth time that's happened to me since I started working here seven days ago. Customers are always calling back wanting refunds. I read the telephone script just as its written so I haven't made any mistakes. Itinerary's packets must say something different than what I tell people. I'd like to take a look at it so I could explain things to customers." Blair shot back, "And you'll never see it. Just read your cards and do your job. If we told them the truth, we wouldn't have Itinerary or a job."

Discussion Questions

1. Has anything illegal been done with the Itinerary telemarketing plan?
2. Are the postcard and follow-up phone calls deceptive?
3. If you were Sheila, would you continue to do the work? Suppose your family was dependent upon your income, would you continue the job?
4. If you were an executive at a credit card firm that had received a number of complaints on Itinerary, would you take action? Would you investigate?

4.8 Bungee Ads: A Big Jump

Nike and Reebok International are shoe manufacturers who are intense competitors, particularly in the hightop tennis shoe market. Nike manufacturers Air hightops and Reebok manufactures the Pump, a hightop tennis shoe.

Reebok's ad agency, Chiat/Day/Mojo of San Francisco developed a comparison ad with bungee jumpers. Bungee jumping is a "sport" with growing popularity in which people are tethered at the ankles with large elastic ropes and then jump from high places. The participant feels the thrill of free falling but is caught just above the ground by the exhausted length of the elastic ropes.

In the Reebok ad, one jumper is wearing the Reebok Pumps while the other jumper is wearing Nike Air hightops. Both jump from a Seattle bridge from 180 feet above rocks and water in the Seattle bay area. The commercial follows the jumps with the sound of the wind, their clothes and the tightening of the ropes. After the jump, the Reebok wearer is safely hanging by the bungee ropes just above the water. The Nike jumper is gone and the commercial shows only his shoes in the bungee ropes.

The announcer then states:

"The Pump from Reebok. It fits a little better than your ordinary athletic shoe."

By the end of the first week, NBC refused to run the ad. Public and professional ad industry outcry over the ad was so extensive that the other broadcasters followed and the ad was withdrawn.

Discussion Questions

1. Is the ad just a comparative ad that uses shock value?
2. Does the concept in the commercial contain humor that is too dark to be acceptable?
3. Is the ad a clever advertising ploy?
4. Is anyone really harmed by the ad?
5. Would you be offended by the ad?
6. Would you have continued to run the ad?

Sources

Garfield, Bob. "Good Taste Takes Deep Dive in Bungee Ad for Reebok Pump." *Advertising Age* Mar. 26, 1990, 52.

Grimm, Matthew. *Adweek's Marketing Week* Mar. 26, 1990, 5.

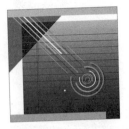

SECTION B
APPROPRIATION OF OTHERS' IDEAS

What belongs to whom? When does an idea belong to someone else? Laws on patents and copyrights afford protection in some cases, but others are too close to call, or are they?

4.9 THE OBVIOUS IDEA AND A PARTING OF THE WAYS

In 1986, aerobics instructor, Gin Miller, tore a knee ligament. At the suggestion of her physical therapist, Ms. Miller resumed her exercise program after the injury by stepping up and down on a wooden step. She added music to her recovery work-out and developed additional moves for the stepping process. She called her new step-up routines "Bench Blast," and her students in classes and gyms throughout Atlanta immediately took to the new technique. Ms. Miller's involvement is, as they say, urban legend and it is unclear if Ms. Miller was alone in the development of the step and its development was uniquely hers.

By 1989, the growing popularity of Miller's step-up caught the attention of Richard Boggs, the owner of seven Atlanta health clubs. Boggs and several partners created Sports Step and began marketing a new plastic platform in lieu of the original Miller wooden stool. It was called "The Step" and was produced in three versions ranging in price from $59 to $199 including accompanying video tapes.

At the time of the Boggs' partnership, the aerobic industry was flat. Sales for 1990 were the same as sales for 1987 according to figures of the Sporting Goods Manufacturers Association.

Reebok discovered the step and began researching its health benefits and developing shoes for the step workout as well as training programs for step instructors.

In 1990, Reebok and Boggs agreed to a joint venture. Reebok's name would be put on all steps sold in health clubs. Reebok agreed to use the step in its ads and promotions, with Reebok's benefit coming from increased sales in apparel and footwear.

As with all aerobic partnerships in which a small firm with a good idea latches onto the marketing power of a large firm, the alliance was successful. Reebok spent $7 million for ads, but its shoe sales increased 10 percent following two years of flat sales. Sports Step's sales went from $7.8 million in 1990 to $19 million in 1991. Sales in 1992 are predicted to be $40 million. Currently, 40 percent of the country's health clubs have the step as equipment. There are 27,000 health clubs nationwide.

Approximately 7.3 million Americans participate in step aerobics. There are ten manufacturers of steps, but Reebok enjoys name recognition and an association with this form of aerobics.

Future growth in the market is expected to come from sales to consumers who exercise or want to exercise at home. Sports Step would like to sell its step to the home market sans the Reebok label. Reebok is developing its own step for home market sales. Sports Step has stopped using the Reebok name on health club sales. The parties are currently in litigation over all of these disputes.

Discussion Questions

1. Is the idea of a "step" for workouts too generic to be entitled to protection?
2. Should Reebok and Sports Step be permitted to pursue their markets independently?
3. It is unethical to depart from an unclear contract?

SOURCE

Grossman, Laurie. "Teaming Up With a Big Player May Not Assure a Win." *Wall Street Journal* Mar. 18, 1992, B2.

4.10 RAGU THICK AND ZESTY

Ragu Foods, Inc.'s spaghetti sauce has been the leading seller of prepared spaghetti sauce in the United States since 1972. By 1973, Ragu held over 60 percent of the market. It was late in 1973 that Hunt-Wesson Foods, Inc., made the decision to enter the prepared spaghetti sauce market.

Hunt's entry into the market place was its "Prima Salsa" spaghetti sauce. Hunt's marketing campaign for its new sauce featured the phrase, "Extra Thick and Zesty." Hunt's introduced its new sauce, after extensive marketing and taste studies in 1976, using that slogan.

Just before Hunt's launched its national campaign on "Prima Salsa," Ragu introduced a new sauce to its line that it called, "Ragu Extra Thick and Zesty". Ragu's advertising campaign used a photo similar to Hunt's ad photo of a ladle of sauce being poured over a bed of noodles. The Ragu new sauce entry was thickened with starch, whereas the Hunt's Prima Salsa was thickened through a longer cooking process. The label on the Ragu sauce did not make the distinction clear.

Hunt's executives claimed the introduction of the Ragu sauce appropriated all their work and research and created product confusion in the minds of the consuming public. Ragu held over 65 percent of the market in 1975, the year the Prima Salsa product was introduced.

Ragu maintains that its product was simply a response to competition and good business strategy. Hunt's claims there can be no competition because of Ragu's domination of the market. Hunt's feels Ragu's methods are unfair.

Discussion Questions

1. Is Ragu just an aggressive competitor, or has Ragu appropriated ideas?
2. Are any moral standards violated by Ragu's conduct?
3. Would you feel comfortable with the new sauce's name if you were a marketing executive with Ragu?
4. Is product confusion a fair method of competition?
5. Aren't companies free to meet the market with their product lines?

SOURCE

Hunt-Wesson Foods, Inc. v. Ragu Foods, Inc., 627 F.2d 919 (9th Cir. 1980).

4.11 THE LITTLE INTERMITTENT WINDSHIELD WIPER AND ITS LITTLE INVENTOR

Robert W. Kearns obtained a patent for his first intermittent car windshield wiper system in 1967. The intermittent windshield wiper system began appearing on the major automakers' cars and those of Japanese cars during the 1970s. The systems were put on the cars without any payment to Mr. Kearns. The auto manufacturers maintained that the idea was an obvious one and that it was only a matter of time before their engineers developed the same type of system. The manufacturers also maintained that their systems were different from Kearns in design and function.

Kearns filed suit against Ford, General Motors, Chrysler, Fiat, Toyota and most other Japanese auto manufacturers. Kearns had planned to open his own manufacturing firm to supply the intermittent windshield washer systems to all the car manufacturers but was unable to do so after the companies manufactured the systems in-house.

In November 1990, Kearns settled his case with Ford Motor Company for $10.2 million which amounted to thirty cents per car sold by Ford with the intermittent windshield wiper systems. In June, 1992, a jury awarded Kearns $11.3 million in damages from the Chrysler corporation or about ninety cents per car for Chrysler's infringement of Kearns' patent. Chrysler had sold 12,564,107 vehicles with the device. Kearns had originally asked for $3-$30 per car or damages ranging from $37.7 million to $377 million because of the treble damage provisions of the infringement laws.

Kearns still has suits pending against the other car companies. He spent $4 million in legal fees in the Ford case and expects to spend $5.5 million on the Chrysler case before it is completed because of Chrysler's announcement that it will appeal an "unreasonable and excessive" verdict.

Kearns says that his success should be an inspiration for other inventors because they can see they can win when they go up against large corporations that have used their ideas without reimbursement.

Discussion Questions

1. Is it ethical to use an idea based on the risk analysis that the owner of that idea simply cannot afford to litigate the matter?
2. Why was the intermittent system so important to the car dealers?
3. Could Kearns have done anything further to protect himself?
4. If you were an executive with one of the car companies still in pending litigation against Kearns, would you settle the case? Why or why not?

SOURCES

"Chrysler Told to Pay Inventor $11.3 Million." *New York Times* June 12, 1992, C3.

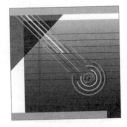

SECTION C
PRODUCT PRICING

What price is fair? Is a price always the most a customer is willing to pay? Should businesses afford special discounts for nonprofit buyers?

4.12 CATERERS AND THE DUPLICATION OF OVERHEAD RECOVERY

Carts, Candies and Caviar, Inc., (CCC) is a catering business based in Phoenix, Arizona. CCC has enjoyed nearly exponential growth since it was founded in 1974 by Cindy Callstone. With sales over $1 million for 1991, Cindy was looking toward a bright future. Cindy also realized she needed assistance with financial planning. In 1992, through a relationship with one of the local universities, Cindy took on two senior business students as interns. Their assigned task was to develop a plan for financing Cindy's expansion plans including the construction of new kitchen facilities.

The two students, Vera Dickerson and Ralph Dunn, were given full access to Cindy's books, records and contracts. In the course of their review work, Vera and Ralph discovered what Vera called "interesting business practices" in billing. For example, Cindy billed all of her computer time to all customers who were "cost plus" customers. These customers had contracts in which they agreed to pay all catering costs plus a certain percentage profit for Cindy. In one month, Cindy recovered all of her computer time from fifteen different customers.

Cindy billed full "kitchen time" to the same cost plus customers. Kitchen time is an overhead amount for Cindy's kitchen facilities computed on a per day or per hour basis. For example, if a dinner preparation takes a full day, Cindy bills the customer for 1/30 of the monthly cost of her kitchen facility. However, it would be rare for Cindy to devote the kitchen solely to one customer. In many cases, the same dinner is prepared simultaneously for eight to ten customers. All the customers would be billed for a full day.

Cindy has negotiated discount arrangements with soda vendors. For example, for every catered event where she uses Sparkle Soda. Sparkle gives her a 15 percent discount because Sparkle views the catered event as a means of advertising. Cindy does not reflect the 15 percent discount in her billing. Vera found some instances where the customer chose its soda vendor and paid the vendor directly, but Cindy's bill to those customers still included charges for the soda. Vera asked Cindy about the bills for the soda and Cindy replied, "If they catch it, we'll pay them back, otherwise don't worry about it. This is just the way things are done in this business."

After their review of the financial records, Vera and Ralph met to discuss their proposed financial strategy. Vera began by commenting, "She's ripping off the customers and they don't even know it!" Ralph responded, "Look, my uncle is in the catering business. They all operate this way. They get as much into the bill as they can. Maybe the customers will catch it. If they do, you admit the mistake and refund it. If they don't, you make more money. It's no big deal. And besides, look how successful she is. No one is crying 'foul'! They're just giving her more business."

Discussion Questions

1. Evaluate all of Cindy's billing practices from an accounting perspective.
2. Evaluate all of Cindy's billing practices from an ethical perspective.
3. Cindy claims she is just following industry practice. Is this a proper moral standard for her operation?
4. Could Cindy's practices prove costly in the future?
5. If you were Vera, what would you do?

4.13 NURSING HOMES, THE ELDERLY AND VIDEO CASSETTES FOR "HOME-VIEWING"

The Motion Picture Licensing Corporation (MPLC) is the organization responsible for the licensing of motion pictures and the collection of royalties for showings of the motion pictures. Their licensing jurisdiction runs to all levels from "big screen" distribution to video cassette rentals. The MPLC registers the movies and then collects royalties and distributes them to the appropriate parties. The MPLC is a creation of the major studios and simply acts as an agent for all studios in the distribution of films and collection of revenues. At one time, MPLC's task was relatively uncomplicated since film distribution was either for "big screen" or television use. However, with the advent of the video rental business, the MPLC's control of distribution became increasingly difficult.

In 1984, the video rental store industry began a period of tremendous growth that would eventually culminate in a "video store on every corner." The ease of access and reasonable video fees prompted directors of hospices and nursing homes to offer video tape showings in the nursing homes. Many of the incapacitated and disabled elderly in these homes would be unable to go to a theater and many could not visit homes of relatives and friends. The videotapes were shown in the common rooms of these homes and hospices.

In 1987, the MPLC learned of the practices of the nursing homes. Taking the position that the showing of the tapes in the homes was a "public performance" under the copyright laws and that the homes needed a "public performance license," the MPLC began taking enforcement action. In July 1987, the MPLC budgeted $3.5 million for a two-year campaign designed to educate nursing home and hospice operators about the rights of film copyright owners.

A notice was distributed to nearly all nursing homes and hospices on the east coast notifying directors that the showing of the videos was illegal. One home received a bill for unpaid license fees in the amount of $16,975.00. Others were notified of the civil damages of $250 per showing for violation of MPLC's rights.

A nursing home resident wrote a letter of protest regarding the actions of MPLC to Senator Roth of Delaware. An excerpt appears below:

> Emily P. Bissell Hospital is our home, just as other nursing care facilities are home for their residents. It is not by choice that we are here, but we are, and our lives are now changed in many, many ways. For the most part we are not able to get out into the community to do the things that most people take for granted, such as going to the movies, or going to the video store. If the staff from our Activity Department could show us some of the movies available on video cassettes, however, it would certainly bring us a lot of pleasure, and we do not see how this type of situation could be defined as a 'public showing' as the law currently sees it.

As a result of the letter, Senator Roth proposed an amendment to the copyright laws which would grant a carefully drawn exemption for showings in a hospital, hospice, nursing home, retirement home, or other such facility providing health-related care on a regular basis. Representative Benjamin Cardin of Maryland has introduced a companion bill in the House.

The MPLC, along with all the major studios, is opposing the bill. However, some of the studios are attempting to resolve the problem sans legislation. Disney is offering a twenty-year, royalty-free license agreement to any eligible facility in exchange for a $10 contribution in Disney's name to the United Way. Time-Warner is offering a similar deal but for twenty-five years. Columbia Pictures will grant the licenses for $1 per year. However, all the studies are opposing the bill which they have labeled a "serious erosion of the public performance doctrine."

Discussion Questions

1. What rights is MPLC trying to protect?
2. Are the nursing homes and hospices violating the rights of MPLC?
3. Are there situations you have seen that would also constitute violations of the public performance license requirements?
4. Does it really harm anyone if a nursing home shows a video tape?
5. Doesn't everyone violate copyright laws with VCRs?

4.14 SALOMON BROTHERS AND BOND PRICING

Salomon Brothers is an eighty-one-year-old investment banking firm that was, prior to the summer of 1991, the most powerful government bond dealer on Wall Street. The U.S. government bond market is a $2.3 trillion market.

Regulations in the bond market prohibit any firm from acquiring more than 35 percent of the Treasury notes and bonds at government auctions. Known as the 35 percent rule, it exists to prevent one firm from buying enough of the market to unilaterally dictate the prices of the instruments.

On August 9, 1991, Salomon announced it was suspending two managing directors, Paul Mozer and Thomas Murphy, along with two other employees for violations of the 35 percent rule. However, the suspension led to the discovery of several problems with regard to the 35 percent rule.

In December 1990, Salomon bought 35 percent of a $8.5 billion four-year note Treasury auction item and also submitted, through a customer another $1 billion bid on the same notes. The $1 billion was really for Salomon and it ended up with 46 percent of the offering. Salomon had placed a "squeeze" on the market; huge distortions in supply caused by Salomon forced the payment of high prices.

For example, in February 1991, Mozer had a customer, Mercury Asset Management, a branch of S. G. Warburg, place a $1 billion order for thirty-year Treasury bonds. Mozer meant the order to be bogus in order to surprise a new employee trader. However, the deal went through and was booked to Salomon. Rigged bids were discovered in three Treasury auctions during 1991, including the one described early in May, 1991.

At the Treasury auction on May 22, 1991, Salomon Brothers bought nearly 90 percent of the two-year note instruments valued at $12.26 billion through hedge funds, or large partnerships. Prices for the instruments skyrocketed as a result. Salomon denied there was any collusion with the hedge funds but a government investigation was launched.

The result of Salomon's cornering of the Treasury market was that small bond-trading housing and commercial banks experienced substantial losses; $100 million from the May auction alone. A Texas Christian University MBA graduate, Michael Irelan, was fired from his job at Boatmen's National Bank in St. Louis when he lost $400,000 in the Salomon May "squeeze." "I liked my job and believe I had become a good sound trader. But now, who knows if I will be able to do this again."[1]

Hickey Securities, Inc., lost several million dollars in the May "squeeze" and their investors defected, causing their assets to fall from $100 to $30 million in a four-month period.

Richard Breeden, Chairman of the SEC said that there weren't just a few bad apples in the Treasury market but that the structure of the market was wrong. "It's very important that we ... take a cold, hard look at: Do the intermediaries, the people who stand behind the Treasury and the ultimate purchasers of these

---

1. Constance Mitchell, "Salomon's 'Squeeze' In May Auction Left Many Players Reeling," *Wall Street Journal* (Oct. 31, 1991): A10.

bonds, have too much power?"[2] For some time, dealers, like Salomon, had been advising the Treasury on how to run the market. The primary dealers, like Salomon could corner the market as follows:

1. The firm puts in a bid for its maximum 35 percent share of the government bonds being auctioned. To ensure that the bid is accepted, it is made slightly above the going price of the bonds already being quoted in the 'when-issued' market.
2. The firm simultaneously puts in a bid, at a similarly high price, for more bonds on behalf of its major customers.
3. The bids are accepted by the Treasury Department.
4. In a prearranged transaction, the firm purchases at cost the bonds it bought on behalf of its customers. When the firm has enough bonds to control the supply, it has 'cornered' the market.
5. When other bond dealers want to buy the bonds, perhaps to cover short positions (bonds they sold that they didn't own), the firm can name its price.[3]

Up until the trading scandal broke, Salomon had the top profits of all the Wall Street firms: $451 million for the first half of 1991. After the scandal broke, Salomon's stock went from $36 per share in August to $23 by the end of September, a 30 percent drop.

Clients of Salomon began looking elsewhere. By mid-September, the state of Maryland's $13 billion state pension fund was talking with Goldman Sachs and other firms. Salomon sold $40 billion in securities between May 1991 and September 1991, reducing its assets to $105 billion.

Estimates of accounting reserves for litigation by Treasury investors, Salomon shareholders and competitors were put at $1 billion or one-third of Salomon's net worth. Salomon took a conservative $200 million reserve in October, with the resulting reduction in earnings in what was otherwise a banner year.

Warren E. Buffet, whose firm owns $700 million in Salomon convertible shares, was named interim chairman in August, 1991. He went before the House Subcommittee on Telecommunications & Finance and confirmed misdeeds by the firm. His testimony indicated Salomon had $10.6 billion or 94 percent of the May 1991 Treasury-note auction. Buffet's steps were viewed favorably by prosecutors: "The unquestionably substantial steps taken by Salomon inevitably reduce the government's need to punish,"[4] was the comment by Bruce Baird, the prosecutor in the Drexel Burnham Lambert, Inc., junk bond case.

In May 1992, Salomon settled with the SEC for a $290 penalty and a two-month suspension from June 1 to August 3, 1992. Drexel Burnham Lambert paid $600 million in penalties in 1989. Former Treasury secretary, William E. Simon, stated, "It's an absolutely startling number. If I understood the infractions, this is an extremely severe penalty against the firm and will most certainly send a message to Wall Street that infractions are going to be dealt with in very harsh

---

2. David Wessel, "Treasury and the Fed Have Long Caved In To 'Primary Dealers'," *Wall Street Journal* (Sept. 25, 1991): A7.

3. Gary Weiss, et al., "The Salomon Shocker: How Bad Will Its Get?" *Business Week* (Aug. 26, 1991): 54–57.

4. Michael Galen, "Salomon: Honesty is the Gutsiest Policy," *Business Week* (Sept. 16, 1991): 100.

ways."[5] No criminal charges will be brought against the firm, but former senior officials at Salomon will be investigated.

Salomon remains on Standard & Poor's credit watch and reported a loss of $29 million for the fourth quarter of 1991. Salomon continues to suffer from the setbacks of many executives departing with a resulting brain drain. While Congress is considering restructuring the auction market, the Treasury has changed auction operational procedures, including a requirement of verification of large bids and actual receipt of bonds.

Discussion Questions

1. Was Salomon's conduct harmful to others?
2. Salomon's earnings for 1991 were still $507 million despite third and fourth quarter losses. Should the earnings be forfeited?
3. Was the SEC penalty sufficient?
4. Why didn't someone disclose Salomon's practices prior to the Congressional hearings?
5. Can people like Michael Irelan ever be adequately compensated?
6. In mid–1992, Salomon named Charles Williams, a well-known Wall Street troubleshooter as its chief of fixed-income compliance. Salomon is said to want "suspenders on top of belts" in its compliance units. Mr. Williams reportedly received a $200,000 pay package. Is this the cost of ethics or the price of ethical violations?

SOURCES

Labaton, Steven. "Wall Street Opposing Bond Rules." *New York Times* June 1, 1992, C1.

Siconolfi, Michael. "Scandal at Salomon Leaves Its Mark on the Bottom Line." *Wall Street Journal* Feb. 7, 1992, C1.

Salwen, Kevin, and Tom Herman. "Freddie Mac Fines Firms for Inflated Orders." *Wall Street Journal* Oct. 4, 1991, C1.

Salwen, Kevin. "Salomon's Dealer Role is Supported." *Wall Street Journal* Sept. 27, 1991, C1 and C17.

Weiss, Gary, et al. "How Bad Will it Get?" *Business Week* Oct. 7, 1991, 122-124.

Spiro, Leah Nathans. "The Bomb Shelter Salomon Built." *Business Week* Sept. 9, 1991, 78–80.

Salwen, Kevin, and John Connor. "SEC Mulls Penalties for Street." *Wall Street Journal* Oct. 2, 1991, C1.

Weiss, Gary. "Behind the Happy Talk at Salomon." *Business Week* Nov. 11, 1991, 150–152.

Power, William. "Salomon's Big Loss Could Well Become Goldman Sach's Gain." *Wall Street Journal* Sept. 10, 1991, A1 and A8.

Baumohl, Bernard. "Swaggering Into Trouble." *Time* Aug. 26, 1991, 41.

---

5. Michael Siconolfi, et al., "Salomon Is Breathing Easier After Accepting Huge Fine in Scandal," *Wall Street Journal* (May 21, 1992): A1.

Weiss, Gary, et al. "Clearing the Wreckage." *Business Week* Sept. 2, 1991, 66–68.

McNamee, Mike. "The Judgment of Salomon: An Anticlimax." *Business Week* June 1, 1992, 106.

Cohen, Laurie P. "Ex-Salomon Trader Supplied Information to Prosecutors." *Wall Street Journal* May 28, 1992, C1.

"The Salomon Scandal In Bondage." *The Economist* Sept. 14, 1991, 92–93.

Siconolfi, Michael. "Salomon Names Charles Williams A Compliance Chief." *Wall Street Journal* June 16, 1992, B14.

Eichenwald, Kurt. "Salomon Still Struggling to Diversify Its Business." *New York Times* Sept. 8, 1992, C1, C4.

Hertzberg, Daniel, and Laurie P. Cohen. "Scandal Is Fading Away for Salomon, But not for Trader Paul Mozer." *Wall Street Journal* Aug. 7, 1992, A1.

Eichenwald, Kurt. "Outside Lawyer Appointed General Counsel at Salomon." *New York Times* Sept. 2, 1992, C3.

Salwen, Kevin. "House Panel Seeks to Amend Securities Bill." *Wall Street Journal* Aug. 7, 1992, A5.

UNIT FIVE
BUSINESS AND ITS
PRODUCT

Quality, safety, service and social responsibility. Customers want these qualities
in a product and a company. Does the profit motivation interfere with these
traits?

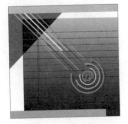

SECTION A
CONTRACT RELATIONS

The law of contracts is detailed, but ethical discussions center on the fairness of treatment and the balance of the agreement.

5.1 JOSEPH HORNE COMPANY AND THE DILLARD'S PREMATURE TAKEOVER

Joseph Horne Company is a Pittsburgh department store chain. In 1986, Horne's was the target of a management leveraged buy-out and was suffering with the resultant $160 million in debt.

Horne's executives were relieved when in 1988, Dillard Department Stores, Inc., and mall developer Edward J. DeBartolo agreed to buy Horne's stock for $74 million as well as assume the heavy debt from the 1986 buy-out.

Dillard's was permitted to infiltrate Horne's fourteen stores. Dillard's installed data lines and computers in Horne's to prepare for the consolidation. Horne's stores were thus hooked to Dillard's Little Rock headquarters and Dillard's assumed control of Horne's merchandise purchasing.

Dillard's executives wanted financial and purchasing control to be able to conduct their pre-closing due diligence with respect to the company records. The contract price was contingent upon a finding that Horne's financial statements were accurate. Horne's CEO, Robert A. O'Connell, discussed with E. Ray Kemp, Dillard's vice chairman, his concerns about the extent of Dillard's control and its rapidity. Kemp told O'Connell, "Trust me, it would take an act of God for this deal not to go through."[1]

---

1. M. Schroeder, and W. Zellner, "Hell Hath No Fury Like a Big Store Scorned," *Business Week* (Sept. 23, 1991): 39–40.

Dillard's has been acquiring department stores like Horne's all over the country, adding 196 stores in the last five years. Dillard's pursues financially troubled firms and has experienced a 20 percent increase in earnings for each of the past four years.

Eventually (in 1990), the Dillard/Horne deal fell through and Horne filed suit against Dillard's and DeBartolo for breach of contract and fraud. Horne's suit states that Dillard's plan in taking over the buying and data was to decrease the value of Horne's to get a bargain price.

Experts in the industry indicate that Horne's demonstrated inexperience by allowing Dillard's rapid infiltration. The contract provided that Horne's could veto any proposal for Dillard activity in Horne's business.

During the time between the negotiation of the contract and Dillard's cancellation of the agreement, Dillard's executives found that some Horne accounting practices were questionable. But some industry experts and Horne executives say Dillard's often "nickels-and-dimes" sellers to bring down the price.[2]

Horne's suit also alleges that Dillard's told five hundred employees their jobs would be gone after the takeover. Thirty percent of those five hundred quit before Dillard's and DeBartolo withdrew. Because Dillard's took over merchandise buying, Horne's suit maintains that its deliveries of merchandise were late and that it had the wrong merchandise for critical periods like the holiday season.

Currently, Horne's is working with lenders for its survival. An officer at Pittsburgh National Bank testified in his deposition in the suit that a Dillard's executive told him in 1988 that Dillard's might wait until Horne's bankruptcy to buy the company. Dillard's denies the statement and the plan. In 1992, Dillard's and Horne's reached a settlement on the litigation.

Discussion Questions

1. Were the damages Horne's experienced just a consequence of a failed business deal?
2. Did Dillard's take advantage of a debt-ridden company?
3. What obligations do takeover targets have with respect to financial disclosures?
4. Did Dillard's have any special obligations because of its access to Horne's data and buying power?

---

2. *Ibid.*

5.2 Hidden Car Rental Fees

There are six major players in the global rental car market with each firm's share listed below (in billions):

Hertz	$4.0
Avis	3.2
Budget	2.5
National	2.5
Alamo	0.6
Dollar	0.5
Other	2.5[1]

Customers who rent cars are often perplexed by the variety of rates quoted and the additional charges that confront them as they stand at the rental car counter. All the national firms have daily rates, weekend rates and weekly rates. Some firms offer unlimited free mileage while others offer one hundred free miles with a subsequent charge per mile.

Additional charges vary, but can include charges for a second driver, a child seat, remote drop-off, and charges for four or more forms of insurance including the collision/damage waiver (CDW), liability insurance, personal effects coverage and personal accident insurance. A customer at National Car Rental in Boston in 1987 paid $9 a day atop his $60 per day rental fees and said, "It's expensive, but I figure you get in a crack-up and you're going to get nailed if you don't have it."[2]

In 1988, regulatory and legislative bodies began taking action with respect to rental car practices. Some states took the position that rental car agents should be licensed as insurance agents. In August 1988, a U.S. District Court in New York ordered Hertz Corporation to refund $13 million to rental car customers after the company pleaded guilty to criminal charges in connection with overcharging customers to repair vehicles which had been damaged, but for which there was no CDW.

On September 4, 1988, the National Association of Attorneys General appointed a task force headed by Kansas Attorney General Bob Stephan to study deceptive and unfair practices in the car rental industry.

In August 1988, the FTC cited both large and small companies for using deceptive practices in advertising. Clinton Krislov, a Chicago lawyer who represented consumers in class-actions lawsuits against rental agencies in Chicago and Des Moines, made the following statement:

> This is sort of like trying to judge an ugly contest among frogs. There are, I suppose, some pockets of honesty in this business, but ...[3]

---

1. M. Wald, "Hertz to New York: Pay More," *New York Times* (Jan. 19, 1992): F10.

2. Corie Brown, "Cracking Down on a Costly Car-Rental Option," *Business Week* (Nov. 30, 1987): 135.

3. A. Taylor, III, "Why Car Rentals Drive You Nuts," *Fortune* (Aug. 31, 1987): 74.

In addition, the FTC has proposed a regulation that would require the use of a standard rental car contract and disclosure in all ads of full rental charges, including gas charges, collision protection fees, and repair charges. The regulation would also limit customer charges for collisions and theft to $100.

In some cases, renters who refuse CDW have been told no cars are available. In other cases, renters have had $1,000 to $3,000 frozen on their credit cards because they did not take the CDW.

During 1989 several states considered legislation which would ban the CDWs. California did pass a CDW bill that limits the waiver fee to $9 per day and requires disclosure to the customer about its purposes (including disclosure in ads for rental charges). New York and Illinois passed statutes that limit the charges for car damage to $100 and $200. These low damage charges eliminate the need for most renters to buy CDW.

CDW is the money-maker for the smaller car agencies. The agencies offer lower base rental rates and make their profits through the hidden extras like CDW. The smaller companies maintain that without CDW, they will be unable to compete. Reliance on the 90 percent of their customers who take CDW is their means of survival. Without it, they assert, prices will simply go up.

In 1992, the FTC brought charges against Dollar Rent-A-Car Systems, Inc., and Value Rent-A-Car, Inc., alleging their failure to fully disclose information on charges to customers.

Assume you are the public affairs vice president for one of the top six rental car companies as you answer the following questions.

Discussion Questions

1. Would you change any of your policies with respect to CDW?
2. Would you change your advertising to disclose CDW?
3. Would you instruct your counter agents to explain that the CDW coverage may be duplicative?
4. Would you change any of the other extra charges typical in the industry? (i.e., Would you revamp your pricing policy?) Would such a change hurt or help you competitively speaking?

SOURCES

Taylor, III, A. "Why Car Rentals Drive You Nuts." *Fortune* Aug. 31, 1987, 74.

Wald, M. "Hertz to New York: Pay More." *The New York Times* Jan. 19, 1992, F10.

Dahl, J., and C. Winans. "States, Car-Rental Firms Collide Over Damage Waivers." *Wall Street Journal* Aug. 14, 1989, B1.

Golz, E. "Hidden Auto Rental Charges, Fees Can Take You For a Ride." The *Mesa Tribune* Feb. 21, 1989, D1.

Jones, David. "Illinois Moves to Ban Rental Car Waivers." *National Underwriter* July 11, 1988, 3 and 79.

Katz, Michael. "FTC Forces Car Rental Firms to Reveal All." *Wall Street Journal* Aug. 14, 1992, B1.

5.3 THINNING DIET INDUSTRY

Oprah Winfrey started the latest diet craze when she appeared on her television show in 1988 in her size 10 Calvin Klein jeans boasting a sixty-seven-pound weight loss from use of Sandoz Nutrition Corporation's Optifast. The preventive medicine center at Graduate Hospital in Philadelphia, Pennsylvania had five hundred calls about Optifast the day Oprah appeared on television. The diet industry has grown 15 percent per year since Oprah made her infamous appearance. The industry's total revenues now top $3 billion with the major competitors listed below:

Weight Watchers International	$ 1.3 billion
Nutri/System, Inc.	$764 million
Diet Center, Inc.	$275 million
Thompson Medical Co. (Slim-Fast)	$260 million
Sandoz Nutrition (Optifast)	$120 million

Diet programs are sold through celebrity endorsements and before and after ads. Lynn Redgrave has been the Weight Watchers spokesperson while Susan Saint James has appeared for Diet Center. Christina Ferrara, Tommy Lasorda, Kathie Lee Gifford and others have appeared for Slim-Fast and Ultra-Slim-Fast. Nutri/System has relied on radio disc jockeys to use its programs and then talk about their weight loss on the air.

Weight Watchers' CEO likened the diet craze to the excesses of the 1980s on Wall Street: everything is more and more extreme. By mid-year 1990, Representative Ron Wyden of Oregon, the chair of the House Small Business Subcommittee asked representatives of the industry to come to hearings to explain their hard-sell tactics. Wyden's hearings brought out evidence that fully 90 percent of those who lose weight rapidly on the quick-loss programs regain the lost weight within two years and often more. Wyden also asked why employees in these programs were referred to as weight loss specialists when in fact they had no expertise and were really sales personnel. Charles Berger of Weight Watchers, International (CEO) testified:

"Without touching on the issue of greed, some companies in our field have over-promised quick weight loss. And the promises have grown increasingly excessive."[1]

Just prior to the House hearings, nineteen lawsuits were filed in Dade County Florida by nineteen women who alleged gallbladder damage. Seventeen of the women had had their gallbladders removed after participating in the Nutri/System program, even though there was no previous diagnosis of gallbladder difficulties. Jenny Craig, Inc., was also a target of the gallbladder lawsuits.

Nutri/System responded to the suits and in the hearings by stating that obese people who respond to Nutri/System ads and enter the program are going to be

---

1. Julie Johnson, "Bringing Sanity to the Diet Craze," *Time* (May 21, 1990): 74.

vulnerable to a variety of ailments, including gallbladder disease. The suits were referred to by the company as "without merit" and "a carefully orchestrated" campaign by the lawyers for the nineteen women.

A marketing consultant has observed about the diet industry:

> "There is such a market for faddish nutritional services that even if you lose some customers you'll get new ones. To some extent in this industry, a lot more depends on how good your marketing is than your product."[2]

In 1991, the Federal Trade Commission charged Optifast 70, Medifast 70 and Ultrafast with deceptive claims in their marketing, calling the claims made "unsubstantiated hype". The agency cited the statement, "you'll have all you need to control your weight for the rest of your life," as unsubstantiated. The FTC also announced it was investigating other diet programs. Representative Wyden said the FTC's complaints against the three companies was only "the tail of the elephant; the real test is whether these standards will be applied throughout the industry."[3]

By mid–1992, and in response to Representative Wyden's hearings, the FTC completed its investigation of misleading advertising by more than one dozen diet chains and announced its plans to promulgate advertising rules for the diet chains. The before-and-after testimonials will be required to include pictures of typical clients, not just the most successful ones. Documentation of claims of keeping the weight off will also be required. The FTC's rule proposal in this area was the result of the National Institutes of Health's report that, within a year, virtually all dieters regain two-thirds of their weight and within five years, regain it all.

At the same time as the FTC's announcements, the Food and Drug Administration announced that it would decide whether PPA (phenyl-propanolamine), the amphetamine-like stimulant, may still be included in appetite-suppressant products such as Acutrim and Dexatrim.

Meanwhile, Oprah announced that she would never go back to a liquid diet program and the mother of a twenty-three-year old bride-to-be who died of heart failure after six weeks and a twenty-one-pound weight loss at Physicians' Weight Loss Center was awarded $15 million by an Alabama jury.

The sociological issues in weight loss abound. Susie Orbach, author of *Fat is a Feminist Issue*, explains that fifty million Americans begin diets every year and notes, "When I started working in this field 22 years ago, eating problems affected a limited group, women in their 30s and 40s. Now, we know from studies that girls of 9 and women of 60 are all obsessed with the way they look."[4]

---

2. Alix Freedman, and Udayan Gupta, "Lawsuits May Trim Diet Firms," *Wall Street Journal* (Mar. 23, 1990): B1.

3. Jeanne Saddler, "FTC Targets Thin Claims of Liquid Diets," *Wall Street Journal* (Oct. 17, 1991): B1 and B6.

4. Larry Armstrong, and Maria Mallory, "The Diet Business Starts Sweating," *Business Week* (June 22, 1992): 32–33.

Five of the industry members (Jenny Craig, Nutrisystem, Physician's Weight Loss Center, Diet Center and Weight Watchers) petitioned the FTC in August 1992 to establish standards in advertising for the industry.[5]

Discussion Questions

1. Assume that you are able to land a part-time job as a "weight counselor" with a quick-weight loss program. Would you have any ethical constraints on performing your job?
2. Don't people just want to lose weight quickly? What if you told them they would gain it back and that there were health risks and they decided to go forward anyway? Would you and your product be adhering to a proper moral standard of full disclosure and freedom of choice?
3. Does the diet industry make money from temporary motivation? Or does the diet industry only provide temporary motivation?
4. Are the ads misleading?
5. Should the proposed FTC regulations and disclosure requirements be imposed? Would you propose any alternatives to the FTC proposals?

SOURCES

Schroder, Michael. "The Diet Business Is Getting a Lot Skinnier." *Business Week* June 24, 1991, 132–34.

Freedman, Alix, and U. Gupta. "Lawsuits May Trim Diet Firms." *Wall Street Journal* March 23, 1990, B1 and B2.

Johnson, Julie. "Bringing Sanity to the Diet Craze." *Time* May 21, 1990, 74.

Weber, Joseph. "The Diet Business Takes It On the Chin." *Business Week* April 16, 1990, 86–87.

---

5. Molly O'Neill, "5 Diet Companies Ask U.S. for Uniform Rules on Ads," *New York Times* (Aug. 25, 1992): C1, C2.

5.4 THE SURE SALE OF THE PAPER BAGS

Smith-Scharff Paper is a Missouri corporation in the business of distributing paper products. Smith-Scharff has had a business relationship with P.N. Hirsch, a subsidiary of Interco Incorporated, since 1947.

The business relationship involved the sale of paper bags with the P.N. Hirsch logo by Smith-Scharff to P.N. Hirsch. To be able to meet Hirsch's orders on demand, Smith-Scharff kept a supply of the imprinted bags on hand. Smith-Scharff ordered the bags from a supplier in quantities that were based on Hirsch's historical sales.

The relationship was nearly continuous from 1947–1983 with only one interruption for one year some time during the 50s or 60s. During this one-year interruption, Hirsch purchased its bags from another distributor, but before switching to the new distributor, Hirsch bought all the bags Smith-Scharff had on hand.

In 1983, P.N. Hirsch was liquidated and Dollar General purchased its retail outlets. When Arthur L. Scharff, the president of Smith-Scharff, learned of the sale, he wrote to Bernard Mayer, the president of P.N. Hirsch to demand assurance that the bags with the P.N. Hirsch logo that Smith-Scharff had on hand would be purchased.

Bernard Mayer assured Arthur Scharff that P.N. Hirsch would honor all commitments and that the company's integrity should not be questioned. At that time, Smith-Scharff had $65,000 worth of P.N. Hirsch bags on hand and Scharff sent Mayer a bill for that amount.

Between 1983 and 1984, P.N. Hirsch paid for $45,000 in bags. Smith-Scharff was left with $20,679.46 in bags and filed suit against P.N. Hirsch for that amount.

P.N. Hirsch says that a written contract was necessary. Smith-Scharff says that it relied on an on-going business relationship and that it had specially manufactured bags that could not be used or sold by anyone else.

Discussion Questions

1. Were any moral standards violated by either party?
2. Did ethical commitments arise because of reliance by Smith-Scharff?
3. What did Mayer mean when he stated that P.N. Hirsch's integrity should not be questioned?
4. Did Smith-Scharff have any alternative uses for the bags?
5. Do ethical obligations arise even when the legal requirements for a contract are not met?

SOURCES

Smith-Scharff Paper v. P.N. Hirsch & Co., 754 S.W.2d 928 (Mo. 1988).
Adapted from Jennings, M. *Legal Environment of Business.* 2d ed. 1991, 382–83.

5.5 THE CLUTTERED APPLE POWDER

Schulze and Burch Biscuit Company uses dehydrated apple powder to make strawberry and blueberry Toastettes, sold by Nabisco.

E. Edward Park, Schulze and Burch's Director of Procurement, entered into negotiations with Rudolph Brady, a broker for Tree Top, Inc., a producer of apple juice, apple sauce and other apple products.

A by-product of Tree Top's juice production is apple powder, and Park negotiated with Brady for the purchase of the apple powder from Tree Top. The two were able to successfully negotiate nine contracts for the sale of the apple powder. The front of Schulze and Burch's purchase order included the following restriction which limited the terms of the apple powder contract to the terms on Schulze and Burch's purchase order:

> **IMPORTANT**
> The fulfillment of this order or any part of it obligates the Seller to abide by the terms, conditions and instructions on both sides of this order. Additional or substitute terms will not become part of this contract unless expressly accepted by Buyer; Seller's acceptance is limited to the terms of this order, and no contract will be formed except on these terms.

Also, in each of the nine contracts, Brady sent back Tree Top's confirmation which included the following section that requires disputes on the contract to be submitted to arbitration:

> SELLER GUARANTEES TO CONFORM TO THE NATIONAL PURE FOOD LAWS. ALL DISPUTES UNDER THIS TRANSACTION SHALL BE ARBITRATED IN THE USUAL MANNER. THIS CONFIRMATION SHALL BE SUBORDINATE TO MORE FORMAL CONTRACT, WHEN AND IF SUCH CONTRACT IS EXECUTED. IN THE ABSENCE OF SUCH CONTRACT, THIS CONFIRMATION REPRESENTS THE CONTRACT OF THE PARTIES. IF INCORRECT, PLEASE ADVISE IMMEDIATELY.

Neither Park nor Brady discussed either of the clauses during the course of their nine-contract relationship.

With the last contract, Schulze and Burch said that the dehydrated apple powder was full of stems and wood splinters. The result of the clutter was that Schulze and Burch's machinery for Toastette manufacture became clogged. Because of the clogging, the production line was shut down and Schulze and Burch experienced financial losses.

When Schulze and Burch complained to Tree Top, Tree Top said that under their confirmation, Schulze and Burch had to submit the matter to arbitration. Schulze and Burch filed suit against Tree Top to recover its income losses and other damages caused by the cluttered powder.

Discussion Questions

1. Did the parties really understand the terms of their agreement?
2. Does it matter whether arbitration is required? Shouldn't Tree Top correct the problems with the apple powder?

3. Are legal technicalities interfering with a defective product and the buyer's resulting losses?

4. Should Tree Top offer to remedy the problem?

5. Suppose Tree Top had no legal obligation to provide clutter-free powder. Does it have an ethical obligation to do so?

SOURCES

Schulze and Burch Co. v. Tree Top, Inc., 831 F.2d 709 (7th Cir. 1987).

Adapted from Jennings, M. *Legal Environment of Business*. 2d ed. 1991, 387–89.

5.6 SEARS AND HIGH COST AUTO REPAIRS

In 1991, the California Department of Consumer Affairs began an investigation of Sears Auto Repair Centers. Sears' automotive unit of its merchandise group is responsible for 9 percent of the group's $19.4 billion in revenues. The automotive unit has been one of the fastest-growing and most profitable wings of the Sears' business over the past two years. Sears has 850 automotive repair shops nationwide.

The California investigation used office agents in an undercover operation. The agents posed as customers at thirty-three of the seventy-two Sears automotive repair shops located from Los Angeles to Sacramento. The investigation found that the car owner/agents were overcharged 90 percent of the time by an average of $223. The investigation consisted of two phases. In the first phase, the agents took thirty-eight cars with worn-out brakes but no other mechanical problems to twenty-seven Sears' units from December 1990 to December 1991. In thirty-four of the cases, the agents were told that their cars needed additional work. An agent who was sent to the Concord shop, located in a San Francisco suburb, was overcharged $585 when the front brake pads, front and rear springs and control-arm bushings were replaced. Sears' advertisements listed brake jobs at prices of $48 and $58.

In the second phase of the investigation, Sears was alerted of the investigation and ten units were targeted. In seven of those cases, the agents were overcharged. There were no springs and shock sales in these cases, but the average overcharge was $100 per agent.

Up until 1990, Sears paid its service advisors (automotive shop employees) by the hour rather than by the amount of work. But in February 1990, Sears instituted a new policy which included an incentive compensation policy. That incentive policy paid employees on the basis of the amount of repairs customers authorize. In addition, the service advisors were given sales quotas on specific auto parts. Employees who did not meet the quotas often had their hours reduced or were assigned to work in other departments in the Sears stores. California regulators indicated the complaint levels at their offices increased dramatically once the commission structure was implemented.

The California Department of Consumer Affairs charged all seventy-two Sears automotive units in the state with fraud, false advertising, and the failure to clearly state parts and labor on invoices.

Jim Conran, the director of the Department stated:

> This is a flagrant breach of the trust and confidence the people of California have placed in Sears for generations. Sears has used trust as a marketing tool, and we don't believe they've lived up to that trust. The violation of the faith that was placed in Sears cannot be allowed to continue, and for past violations of law, a penalty must be paid.[1]

Dick Schenkkan, a San Francisco lawyer representing Sears stated that Mr. Conran issued the complaint in response to bipartisan legislative efforts to cut

---

1. Lawrence M. Fisher, "Accusation of Fraud at Sears," *New York Times* (June 12, 1992): C2 and C12.

his agency's funding because of a state budget crunch and noted, "He is garnering as much publicity as he can as quickly as he can. If you wanted to embark on a massive publicity campaign to demonstrate how aggressive you are and how much need there is for your services in the state, what better target than a big, respected business that would guarantee massive press coverage?"[2]

Richard Kessel, the executive director of the New York State Consumer Protection Board stated that he "has some real problems" with Sear's policy of paying people by commission, "If that's the policy, that in my mind could certainly lead to abuses in car repairs."[3]

In a prepared statement issued immediately following the complaint, Sears stated that California's investigation was "very seriously flawed and simply does not support the allegations. The service we recommend and the work we perform are in accordance with the highest industry standards."[4]

Shortly after the announcement of the complaint, Sears ran the following ad:

> With over two million automotive customers serviced last year in California alone, mistakes may have occurred. However, Sears wants you to know that we would never intentionally violate the trust customers have shown in our company for 105 years."

Ten days after the complaint was announced, the chairman of Sears, Edward A. Brennan, announced that Sears was eliminating the commission-based pay structure for employees who propose auto repairs. Brennan conceded that the pay structure may have created an environment in which mistakes were made because of rigid attention to goals. Brennan announced the compensation system would be replaced with one in which customer satisfaction will be the primary factor in determining service personnel rewards. Brennan said the shift would be away from quantity to quality. An outside firm would be hired to conduct unannounced shopping audits of Sears auto centers to be certain the hard sells are eliminated. Further, the sales quotas on parts would be discontinued. Brennan did not admit there was any scheme to recommend unnecessary repairs but emphasized that the system encouraged mistakes. However, Brennan accepted full responsibility for the policies stating, "The buck stops with me."[5]

Class action lawsuits by Sears auto repair customers are pending in California and a New Jersey undercover investigation has produced findings similar to those in the California operation. New Jersey officials found that one hundred percent of the Sears stores in its investigation recommended unneeded work vs. sixteen percent of non-Sears stores. Brennan's signature appeared on a full-page ad that appeared in all major newspapers throughout the country on June 25, 1992. The ad/letter had the following text:

---

2. *Ibid.*

3. *Ibid.*

4. Tung Yin, "Sears is Accused of Billing Fraud at Auto Centers," *Wall Street Journal* (June 12, 1992): B1.

5. Gregory A. Patterson, "Sear's Brennan Accepts Blame for Auto Flap," *Wall Street Journal* (June 23, 1992): B1.

An Open Letter to Sears Customers:

You may have heard recent allegations that some Sears Auto Centers in California and New Jersey have sold customers parts and services they didn't need. We take such charges very seriously, because they strike at the core of our company — our reputation for trust and integrity.

We are confident that our Auto Center customers satisfaction rate is among the highest in the industry. But after an extensive review, we have concluded that our incentive compensation and goal-setting program inadvertently created an environment in which mistakes have occurred. We are moving quickly and aggressively to eliminate that environment.

To guard against such things happening in the future, we're taking significant action:

- We have eliminated incentive compensation and goal-setting systems for automotive service advisors — the folks who diagnose problems and recommend repairs to you. We have replaced these practices with a new non-commission program designed to achieve even higher levels of customer satisfaction. Rewards will now be based on customer satisfaction.
- We're augmenting our own quality control efforts by retaining an independent organization to conduct ongoing, unannounced "shopping audits" of our automotive services to ensure that company policies are being met.
- We have written to all state attorneys general, inviting them to compare our auto repair standards and practices with those of their states in order to determine whether differences exist.
- And we are helping to organize and fund a joint industry-consumer-government effort to review current auto repair practices and recommend uniform industry standards.

We're taking these actions so you'll continue to come to Sears with complete confidence. However, one thing we will never change is our commitment to customer safety. Our policy of preventive maintenance — recommending replacement of worn parts before they fail — has been criticized by the California Bureau of Automotive Repair as constituting unneeded repairs. We don't see it that way. We recommend preventive maintenance because that's what our customers want, and because it makes for safer cars on the road. In fact, 75 percent of the consumers we talked to in a nationwide survey last weekend told us that auto repair centers should recommend replacement parts for preventive maintenance. As always, no work will ever be performed without your approval.

We understand that when your car needs service, you look for, above all, someone you can trust. And when trust is at stake, you can't merely react, we must overreact.

We at Sears are totally committed to maintaining your confidence. You have my word on it.

> Ed Brennan
> Chairman and Chief Executive Officer
> Sears, Roebuck and Co.

On September 2, 1992, Sears agreed to pay $8 million to resolve the claims on overcharging in California. The $8 million included reimbursement costs, new employee training, and coupons for discounts at the service center.

Discussion Questions

1. What temptations did the employee compensation system present?
2. Suppose you had been a service advisor, would you have felt comfortable recommending repairs that were not immediately necessary but would be eventually?
3. What costs will Sears experience as a result of the complaint, regardless of its eventual disposition?
4. Is Brennan acknowledging moral responsibility for the overcharges?
5. Does it matter whether the overcharges were intentional or part of business incentives?

SOURCES

Healty, James R. "Shops Under Pressure to Boost Profits." *USA Today* July 14, 1992, 1A.

Stevenson, Richard W. "Sear's Crisis: How Did It Do?" *New York Times* June 17, 1992, C1.

Healey, James R. "Sears Auto Cuts Commissions" *USA Today* June 23, 1992, 2B.

Fisher, Lawrence M. "Sear's Auto Centers to Halt Commissions." *New York Times* June 23, 1992, C1.

Patterson, Gregory A. "Distressed Shoppers, Disaffected Workers Prompt Stores to Alter Sales Commissions." *Wall Street Journal* July 1, 1992, B1 and B4.

"Open Letter." *Arizona Republic* June 25, 1992, A9.

"Sears Gets Handed a Huge Repair Bill." *Business Week* Sept. 14, 1992, 38.

Miller, James. "Sears Roebuck Expects Loss in 3rd Period." *Wall Street Journal* Sept. 8, 1992, A3.

Flynn, Julia, et al. "Did Sears Take Other Customers For a Ride?" *Business Week* Aug. 3, 1992, 24–25.

Section B
Product Safety

Only a manufacturer knows the results of its safety tests on a product. Only the manufacturer has the ability to correct defects or recall dangerous products. The decision to act on safety tests or recall a product is costly. There are no earnings on recalls unless the company's reputation is preserved.

5.7 Ford and its Pinto

A. The Pinto's Development

In 1968, Ford began designing a new subcompact automobile which ultimately became the Pinto. Mr. Lee Iacocca, then a Ford vice president, conceived the project and was its moving force. Ford's objective was to build a car at or below 2,000 pounds to sell for no more than $2,000. At that time, prices for gasoline were increasing and the American auto industry was losing competitive ground to the small vehicles of Japanese and German manufacturers.

Ordinarily marketing surveys and preliminary engineering precede the styling of a new automobile line. Pinto, however, was a rush project, so that styling preceded engineering and dictated engineering design to a greater degree than usual. Among the engineering decisions dictated by styling was the placement of the fuel tank. It was then preferred practice in Europe and Japan to locate the gas tank over the rear axle in subcompacts because a small vehicle has less "crush space" between the rear axle and the bumper than larger cars. The Pinto's styling, however, required the tank to be placed behind the rear axle leaving only nine or ten inches of "crush space" — far less than in any other American automobile or Ford overseas subcompact. In addition, the Pinto was designed so that its bumper was little more than a chrome strip, less substantial than the bumper of any other American car produced then or later. The Pinto's rear structure also lacked reinforcing members known as "hat sections" (two longitudinal side members) and horizontal cross-members running between them such as were found in cars of larger unitized construction and in all automobiles produced by Ford's overseas operations. The absence of the reinforcing members rendered the Pinto less crush resistant than other vehicles. Finally, the differential housing selected for the Pinto had an exposed flange and line of exposed bolt heads. These protrusions were sufficient to puncture a gas tank driven forward against the differential upon rear impact.

During the development of the Pinto, prototypes were built and tested. Some were "mechanical prototypes" which duplicated mechanical features of the design but not its appearance while others, referred to as "engineering prototypes," were true duplicates of the design car. These prototypes as well as two production Pintos were crash tested by Ford to determine, among other things, the integrity of the fuel system in rear-end accidents. Ford also conducted the tests to see if the Pinto as designed would meet a proposed federal regulation requiring all automobiles manufactured in 1972 to be able to withstand a twenty-mile-per-hour fixed barrier impact without significant fuel spillage and all automobiles manufactured after January 1, 1973, to withstand a thirty-mile-per-hour fixed barrier impact without significant fuel spillage.

The crash tests revealed that the Pinto's fuel system as designed could not meet the twenty-mile-per hour proposed standard. Mechanical prototypes struck from the rear with a moving barrier at twenty-one-miles-per-hour caused the fuel tank to be driven forward and to be punctured, causing fuel leakage in excess of the standard prescribed by the proposed regulation. A production Pinto crash tested at twenty-one-miles-per-hour into a fixed barrier caused the fuel neck to be torn from the gas tank and the tank to be punctured by a bolt head on the differential housing. In at least one test, spilled fuel entered the driver's compartment through gaps resulting from the separation of the seams joining the rear wheel wells to the floor pan. The seam separation was occasioned by the lack of reinforcement in the rear structure and insufficient welds of the wheel wells to the floor plan.

Tests conducted by Ford on other vehicles, including modified or reinforced mechanical Pinto prototypes, proved safe at speeds at which the Pinto failed. Where rubber bladders had been installed in the tank, crash tests into fixed barriers at twenty-one-miles-per-hour withstood leakage from punctures in the gas tank. Vehicles with fuel tanks installed above rather than behind the rear axle passed the fuel system integrity test at thirty-one-miles-per-hour against a fixed barrier. A Pinto with two longitudinal hat sections added to firm up the rear structure passed a twenty-mile-per-hour impact fixed barrier test with no fuel leakage.

When a prototype failed the fuel system integrity test, the standard of care for engineers in the industry was to redesign and retest it. The vulnerability of the production Pinto's fuel tank at speeds of twenty and thirty-miles-per-hour in fixed barrier tests could have been remedied by inexpensive "fixes," but Ford produced and sold the Pinto to the public without doing anything to remedy the defects. Design changes that would have enhanced the integrity of the fuel tank system at relatively little cost per car included the following: Longitudinal side members and cross members at $2.40 and $1.80, respectively; a single shock absorbent "flak suit" to protect the tank at $4; a tank within a tank and placement of the tank over the axle at $5.08 to $5.79; a nylon bladder within the tank at $5.25 to $8; placement of the tank over the axle surrounded with a protective barrier at a cost of $9.59 per car; imposition of a protective shield between the differential housing and the tank at $2.35; improvement and reinforcement of the bumper at $2.60; addition of eight inches of crush space at a cost of $6.40. Equipping the car with a reinforced rear structure, smooth axle, improved bumper and additional crush space at a total of $15.30 would have made the fuel tank safe in a thirty-four to thirty-eight-mile-per-hour rear end collision by a vehicle the size of the Ford Galaxie. If, in addition to the foregoing, a bladder or tank within a tank had been used or if the tank had been protected with a shield, it would have been safe in a forty- to forty-five-mile-per-hour rear impact. If the tank had been located over the rear axle, it would have been safe in a rear impact at fifty miles per hour or more.

The idea for the Pinto, as has been noted, was conceived by Mr. Lee Iacocca, then executive vice president of Ford. The feasibility study was conducted under the supervision of Mr. Robert Alexander, vice president of car engineering. Ford's Product Planning Committee, whose members included Mr. Iacocca, Mr. Robert Alexander, and Mr. Harold MacDonald, Ford's group vice president of car engineering, approved the Pinto's concept and made the decision to go forward with the project. During the course of the project, regular product review meetings were held which were chaired by Mr. MacDonald and attended by Mr. Alexander. As the project approached actual production, the engineers responsible for the components of the project "signed off" to their immediate supervisors who in turn "signed off" to their superiors and so on up the chain of command until the entire project was approved for public release by vice president Alexander, MacDonald, and ultimately Mr. Iacocca. The Pinto crash tests results had been forwarded up the chain of command to the ultimate decision-makers and were known to the Ford officials who decided to go forward with production.

B. Analysis of the Gas Tank Issues

Harley Copp, a former Ford engineer and executive in charge of the crash testing program, testified that the highest level of Ford's management made the decision to go forward with the production of the Pinto, knowing that the gas tank was vulnerable to puncture and rupture at low rear impact speeds creating a significant risk of death or injury from fire and knowing that "fixes" were feasible at nominal cost. He testified that management's decision was based on the cost savings which Ford would incur from omitting or delaying the "fixes."

Mr. Copp's testimony concerning management's awareness of the crash tests results and the vulnerability of the Pinto fuel system was corroborated by other evidence. At an April 1971 product review meeting chaired by Mr. MacDonald, those present received and discussed a report prepared by Ford engineers pertaining to the financial impact of a proposed federal standard on fuel system integrity and the cost savings which would accrue from deferring even minimal "fixes." It is reasonable to infer that the report was prepared for and known to Ford officials in policy-making positions.

Finally, Mr. Copp testified to conversations in late 1968 or early 1969 with the chief assistant research engineer in charge of cost-weight evaluation of the Pinto, and to a later conversation with the chief chassis engineer who was then in charge of crash testing the early prototype. In these conversations, both men

TABLE 5-1
Costs of the 1970 Potential Design Modification Strategy: Low Estimate[1]

Calendar Year	Sales (1,000)	Estimated Unit Cost ($)	Estimated Total Cost ($ million)	Present Value of Estimated Costs in 1970 ($ million)
1970	76	8.00	.608	.608
1971	328	8.00	2.624	2.385
1972	287	8.00	2.296	1.897
1973	268	8.00	2.144	1.611
1974	192	8.00	1.536	1.049
1975	170	8.00	1.360	.844
1976	106	8.00	.848	.479
Total				8.873

TABLE 5-2
Costs of the 1970 Potential Design Modification Strategy: High Estimate[1]

Calendar Year	Sales (1,000)	Estimated Unit Cost ($)	Estimated Total Cost ($ million)	Present Value of Estimated Costs in 1970 ($ million)
1970	76	18.66	1.418	1.418
1971	328	18.66	6.120	5.564
1972	287	18.66	5.355	4.425
1973	268	18.66	5.001	3.757
1974	192	18.66	3.583	2.447
1975	170	18.66	3.172	1.969
1976	106	18.66	1.978	1.116
Total				20.696

expressed concern about the integrity of the Pinto's fuel system and complained about management's unwillingness to deviate from the design if the change would cost money. Table 5-1 and Table 5-2 reflect the computed costs of modification.

J. C. Echold, the director of automotive safety for Ford conducted a study for Ford on the issue of gas tank design in anticipation of government regulations requiring modification called, "Fatalities Associated with Crash Induced Fuel Leakage and Fires". The study included the following cost/benefit analysis:

The total benefit is shown to be just under $50 million, while the associated cost is $137 million. Thus, the cost is almost three times the benefits, even using a number of highly favorable benefit assumptions.

---

1. *Automotive News*, Almanac Issues for 1971–1979, Slocum Publishing Company, Detroit, 1971, and Marketing Services, Inc., Detroit, 1972–1979.

Benefits:

Savings   — 180 burn deaths, 180 serious burn injuries, 2,100 burned vehicles.

Unit cost   — $200,000 per death, $67,000 per injury, $700 per vehicle.

Total Benefits   — 180 x ($200,000) plus
180 x ($67,000) plus
2100 x ($700) = $49.15 million

Costs:

Sales   — 11 million cars, 1.5 million light trucks

Unit Cost   — $11 per car, $11 per truck

Total Costs   — 11,000,000 x ($11) plus
1,500,000 x ($11) = $137 million[1]

Ford's $200,000 figure for life was based on a figure from the National Highway Traffic Safety Administration which was developed as follows:

Component	1971 Costs
Future Productivity Losses	
Direct	$132,000
Indirect	41,300
Medical Costs	
Hospital	700
Other	425
Property Damage	1,500
Insurance Administration	4,700
Legal and Court	3,000
Employer Losses	1,000
Victim's Pain and Suffering	10,000
Funeral	900
Assets (Lost Consumption)	5,000
Miscellaneous Accident Cost	200
TOTAL PER FATALITY:	$200,725[2]

C. A Gas Tank Tragedy

In November 1971, the Grays purchased a new 1972 Pinto hatchback manufactured by Ford in October 1971. The Grays had trouble with the car from the outset. During the first few months of ownership, they had to return the car to the dealer for repairs a number of times. Their car problems included excessive gas and oil consumption, down shifting of the automatic transmission, lack of power, and occasional stalling. It was later learned that the stalling and excessive fuel consumption were caused by a heavy carburetor float.

On May 28, 1972, Mrs. Gray, accompanied by thirteen-year-old Richard Grimshaw, set out in the Pinto from Anaheim for Barstow to meet Mr. Gray. The

---

1. Ralph Drayton, "One Manufacturer's Approach to Automobile Safety Standards," *CTLA News* VIII, no. 2 (February 1968): 11.

2. Mark Dowie, "Pinto Madness," *Mother Jones* (September/October, 1977): 28.

Pinto was then six months old and had been driven approximately three thousand miles. Mrs. Gray stopped in San Bernadino for gasoline, got back onto the freeway (Interstate 15) and proceeded toward her destination at sixty to sixty-five miles per hour. As she approached the Route 30 off-ramp where traffic was congested, she moved from the out fast lane to the middle lane of the freeway. Shortly after this lane change, the Pinto suddenly stalled and coasted to a halt in the middle lane. It was later established that the carburetor float had become so saturated with gasoline that it suddenly sank, opening the float chamber and causing the engine to flood the stall. A car traveling immediately behind the Pinto was able to swerve and pass it but the driver of a 1962 Ford Galaxie was unable to avoid colliding with the Pinto. The Galaxie had been traveling from fifty to fifty-five miles per hour but before the impact had been braked to a speed of from twenty-eight to thirty-seven miles per hour.

At the moment of impact, the Pinto caught fire and its interior was engulfed in flames. According to plaintiff's expert, the impact of the Galaxie had driven the Pinto's gas tank forward and caused it to be punctured by the flange or one of the bolts on the differential housing so that fuel sprayed from the punctured tank and entered the passenger compartment through gaps opening between the rear wheel well sections and the floor pan. By the time the Pinto came to rest after the collision, both occupants had sustained serious burns. When they emerged from the vehicle, their clothing was almost completely burned off. Mrs. Gray died a few days later of congestive heart failure as a result of the burns. Grimshaw managed to survive, but only through heroic medical measures. He had undergone numerous and extensive surgeries and skin grafts and must undergo additional surgeries over the next ten years. He lost portions of several fingers on his left hand and portions of his left ear, while his face required many skin grafts from various portions of his body.[3]

D. Aftermath of the Pinto: Criminal and Civil Liability

Ford continued to litigate Pinto suits with verdicts reaching $6 million by 1980. In 1979, the State of Indiana filed criminal charges against Ford for reckless homicide. The indictment appears below:

STATE V. FORD MOTOR CO.
INDICTMENT IN FOUR COUNTS CHARGING THREE COUNTS OF RECKLESS HOMICIDE, A CLASS D FELONY AND ONE COUNT OF CRIMINAL RECKLESSNESS, A CLASS A MISDEMEANOR

NO. 5324 (1979)

INDIANA SUPERIOR COURT, ELKHART COUNTY, INDIANA

The Grand Jurors of Elkhart County, State of Indiana, being first duly sworn upon their oaths do present and say:

---

3. Portions excerpted from *Grimshaw v. Ford Motor Co.*, 174 Cal. Rptr. 348 (1981).

COUNT I

That Ford Motor Company, a corporation, on or about the 10th day of August, 1978, in the County of Elkhart, State of Indiana, did then and there through the acts and omissions of its agents and employees acting within the scope of their authority with said corporation recklessly cause the death of Judy Ann Ulrich, a human being, to-wit: that the Ford Motor Company, a corporation, did recklessly authorize and approve the design, and did recklessly design and manufacture a certain 1973 Pinto automobile, Serial Number F3T10X298722F, in such a manner as would likely cause said automobile to flame and burn upon rear-end impact; and the said Ford Motor Company permitted said Pinto automobile to remain upon the highways and roadways of Elkhart County, State of Indiana, to-wit: U.S. Highway Number 33, in said County and State; and the said Ford Motor Company did fail to repair and modify said Pinto automobile; and thereafter on said date as a proximate contributing cause of said reckless disregard for the safety of other persons within said automobile, including, the said Judy Ann Ulrich, a rear-end impact involving said Pinto automobile did occur creating fire and flame which did then and there and thereby inflict mortal injuries upon the said Judy Ann Ulrich, and the said Judy Ann Ulrich did then languish and die by incineration in Allen County, State of Indiana, on or about the 11th day of August, 1978.

And so the Grand Jurors aforesaid, upon their oaths aforesaid, do say and charge that the said Ford Motor Company, a corporation, did recklessly cause the death of the said Judy Ann Ulrich, a human being, in the manner and form aforesaid, and contrary to the form of the statutes in such cases made and provided, to-wit: Burns Indiana Statutes, Indiana Code Section 35-42-1-5; and against the peace and dignity of the State of Indiana.

COUNTS II AND III

[Counts II and III repeat the allegations of Count I as to the deaths of Donna M. Ulrich and Lynn M. Ulrich, respectively.]

COUNT IV

That Ford Motor Company, a corporation, on or about the 10th day of August, 1978, and diverse days prior thereto, in the County of Elkhart, State of Indiana, did through the acts and omissions of its agents and employees acting within the scope of their authority with said corporation, recklessly create a substantial risk of bodily injury to the persons of Judy Ann Ulrich, Donna M. Ulrich and Lynn M. Ulrich, human beings, and each of them, to-wit: that the Ford Motor Company, a corporation, did recklessly permit a certain 1973 Pinto automobile, Serial Number F3T10X298722F, designed and manufactured by the said Ford Motor Company to remain upon the highways and roadways of Elkhart County, State of Indiana, to-wit: U.S. Highway Number 33 in said County and State; and said Pinto automobile being recklessly designed and manufactured in such a manner as would likely cause said automobile to flame and burn upon rear-end impact; and that the said Ford Motor Company had a legal duty to warn the general public and certain occupants of said Pinto automobile, namely: Judy Ann Ulrich, Donna M. Ulrich and Lynn M. Ulrich of the dangerous tendency of said Pinto automobile to flame and burn upon rear-end impact; and the said Ford Motor Company did fail to repair and modify said Pinto automobile; and that as a proximate contributing cause of said Ford Motor Company's acts, omissions and reckless disregard for the safety of other persons within said Pinto automobile, including the said Judy Ann Ulrich, Donna M. Ulrich and Lynn M. Ulrich, a rear-end impact involving said Pinto automobile did occur on or about

August 10, 1978, in Elkhart County, Indiana, creating fire and flame which did then and there and thereby inflict bodily injury upon the persons of the said Judy Ann Ulrich, Donna M. Ulrich and Lynn M. Ulrich, human beings, and each of them.

And so the Grand Jurors aforesaid, upon their oaths aforesaid, do say and charge that the said Ford Motor Company, a corporation, did recklessly create a substantial risk of bodily injury to the persons of Judy Ann Ulrich, Donna M. Ulrich and Lynn M. Ulrich, human beings, and each of them, in the manner and form aforesaid, and contrary to the form of the Statutes in such cases made and provided, to-wit: Burns Indiana Statutes, Indiana Code Section 35-42-2-2, and against the peace and dignity of the State of Indiana.

A true bill.

Discussion Questions:

1. Give the total cost involved if all the "fixes" were done for the Pinto "gas tank problem".
2. What was management's position on the fixes?
3. Who was responsible for the Grimshaw's injury? Would Mr. Copp have moral responsibility for the accident, death and injuries?
4. Was the Pinto design in violation of any laws?
5. Was Ford simply answering a public demand for a small, fuel-efficient and inexpensive auto?
6. Aren't all automobiles dangerous and subject to damage and resultant injuries? Do we assume risks in driving and buying an automobile?
7. If you had held Copp's position, what would you have done differently?
8. Today the Pinto has become a popular car in stock-car racing. The recalled Pintos can be purchased for $50 from a junkyard. Should Ford be concerned about such use?

SOURCES

Patterson, Gregory A. "Downscale Racer: The Pinto is Junk, But it Sure is Fast." *Wall Street Journal* June 14, 1990, A1.

"Who Pays for the Damage?" *Time* Jan. 21, 1980, 61.

Dardis, Rachel, and Claudia Zent. "The Economics of the Pinto Recall." *Journal of Consumer Affairs* Winter, 1982, 261–277.

5.8 A. H. Robins and its Dalkon Shield

The Dalkon Shield was designed in 1968 by a doctor and engineer who then incorporated and commercially introduced the device to the medical profession in 1969. The shield was a new form of contraception designed to eliminate the dangers associated with the use of birth control pills. Both the Dalkon Shield and the Lippes Loop were heralded as ideal modern birth control: safe, cheap and effective. Dr. Hugh Davis, the shield inventor declared it, "A first-choice method of contraception control." "Dalkon" is an acronym from Davis' name, his engineer friend, Irwin Lerner and Lerner's lawyer, Robert Cohn. "Shield" evolved because the device looked like a policeman's badge.

In June 1970, A. H. Robins (a 123-year-old Virginia company and the maker of Sergeant's flea and tick collars, Chapstick, Robitussin and Dimetapp) acquired all rights to the Dalkon Shield and sold it on the open market between June 12, 1970 and June 28, 1974. During that period over 2.2 million devices were prescribed for women in the United States (Cost: $4.35; cost to make $.35) and 1.7 million were shipped abroad.

A. H. Robins enjoyed an excellent reputation as a pharmaceutical firm but, prior to the shield, had no experience in the birth control market. When the shield was purchased in 1970 for $750,000 plus consulting fees and 10 percent royalties on sales for Dr. Davis, Robins had never made or sold a medical device or gynecological product and had no ob-gyns on staff. At the time of the purchase, there was evidence that Davis' 1.1 percent contraceptive failure rate for the shield was actually 5 percent. Robins nonetheless used the 1.1 percent figure in its advertising.

In March 1971, Wayne Crowder, the quality control supervisor for the shield, devised crude experiments for the shield and found that the open-ended string on the device could "wick" bacteria from the vagina into the sterile uterus hence resulting in infections and pelvic inflammation [pelvic inflammatory disease (PID)].

Crowder suggested to officers that the tip be heat-sealed or that the string be replaced with a safer monofilament string. Crowder explained that he couldn't "in good conscience" approve of "something that I felt could cause infections." Crowder's boss replied that "conscience didn't pay his salary." Crowder was eventually fired.

In October of 1974, the FDA's Advisory Committee on Obstetrics and Gynecology voted to lift the recommendation and to allow sales to resume. This decision was reversed on November 7, 1974, when new defects in the product were discovered. On December 20, 1974, the FDA acted against the advice of the Advisory Committee and sanctioned the sale of the shield. All of the events were reported in national papers such as the *New York Times* and the *Washington Post*. Most major city newspapers also carried stories.

The Dalkon Shield package and insert did not mention the possible dangers from use and did not recommend a fixed removal date which is customary manufacturer practice.

During the hearings on the Medical Device Amendments of 1973, one physician admonished:

I would like to point out without reservation that it is not only time for regulation of IUD testing, manufacture, and advertising, but it is long overdue. Parenthetically, I must question how 14 years have elapsed since the introduction of the plastic IUDs into women commenced without responsible organizations and experts demanding regulatory standards.

It remains even more astonishing that because of the benign silence of these usually concerned parties, the protection of women users of IUDs was neglected for over a decade by a Federal agency which has rather specific obligations to deal with the safety of health-related products. The fact that the Food and Drug Administration has never been given specific legislative authority over medical devices is a matter of record, but that seems a mute excuse for inaction.[1]

An estimated 2.8 million shields were sold between 1970 and 1974. The shield produced documented injuries to women including septic abortion, tubal pregnancy, perforation of the uterine wall, PID and death. In many cases, complete hysterectomies were required because of perforations and tissue-masses. Damage to kidneys, intestines and the colon were frequent with a colostomy being a remedy for damage to the colon. The most common injury was PID.

Nearly 11,000 suits were filed against A. H. Robins for injuries from the shield. In one such suit in federal district court in Minnesota, Judge Miles W. Lord, required then-CEO of Robins, E. Claiborne Robins, Jr., Robins' general counsel, William A. Forest, Jr., and Robins' research director to read a speech on ethics in his courtroom. Judge Lord then noted:

> If one poor young man were by some act of his to inflict such damage upon one woman, he would be jailed for a good portion of the rest of his life. And yet your company, without warning to women, invaded their bodies by the millions and caused them injuries by the thousands. And when the time came for these women to make their claims against your company, you attacked their characters ... You have taken the bottom line as your guiding beacon and the low road as your route. This is corporate irresponsibility at its meanest.[2]

In the claims for PID by former Dalkon Shield users, one of Robins' defenses was that PID can be caused by sexually transmitted disease, and probes into the intimate details of the claimants' sex lives were used to establish the defense.

In 1974, the FDA had Robins remove the shield from the market. It was not until 1984 that Robins launched its media campaign urging women, at Robins' expense, to have the shields removed.[3]

By 1984, lawsuits were being filed at a rate of three hundred per month. Robins' stock price had remained depressed since 1984 and Robins establishment of a $615 million reserve for the claims resulted in Robins being the biggest money loser in the Fortune 500 for 1985.

---

1. Medical Device Amendment Hearing Before the Subcommittee on Health of the Committee on Labor and Public Welfare, 93d Cong., 1st Sess. (1973) (statement of Russel J. Thomsen, M.D.) (hereinafter cited as *Device Amendments*).

2. "A. H. Robins Hauls a Judge into Court," *Business Week* (July 16, 1984): 27–28.

3. C. Breslin, "Day of Reckoning," *Ms.* (June, 1984): 46–52.

By the time Robins filed for Chapter 11 bankruptcy in 1985, there were 334,863 pending claims. The raucous atmosphere of the class action litigation [with thirty-eight attorneys just on the Dalkon Shield Claimants' Committee] continued until a new committee of five, including three women claimants, was appointed and A. H. Robins was purchased by American Home Products in January 1988. As part of the takeover, American Home Products agreed to pay $2.375 billion for the Dalkon claimants which permitted the claimants to recover compensatory damages but no punitive damages.[4]

Discussion Questions

1. What moral standards were in conflict?
2. What moral standards would be involved if the banned inventory of the shields were sold to Third World Countries?
3. Explain, from a utilitarian perspective, the long-term benefits and costs of Robins' liability to the women who used the Dalkon Shield.
4. If you were an executive with Robins from 1972–74, would you feel morally responsible for the injuries some women experienced?

SOURCES

406 F. Supp. 540 (Presents a compilation of Dalkon Shield litigation including the general grounds for these suits)

21 U.S.C. §§ 301–392 — Food, Drug and Cosmetic Act

21 C.F.R. § 7.45 (a)

National Confectioners Ass'n v. Califano, 569 F.2d 690 (D.C. Cir. 1978)

Note, *The Intrauterine Device: A Criticism of Governmental Complaisance and an Analysis of Manufacturer and Physician Liability,* 24 Cle. St. L. Rev. 247 (1975)

AMP v. Gardner, 389 F.2d 825 (2d Cir. 1968)

U.S. v. An Article of Drug ... Bacto-Unidisk, 394 U.S. 784 (1969)

In Re A. H. Robins Co., Inc., 850 F.2d 709 (4th Cir. 1989)

Breslin, Catherine. "Day of Reckoning." *Ms.* June 1989, 46.

Geyelin, Milo. "Criminal Investigation of A. H. Robins, Former Law Firm is Dropped by U.S." *Wall Street Journal* Jan. 12, 1990, B3.

Labich, Kenneth. "Lawsuits by the Thousand." *Fortune* April 29, 1985.

Lewin, Tamar. "Pacifying Step in Robins Case." *New York Times* Apr. 1, 1986, 30.

Blustein, Paul. "Out of Court: How 2 Young Lawyers Got Rich by Settling IUD Liability Claims, Appert and Pyle Face Probe of Tactics Used in a Bevy of Dalkon Shield Cases, A Tie to Insurance Adjuster?" *Wall Street Journal* Feb. 24, 1982.

Elmer-DeWitt, Phillip. "A Bitter Pill to Swallow: Birth control in the U.S. is out of date — and getting more so." Reported by Georgia Harbison/New York and Dick Thompson/Washington. *Time* Feb. 26, 1990, 44.

4. K. Labich, "Lawsuits by the Thousand," *Fortune* (Apr. 29, 1985): 258.

5.9 SUICIDE IS PAINLESS

Final Exit: The Practicalities of Self-Deliverance and Assisted Suicide for the Dying is a self-help book on suicide written by Derek Humphry, the founder of the right-to-die Hemlock Society. The book includes detailed discussions about the methods of suicide but advocates death by prescription drugs. The book includes a lethal-drug dosage table and advises taking a travel sickness pill to prevent vomiting. Approximately 25 percent of the book is addressed to doctors and nurses, offering suggestions for helping people commit suicide. Assisting in a suicide is illegal in all states.

The book is published by Carol Publications, a small firm that specializes in the publication of the books of the Hemlock Society.

Susan Wolf, a lawyer at the Hastings Center, a think tank for medical ethics notes:

> The troubling possibility is that people may get a hold of this and kill themselves when they're in the throes of a reversible depression or some other state for which they could get help.
>
> I can see why terminally ill patients would want this information because they have great anxiety about losing control. But a manual on how to end a human life is pretty potent stuff.[1]

Burke Balch, the state legislative director for the National Right to Life Committee states:

> Because of the First Amendment, its difficult to stop the publication of something like this, but there are other ways to proceed. We would call upon those in a position to foster dissemination of this loaded gun — potentially in the hands of children — and urge them to seriously consider refusing to carry it.[2]

Walden Books and B. Dalton chains carry the book. Carol Publishers says its regular client orders are off by 35 percent on the book. Ruth Holkeboer, the owner of Bookworm in Grand Rapids, Michigan has declined to carry the book:

> I don't want to promote book-banning; but there is a higher law, and that is "Thou shalt not kill." If someone was despondent and came into my store and got the book and killed themselves, I would feel responsible. I think this information should be available, but through doctors or medical texts.[3]

The book buyer (self-help and medical books) for the twelve hundred stores in the Waldenbooks chain says:

> I don't order books based on their content but solely on whether [they are] something our customers want.

---

1. M. Cox, "Suicide Manual for Terminally Ill Stirs Heated Debate," *Wall Street Journal* (July 12, 1991): B1.

2. *Ibid.*

3. *Ibid.*

Both B. Dalton and Waldenbooks are still smarting from the criticism received in 1989 when they dropped Salman Rushdie's *Satanic Verses* and were accused of censorship.

Barnes & Noble carries *Final Exit* but keeps it in the diet-and-health section and does no aggressive promotion.

Discussion Questions

1. If you were the owner of a bookstore, would you carry the book in your store?
2. If you were the administrator of a nursing home, would you carry the book in the nursing home library?
3. Suppose that a twenty-two-year old who suffered from depression purchased the book in your bookstore. His family is aware of his depression and is working with him along with a psychiatrist. One night, following the instructions in the book, the young man takes his life. Would you feel morally responsible for his death?
4. Is death with dignity a right?

5.10 A Toy to Die For

Larami Corporation is responsible for the development of 1992's hottest toy: the Super Soaker. The Super Soaker is a high pressure, high volume squirt gun that comes in several sizes and enables its owner (young and old alike are enjoying them) to fire powerful shots of liquid long distances. Currently, Larami holds 70 percent of the market because its air compression system which propels water up to fifty feet away is patented and provides its guns with a competitive edge. The toy is currently Larami's best seller.

With the onset of summer vacation, the toys not only proved to be popular, they proved to be deadly. Young people have loaded the Super Soakers and other similar products, such as Tyco Inc.'s Super Saturator, with not only water, but bleach, ammonia and urine. A fifteen-year-old Boston boy was killed and two other boys wounded in battles with these new-age squirt guns. Larami issued a one-page expression of sympathy for the family of the Boston boy and added that violence and misuse of the gun is "something we cannot control."

Boston's mayor, Raymond Flynn, has asked retailers to stop selling the gun. A bill has been introduced in the Michigan legislature to outlaw the large squirt guns. Woolworth's and Bradlee's have pulled the toys from their shelves and the Sharper Image catalog issued a statement saying it would donate all profits from the sales of the Super Soaker in Boston to charity. A toy industry analyst noted that putting a "Banned in Boston" sticker on the toy may be the best way to sell more of them.

Discussion Questions

1. Should Larami go out of business in response to the death and injuries caused by the guns?
2. Should Larami have a moratorium on production of the gun?
3. Should Larami control the availability of the gun in certain areas?
4. The guns are currently the best sellers for toy stores, even ahead of video games. Should toy stores pull the water guns from their shelves?
5. Is Larami morally responsible for the death of the Boston boy and the injuries to the other boys?

Sources

Pereira, Joseph. "Toy Maker Faces Dilemma as Water Gun Spurs Violence." *Wall Street Journal* June 11, 1992, B1 and B10.

"Squirt, Squirt, You're Dead." *Time* June 22, 1992, 35.

5.11 NESTLÉ INFANT FORMULA

While there is debate in countries like the United States about the merits and problems with breast feeding versus infant formula, there is no such margin for error in the debate in third world nations. Studies done by physicians working in tropical environments in the 1930s demonstrated the difficulties and risks associated with bottle feeding babies in those areas.

First, refrigeration is not generally available so that formula, once it is mixed or opened (in the case of premixed types), cannot be stored properly. Second, the lack of water purification means that formula powder will be mixed with water that will cause the formula-fed infant to have diarrhea or contract disease from organisms in the water. Third, cultural, educational and income differences often lead to the dilution of the powder or formula so that the amount of nutrition reaching the infant is greatly reduced.

Medical evidence and studies also suggest that regardless of the mother's nourishment or sanitation and poverty levels, an infant can be adequately nourished through breast feeding.

In spite of the medical concerns about formula in these countries, some infant formula manufacturers engaged in heavy commercial promotion of bottle feeding for infants.

These promotions, which went largely unchecked through 1970, included mass media promotion with billboards and radio jingles. Posters with photos of healthy, happy infants were distributed along with baby books and samples through the health care systems of various countries.

Also, some firms used "milk nurses" as part of their promotional campaign. "Milk nurses" were women dressed in nurses' uniforms who were assigned to maternity wards by their companies and paid commissions for new customers. "Milk nurses" encouraged new mothers to feed their babies with formula. Any mother who succumbed and began bottle feeding soon discovered that lactation could not be achieved and the commitment to bottle feeding was irreversible.

In the early 1970s, physicians working with the nations where milk nurses were used became vocal about their concerns. For example, Dr. Derrick Jelliffee, the then-director of the Caribbean Food and Nutrition Institute had the Protein-Calorie Advisory Group of the United Nations place the infant formula promotion methods on the agenda for several of its meetings.

Journalist Mike Muller first brought the issue to public awareness with a series of articles in *The New Internationalist* in the 1970s. Muller also wrote a pamphlet called "The Baby Killer", which was published by a British charity, War on Want. The same pamphlet was published in Switzerland but called "Nestlé Kills Babies". Nestlé, based in Switzerland, sued in 1975, and the suit resulted in extensive media coverage.

In response to the bad publicity, the manufacturers of infant formula, representing about 75 percent of the market, formed the International Council of Infant Food Industries (ICIFI) to establish standards for infant formula marketing. The new code banned the milk nurse commissions and required the milk nurses to have some identification to eliminate confusion about their "nurse" status.

The code proved ineffectual in curbing advertising. In fact, distribution of samples increased. By 1977, groups in the United States began a boycott against what Dr. Derrick Jelliffe called "comerciogenic malnutrition" by the formula manufacturers.

One group in the United States, Infant Formula Action Coalition (INFACT) worked with the staff of Senator Edward Kennedy and hearings were held in the Senate Subcommittee on Health and Human Resources which Kennedy chaired. The hearings produced evidence that the worldwide market for infant formula totaled $1.5 billion. Of that, $600 million or 40 percent was in third world countries. No regulation resulted, but certain forms of Congressional aid were tied to requirements that the countries receiving the aid develop pro-breast feeding programs.

Boycotts against Nestlé products began in Switzerland when Muller's pamphlets were published in 1975 and carried over to the United States where they took hold in mid–1977. The boycotts and Senator Kennedy's involvement heightened media interest and coverage. The effect of the media coverage was action by the World Health Organization (WHO). WHO first met in 1979 to debate the issue of infant formula marketing and agreed, at that time, that a code would be drafted.

Through four drafts and two presidential administrations (Carter and Reagan), WHO finally developed a code for infant formula marketing. When the vote of 118 nations was taken on the code, the United States was the sole negative vote because of the Reagan administration's position that the code not be mandatory. In spite of WHO's final position that the code was a recommendation only, the U.S. negative vote was still cast.

Again, the publicity on the vote fueled a continuing boycott of Nestlé which continued until Nestlé announced it would meet the new WHO code standards for infant formula marketing. Nestlé created the Nestlé Infant Formula Audit Commission (NIFAC) to demonstrate its commitment to the WHO code and to ensure implementation of code rules within the company.

In 1988, Nestlé attempted to introduce a new infant formula, Good Start, through its subsidiary, Carnation. As it attempted to break into the then $1.6 billion market, the industry leader, Abbott Laboratories, (54 percent with its Similac brand) made the announcement about Carnation's affiliation. "They are Nestlé," was a statement issued by Robert A. Schoellhorn, Chairman and CEO of Abbott.[1] Schoellhorn also issued a statement disclosing that Nestlé was the owner of Beech-Nut Nutrition Corporation, the company that had officers indicted and convicted (later reversed) for selling adulterated baby apple juice.[2]

Carnation advertised its Good Start in magazines and on television. This direct advertising drew objections from the American Academy of Pediatrics. Grocers were concerned about boycotts.

Carnation's Good Start formula had the letters "H.A." after the name indicating hypoallergenic and Carnation touted it as a medical breakthrough. The formula was made from whey and Carnation advertised it as ideal for colicky babies or babies who had difficulties tolerating milk-based formulas.

1. Rick Reiff, "Baby Bottle Battle," *Forbes* (Nov. 28, 1988): 222–24.

2. For a history of the baby apple juice case, see pp 79.

Good Start was introduced in November of 1988, and by February 1989, the FDA was investigating the formula because of six reported infant reactions (vomiting) to the formula. Carnation agreed not to label the formula hypoallergenic and to include a warning that milk-allergic babies should use Good Start only with a doctor's approval and supervision.

In 1990, with its infant formula marketshare at 2.8 percent, Carnation's president, Timm F. Crull, called on the American Academy of Pediatrics (AAP) to "examine all marketing practices that might hinder breast-feeding."[3] Crull specifically asked the AAP to examine the well-established marketing practices of providing hospitals with education and research grants in exchange for exclusive formula supply rights and sending home free formula with mothers. Some hospitals are supplied free bottles in exchange for exclusive formula rights. Crull also cited formula conferences to which pediatricians are invited and attend expense free.

The AAP began its work and looked into issues such as prohibiting direct marketing of formula to mothers, sending home samples, and accepting cash awards for research from formula manufacturers.

The distribution of samples in third world countries continued during this time. Studies by the United Nations Children's Fund found that a million infants die every year because they are not breast-fed adequately. In many of the cases, the mother has used free formula samples, is unable to buy more, and has had her own milk dry up. The infant starves as a result of no food or receiving only watered-down formula. By the end of 1991, the International Association of Infant Food Manufacturers had agreed to stop distributing infant formula samples by the end of 1992.

Discussion Questions

1. If you had been an executive with Nestlé, would you have changed your marketing approach more after the boycotts began?
2. Did Nestlé suffer long-term damage because of its third-world marketing techniques?
3. How could a marketing plan address the concerns of the AAP and WHO?
4. Is anyone in the infant formula companies morally responsible for the deaths of infants described in the United Nations study?
5. Is the distribution moratorium voluntary? Would your company comply?

SOURCES

Freedman, Alix M. "Nestlé's Bid to Crash Baby-Formula Market in the U.S. Stirs a Row." *Wall Street Journal* Feb. 6, 1989, A1 and A10.

"Breast Milk for the World's Babies." *New York Times* Mar. 12, 1992, A18.

"What's in a Name?" *Time* Mar. 29, 1989, 58.

Star, Marlene G. "Breast is Best." *Vegetarian Times* June 1991, 25–26.

3. Julia F. Siler, and D. Woodruff, "The Furor Over Formula is Coming To a Boil," *Business Week* (Apr. 9, 1990): 52–53.

Garland, Susan B. "Are Formula Makers Putting the Squeeze on the States" *Business Week* June 18, 1990, 31.

Post, James E. "Assessing the Nestlé Boycott: Corporate Accountability and Human Rights." *California Management Review* (1985) 27(2): 113–31.

5.12 THE TOBACCO INDUSTRY

The tobacco industry today faces several major legal/political issues. The first is the emergence of litigation by smokers who have developed cancer and other tobacco-related illnesses. The second is the increasing concern about tobacco advertisements. A third is the exposure of nonsmokers to lung disease through passive smoke. Yet another is the problem of large investors divesting themselves of tobacco company stocks in the name of their ethical commitments.

Since the 1965 ban on television advertising and the ongoing Surgeon General reports on the effects of smoking and secondary smoke, tobacco companies have been faced with increasing challenges with regard to product marketing. Norway and Finland outlawed all forms of tobacco ads in the 1970s, and Canada's ban on all forms of print, media and billboard tobacco ads took effect on January 1, 1989.

To keep the market alive in the United States, tobacco firms currently have over three hundred brands of cigarettes that are somehow different by being slimmer, microfiltered or glitzier. R. J. Reynolds came under fire in early 1990 for its attempted introduction of "Uptown," a cigarette geared to African-American smokers. Only 30.5 percent of white males smoke while 39 percent of black males do. R.J.R. withdrew the proposed test market plans for "Uptown" in the Philadelphia area after intense public pressure and a brutal attack by Louis W. Sullivan, the Health and Human Services Secretary, who noted:

> Uptown's message is more disease, more suffering and more death for a group already bearing more than its share of smoking-related illness and mortality.[1]

Sullivan based his remarks on a study that showed blacks have a lung cancer rate 58 percent higher than whites. A Baltimore survey showed that 20 percent of billboard advertising in white communities is devoted to smoking and drinking ads whereas those ads comprise 78 percent of the billboard space in black neighborhoods.[2]

RJR responded to the criticisms by saying that it intended only to be "upfront" about its intentions:

> We're an honest company, what do you say when the audience is going to be predominantly black?[3]

In February of 1990, after the withdrawal of "Uptown," RJR released plans to introduce a brand of cigarette that targets young, poorly educated white women, referred to as "virile females." The announced brand, "Dakota," targeted the lucrative eighteen to twenty-four-year old woman — the only group of Americans whose rate of smoking is increasing. The advertising campaign focuses on favorite pastimes of these women including: "cruising," "partying," "hot-rod shows," and "tractor pulls."[4]

1. M. Quinn, "Don't Aim That Pack at Us," *Time* (Jan. 29, 1990): 60.

2. "RJR Takes 'Uptown' Ad Out of Pack," *Mesa Tribune* (Jan. 20, 1990): A9.

3. J. Schifman, "Uptown's Fall Bodes Ill for Niche Brands," *Wall Street Journal* (Jan. 22, 1990): B1.

4. "Cigarette's Target: The 'Virile' Female," *The Arizona Republic* (Feb. 17, 1990): A6.

In spite of aggressive marketing plans, sales figures for the tobacco industry look worse than ever. For eight successive years, there has been declining volume in the industry (down 6 percent from 1988). However, the Asian market is a growing one with increased volume of 2.5 percent in 1990.

Aggressive techniques used by antismoking groups have had a significant impact on legislation and investors. Health and Human Services Secretary, Louis Sullivan, proposed that states enact laws banning cigarette machines on college and university campuses to afford protection for minors. In 1988, California voters passed an initiative that added a twenty-five cent per pack tax to cigarettes to fund an antismoking campaign that will have at its disposal $28.6 million from the tax. The ads target teens and appear on television (primarily MTV).

A group called the Tobacco Divestment Group has been active in urging universities to sell their tobacco stock holdings. In May of 1990, then-Harvard president, Derek Bok, announced that Harvard had sold its tobacco holdings. Bok said the university was motivated:

> "by a desire not to be associated as a shareholder with companies engaged in significant sales of products that create a substantial and unjustified risk of harm to other human beings."[5]

City University of New York also divested itself of $3.5 million in tobacco stocks. The Tobacco Divestment Project has become increasingly vocal and has called on all colleges and universities to refuse gifts from tobacco companies, divest themselves of tobacco company holdings and prohibit tobacco company sponsorship of events on campuses. Johns Hopkins University sold its tobacco company holdings because the investments "undermine its efforts to fight cancer."[6]

In April 1990, the Environmental Protection Agency released a study showing that "passive" smoking causes thirty-eight hundred lung cancer deaths each year. "Passive smoking" is inhaling the smoke of smokers around you.[7]

With litigation, the industry has had its share of setbacks. In 1989, Tony Cipollone, the widower of Rose Cipollone (a woman who had lung cancer and continued to smoke) recovered $400,000 in compensatory damages based on the theory that at the time she became addicted, there were inadequate warnings on cigarettes and ads enticed her to smoke by portraying it as safe and embraced by the medical profession.[8] In 1992, the Supreme Court upheld the decision on the grounds that the companies failed to warn of the dangers. One ad praised L & M cigarettes as, "Just What the Doctor Ordered."[9] The verdicts in other tobacco product liability cases vacillate between victories and defeats, but the suits continue with new legal bases as the increasing dangers are announced in new

---

5. K. Deveny, and J. Pereira, "Tobacco Stakes Sold by Harvard," *Wall Street Journal* (May 24, 1990): B1.

6. "University Drops Tobacco Stocks," *Mesa Tribune* (Feb. 23, 1991): A6.

7. B. Rosewicz, and A. Karr, "Smoking Curbs Get a New Lift from EPA Plan," *Wall Street Journal* (June 25, 1990): B1.

8. S. Koepp, "Tobacco's First Loss," *Time* (June 27, 1988): 49–50.

9. L. Tell, and S. Ticer, "A Pothole in Tobacco Road," *Business Week* (June 27, 1988): 32.

studies.[10] The April 1990 EPA study demonstrating a link between higher cancer rates and exposure to secondary smoke offers a new liability theory for nonsmokers. The American Heart Association has recommended that second-hand smoke be treated as an environmental toxin and be banned from offices and public places. Dr. Homayoun Kazemi, a physician who helped prepare the American Heart Association's position stated, "In terms of carcinogenicity, there is nothing even close. The second-closest (environmental) cause of lung cancer would be asbestos."[11]

A 1992 study linked a mother's smoking more than one pack of cigarettes a day to serious behavior problems in children. Another 1992 study confirmed the hazards of passive smoke and resulted in new congressional hearings on the health issues.

Discussion Questions

1. Are there any differences between the "Uptown" and "Dakota" marketing strategies and other consumer-oriented marketing?
2. Is it moral for tobacco companies to sell their products?
3. Evaluate the postures of Harvard, Johns Hopkins and NYU with respect to their divestiture of tobacco company stock.
4. Is freedom of choice an issue in the sale of tobacco? Is it an issue in advertising tobacco products?
5. Evaluate the issue of passive smoke. Are the rights of nonsmokers violated with the presence of passive smoke?

SOURCES

Cippollone v. Liggett Group, 112 S.Ct. 930 (1992).

Dorfman, John R. "Will Tobacco Stocks Burn Out or Stay Hot?" *Wall Street Journal* June 29, 1992, C1.

Geyelin, Milo. "Liability Suits, While Rising, May Not Prevail." *Wall Street Journal* June 26, 1992, B1.

Cox, James. "Decision Unlikely to Snuff Profits." *USA Today* June 25, 1992, 1B.

Snider, Mike. "Passive Smoke Gets New Study." *USA Today* July 21, 1992, 1D.

Elias, Marilyn. "Tying Moms' Smoking to Kids' Behavior." *USA Today* Sept. 9, 1992, 1D.

---

10. W. Glaberson, and P. Engardio, "A Jury Takes Tobacco Companies Off the Hook — For Now," *Business Week* (Jan. 13, 1986): 32. See also, T. Smart, "It Takes More than Black Robes to Scare Tobacco Companies," *Business Week* (April 8, 1991): 34.

11. "Heart Group Urges Ban on Secondhand Smoke," *Mesa Tribune* (June 11, 1992): A1 and A6.

5.13 SUICIDE ATTEMPTS AND THE ANTI-DEPRESSION PRESCRIPTION

In January 1988, Eli Lilly introduced Prozac (fluoxetine), an anti-depressant drug. The drug enjoyed great immediate and continuing success. It was touted as a safer alternative to competing antidepressants and by 1990, its sales of $700 million made it the leading prescription antidepressant. Depression can be lethal with 15 percent of untreated patients committing suicide.

It was also in 1990 that a study appeared in the *American Journal of Psychiatry* that linked Prozac and suicidal behavior. The study reported in the journal was a limited, anecdotal one by Dr. Martin Teicher of Harvard Medical School. The study reported that six of Dr. Teicher's patients developed "serious" suicidal thoughts. Five of the six patients had contemplated suicide in the past, but with the introduction of the patients to Prozac, Dr. Teicher wrote, "the nature of their suicidal thoughts was quantitatively different than it had been in the past. While they were on medication it became an irresistible impulse."[1] Still, Dr. Teicher concluded that if used properly, Prozac is an effective and safe drug.

As a result of Teicher's report, Prozac's market share dipped from 25 percent in 1990 to 21 percent in 1991. Still total sales of Prozac were $900 million worldwide of Lilly's total sales of $5.8 billion. In addition to the medical reports on Prozac, Eli Lilly was coping with massive efforts by the Church of Scientology to ban Prozac. The Church of Scientology actively opposes psychiatry and cited the case of Joseph Wesbecker as evidence that the drug should be banned.

Wesbecker committed a mass murder at the Standard Gravure printing plant in Louisville, Kentucky, in 1989. Wesbecker, who was taking Prozac at the time, killed eight co-workers at the plant, injured twelve others, and then shot himself to death. However, Wesbecker had tried to commit suicide twelve times within the four years preceding the shooting spree. He was diagnosed as a borderline personality and talked about killing his bosses before taking Prozac. He also bought his AK-47 and practiced with it long before he was on the drug.

Still, many members of the medical community praise Prozac because of its results in patients suffering from depression. Frederick K. Goodwin, the U.S. Government's top psychiatrist has stated, "For many, Prozac has truly been a miracle, the first medication to rescue them from the living hell we call depression."[2]

In September 1991, the FDA held hearings on Prozac and the reported suicides and concluded that there was no credible evidence to support the assertions that Prozac causes suicides or violent behavior. The FDA had received 14,100 reports of adverse reactions to Prozac and 500 of those reports involved suicide. Susan Dime-Mennan, the executive director of the National Depressive and Manic Depressive Association testified at the hearings and called the Prozac controversy, "complete fiction organized and funded by an anti-psychiatric group."[3]

---

1. Anastasia Toufexis, "Warnings About a Miracle Drug," *Time* (July 30, 1990): 54.

2. Thomas M. Burton, "Panel Upholds Lilly's Position in Prozac Case," *The Wall Street Journal* (Sept. 23, 1991): B5.

3. *Ibid.*

The FDA also declined to change the label on the drug to require warnings about the suicide and violence side-effects. Dr. John A. Smith, director of the National Mental Health Association stated, "The association is particularly concerned that changing the current label without compelling scientific evidence would discourage physicians from prescribing these life saving medications. [It would also] needlessly frighten potential patients from taking the medication or, even worse, encourage people to stop taking it without consulting their physicians."[4]

Despite the FDA findings, the controversy surrounding Prozac continued. By 1992, there were one hundred Prozac lawsuits against Eli Lilly brought by survivors of suicide victims and those who had attempted suicide while on the drug.

Eli Lilly hired John McGoldrick and Joel Freeman as lawyers for defending these suits. In addition, Eli Lilly developed a strategy of indemnifying physicians who prescribe the drug and offering prosecutors free assistance when they are faced with a defendant alleging a form of the temporary insanity defense — that they committed their crimes while they were under the influence of Prozac.

As the controversy continues, Lilly faces disclosure orders from courts in some of the lawsuits which will require Lilly to produce all documents relating to the testing of Prozac. Also, in early 1992, Pfizer, Inc., introduced its Zoloft antidepressant, priced 7 percent lower than Prozac. With no adverse publicity, Zoloft had captured 4 percent of the antidepressant market by mid–1992.

Discussion Questions

1. In a situation where a company is faced with a question about the safety of its product, should the company do anything?
2. Is the Eli Lilly strategy of defending lawsuits, indemnifying doctors and assisting prosecutors a means of suppressing evidence about the drug Prozac?
3. What moral standards were at issue in deciding whether to change the label on Prozac to include a warning?
4. If you were an executive with Lilly, would you change any of the strategies Lilly had adopted?
5. If you were an executive with Lilly, would you feel morally responsible for any suicides committed while a patient was using Prozac? Would you feel morally responsible for any injuries or deaths the patient causes while using Prozac?

SOURCES

Burton, Thomas M. "Anti-Depression Drug of Eli Lilly Loses Sales After Attack by Sect." *Wall Street Journal* Apr. 19, 1991, A1 and A6.

Flynn, Julia. "Prozac is Making Lilly a Little Edgy." *Business Week* June 22, 1992, 33.

4. "Panel: Data Fail to Link Prozac, Suicidal Actions," *The Arizona Republic* (Sept. 21, 1991): A3.

5.14 ATCs: Danger on Wheels

Honda Motor Co., Ltd., Yamaha Motor Co., Ltd., Suzuki Motors Co., Ltd., Kawasaki Heavy Industries, Ltd., and Polaris Industries were manufacturers of various types of motorcycles and all-terrain vehicles during the 1980s. Honda was the leading seller of all-terrain vehicles (cycles) and had a full range of models available in their three-wheel models. Honda even manufactured a very small three-wheel all-terrain cycle (ATC) that it advertised for children ages four through ten at the height of the ATC market in the mid–1980s.

The ATC was first introduced in 1977 by Honda and the market has grown each year since then. Several of the other manufacturers including Yamaha and Kawasaki entered the market in 1978. Yamaha and Kawasaki models of the ATC have been larger in size and motor capacity and have carried higher price tags than the Honda models. The fat-wheeled vehicles that look like large tricycles were advertised to conquer all land surfaces with great ease. Suzuki's ads said its ATC "will embarrass the wind."

In 1978, based on a complaint from the National Association of Emergency Room Physicians (NAERP) and the American Neurological Society (ANS), the Consumer Product Safety Division began an investigation of the ATCs, their use and misuse. The reports of the CPSD, incorporating information from NAERP and ANS made the following points:

1. Increases in ATC accidents were reflected as follows:

ATV-Related Injuries[1]

	ATV-Related Emergency Room Admissions	Deaths From ATV Accidents
1982	8,600	26
1983	26,900	85
1984	63,900	153
1985	85,900	246
1986	86,400	268

165 of the deaths (for all years) were children ages 11 and younger; 47% of the deaths (for all years) were children ages 16 and younger.

2. 90% of all ATC injuries were in patients under the age of 30 and 70% were in patients under the age of 18;
3. In some areas, ATC-related injuries accounted for 45% of all emergency care on weekends;
4. 90% of all injuries happened to experienced ATC riders/owners (those who had logged more than 25 hours of riding time);
5. Leg injuries were common among the emergency patients with spiral fractures being the most common form of injury;

---

1. Source: Daniel B. Moskowitz, "Why ATVs Could Land in a Heap of Trouble," *Business Week* (Nov. 30, 1987): 38.

6. Many emergencies required treatment for leg burns caused by riders holding their legs too close to ATC engines.

Dr. Ralph R. Fine, M.D., co-director of the National Spinal Cord Injury Statistical Center testified before a House committee about his concerns, "we were seeing a disproportionate number of spinal cord injuries resulting from three wheeler or ATV crashes. These are dangerously deceptive, deceptively dangerous vehicles."[2]

Honda was aware of the report and submitted a study to the Consumer Product Safety Commission that showed the accidents with injuries happened when there was misuse of the ATC. Referred to in the Honda report as "hotdogging," misuse included such conduct as excessive speed; climbing hills at ninety-degree angles; driving through rapidly moving water, and using ramps to enable jumping.

Between 1982 and 1986, there were 559 ATV accident deaths and more than 50,000 injuries. By 1986, there were 2.1 million ATVs in use at an average price of $2,000.00 each. By 1988, the number of injuries had increased to 7,000 per month, and between 1983 and 1988, nine hundred people were killed in ATV accidents. Many of the victims were young children. A Consumer Product Safety Commission report concluded, "Children under 12 years of age are unable to operate any size ATV safely."[3] State attorney generals began regulatory efforts in 1986. Texas Assistant Attorney General Stephen Gardner called for regulation stating, "These are killer machines. They should not be allowed."[4] The CPSC tried to have the industry sales to sixteen-year-olds and younger banned, but was unsuccessful.

After the report, Yamaha introduced a four-wheel model of the ATC, including one that was a two-seater. Yamaha also undertook a dealer education program and had an instruction manual printed with pictures and instructions to encourage responsible operation of their vehicles.

Roy Janson of the American All-Terrain Vehicle Association, a subsidiary of the American Motorcyclist Association, stated at Congressional hearings on ATVs, "Problems result primarily from how a vehicle is used rather than from its design. When ATVs are used as intended, they present no unreasonable risk to their operators. The major problems related to three-wheel ATV injuries are the failure of users to wear proper safety equipment while operating ATVs and using these vehicles in areas not recommended for ATV recreation. User education and information programs are clearly the most effective means for addressing the problems relating to misuse."[5]

In 1980, major rental centers franchised throughout the United States ceased offering ATC rentals because of liability concerns.

The Consumer Product Safety Commission published some proposed regulations for the ATC. The following were the key provisions:

---

2. "Public Safety: All-Terrain Vehicles," *National Safety and Health News* (August 1985): 78–80.

3. Randolph Schmid, "Safety Panel Tackles All-Terrain Cycle Issue," *Phoenix Gazette* (Nov. 19, 1986): A14.

4. Daniel B. Moskowitz, "Why ATVs Could Land in a Heap of Trouble," *Business Week* (Nov. 30, 1987): 38.

5. "Public Safety," 79.

1. No smaller ATCs would be manufactured. The minimum weight for ATC riding would be 100 lbs. and the minimum age sixteen.
2. All ATCs would be equipped with four wheels.
3. All manufacturers would undertake educational ad campaigns on the use and danger of ATCs. No promotional advertising would be permitted in any media form.

During the time the proposed regulations were debated and reviewed (1986–87), the number of ATC accidents continued to climb at a steady rate. Of particular concern was the marked increase in severe injuries (spinal cord and head injuries being more prevalent) in children six to ten years of age. Also during the time of the review of proposed regulations, some manufacturers continued to provide studies to the Consumer Product Safety Commission indicating misuse, and not design, was the primary cause of accidents.

By 1987, the Association of Trial Lawyers of America had established a clearinghouse for the exchange of information on ATV claims and over four hundred lawsuits had been filed. Three-fourths of the suits were being settled for a typical payment of $1 million.

Because of increased, widely publicized objections from consumer groups, as well as a call for action from the American Academy of Pediatrics, in May 1988, the Commission recalled the three-wheel ATCs and halted their future manufacture. The manufacture of the four-wheel vehicle was accelerated and sales continued. Later, after judicial review of the order and agreements by the five manufacturers, the Commission withdrew its recall but successfully implemented the ban on future sales.

However, some consumer groups were not satisfied and felt a recall was necessary. James Florio, a U.S. Representative from New Jersey said, "How can anyone truly concerned with safety in effect say 'Tough Luck' to people who currently own these unsafe vehicles?"[6]

However, the manufacturers did agree to the following provisions regarding existing ATV owners:

- Cash incentives in order to encourage owners of ATVs purchased after Dec. 30, 1987, to enroll in training programs. The agreement requires payment of $50 cash or a $100 U.S. Savings Bond.
- Revised warning labels and owner's manuals, outlining the dangers of vehicle operation.
- A consumer telephone hotline.
- ATVs with engine displacements greater than 90 cc cannot be sold to children under sixteen years of age, and children under twelve years will not be permitted to operate vehicles with engines greater than 70 cc displacement.
- Scrapping a provision in the preliminary agreement that would require ATV purchasers to sign a form acknowledging the risks of operating the vehicle.[7]

Honda sent out the following "Safety Alert" to its ATV owners in January of 1988:

---

6. "Outlawing a Three-Wheeler," *Time* (Jan. 11, 1988): 59.

7. Matt DeLorenzo, "ATV Companies Agree to Warn, Train Owners," *Automotive News* (Mar. 21, 1988): 58.

HONDA

AMERICAN HONDA MOTOR CO., INC.
P.O. BOX 50 — 100 W. ALONDRA BLVD., GARDENA, CALIF. 90247
CABLE ADDRESS — AMEHON, GARDENA, CALIF. (213) 327-8280

January, 1988

ATV SAFETY ALERT

The Consumer Product Safety Commission has concluded that ALL-TERRAIN VEHICLES (ATVs) may present a risk of DEATH or SEVERE INJURY in certain circumstances. While accidents may occur for many reasons:

- Over 900 people, including many children have died in accidents associated with ATVs since 1982.
- Many people have become severely paralyzed or suffered severe internal injuries as a result of accidents associated with ATVs.
- Thousands of people have been treated in hospital emergency rooms every month for injuries received while riding an ATV.

Because of this, the United States Government has filed a lawsuit against all manufacturers and distributors of ATVs asking the Court to declare that ATVs are hazardous and to order the manufacturers and distributors to take actions to protect ATV riders. The distributors, while contesting the validity of the allegations made by the government, are presently engaged in discussions with the government to resolve these issues without litigation.

You should be aware that an ATV IS NOT A TOY AND MAY BE DANGEROUS TO OPERATE. An ATV handles different from other vehicles, including motorcycles and cars. According to the Consumer Product Safety Commission, at ATV can roll over on the rider or violently throw the rider without warning and even hitting a small rock, bump, or hole at low speed can upset the ATV.

TO AVOID DEATH OR SEVERE PERSONAL INJURY:

- NEVER DRIVE AN ATV WITHOUT PROPER INSTRUCTION. TAKE A TRAINING COURSE. BEGINNING DRIVERS SHOULD RECEIVE TRAINING FROM A CERTIFIED INSTRUCTOR. Call 1-800-447-4700 to find out about training course nearest you.
- NEVER LEND YOUR ATV TO ANYONE WHO HAS NOT TAKEN A TRAINING COURSE OR HAS NOT BEEN DRIVING AN ATV FOR AT LEAST A YEAR.
- ALWAYS FOLLOW THESE AGE RECOMMENDATIONS:
    - A CHILD UNDER 12 YEARS OLD SHOULD NEVER DRIVE AN ATV WITH ENGINE SIZE 70 CCD OR GREATER.
    - A CHILD UNDER 16 YEARS OLD SHOULD NEVER DRIVE AN ATV WITH ENGINE SIZE GREATER THAN 90 CCD.
- NEVER ALLOW A CHILD UNDER 16 YEARS OLD TO DRIVE AN ATV WITHOUT ADULT SUPERVISION. CHILDREN NEED TO BE OBSERVED CAREFULLY BECAUSE NOT ALL CHILDREN HAVE THE STRENGTH, SIZE, SKILLS OR JUDGMENT NEEDED TO DRIVE AN ATV SAFELY.
- NEVER DRIVE AN ATV AFTER CONSUMING ALCOHOL OR DRUGS.
- NEVER CARRY A PASSENGER ON AN ATV, CARRYING A PASSENGER MAY UPSET THE BALANCE OF THE ATV AND MAY CAUSE IT TO GO OUT OF CONTROL.

- ■ <u>NEVER</u> DRIVE AN ATV ON PAVEMENT. THE VEHICLE IS NOT DESIGNED TO BE USED ON PAVED SURFACES AND MAY BE DIFFICULT TO CONTROL.
- ■ <u>NEVER</u> DRIVE AN ATV ON A PUBLIC ROAD, EVEN A DIRT OR GRAVEL ONE, BECAUSE YOU MAY NOT BE ABLE TO AVOID COLLIDING WITH OTHER VEHICLES. ALSO, DRIVING ON A PUBLIC ROAD WITH AN ATV MAY BE AGAINST THE LAW.
- ■ <u>NEVER</u> ATTEMPT TO DO "WHEELIES", JUMPS OR OTHER STUNTS.
- ■ <u>NEVER</u> DRIVE AN ATV WITHOUT A GOOD HELMET AND GOGGLES. YOU SHOULD ALSO WEAR BOOTS, GLOVES, HEAVY TROUSERS AND A LONG SLEEVE SHIRT.
- ■ <u>NEVER</u> DRIVE AN ATV AT EXCESSIVE SPEEDS.
- ■ <u>ALWAYS</u> BE EXTREMELY CAREFUL WHEN DRIVING AN ATV, ESPE-CIALLY WHEN APPROACHING HILLS TURNS, AND OBSTACLES AND WHEN DRIVING ON UNFAMILIAR OR ROUGH TERRAIN.
- ■ <u>ALWAYS</u> READ THE OWNER'S MANUAL CAREFULLY AND FOLLOW THE OPERATING PROCEDURES DESCRIBED.

FOR MORE INFORMATION ABOUT ATV SAFETY, CALL THE CONSUMER PRODUCT SAFETY COMMISSION AT 1-800-638-2772, OR THE ATV DISTRIB-UTORS' SAFETY HOTLINE AT 1-800-447-4700.

Discussion Questions

1. Is the product too dangerous to be sold?
2. Are the warnings and the ban on future sales sufficient?
3. If you were in marketing for one of the five firms, could you continue your sales efforts?
4. Should a recall for the three-wheel cycle have been made?
5. Is the cost of a recall just too high?

SOURCES

Isley, Alan R. "Industry is Emphasizing Safety." *USA Today* Nov. 6, 1986, 1B.

"ATV Makers Agree to Warnings, Vehicle Ban." *Arizona Business Gazette* May 9, 1988, Law 3.

"Safety Group Targets Use of ATVs by Young Riders." *The Mesa Tribune* Nov. 20, 1986, A4.

"We Need Regulation of Dangerous ATVs." *USA Today* Nov. 14, 1986, 10A.

"ATV Makers Warned to Halt Sales to Children or Face Ban." *Mesa Tribune* Oct. 2, 1986, A2.

Riggenbach, Jeff. "Regulation Not Needed; Danger is Exaggerated." *USA Today* Nov. 6, 1986, 10A.

Maynard, Frederick M. "Peril in the Path of All-Terrain Vehicles." *Business and Society Review* Winter 1987, 48–52.

Bolger, James. "The High Gravity Risk of ATV's." *Safety & Health* Nov. 1987, 48–49.

5.15 TYLENOL: THE PRODUCT RESCUE

In 1982, twenty-three-year-old Diane Elsroth died after taking a Tylenol capsule laced with cyanide. Within five days of her death, seven more people would die from taking tainted Tylenol purchased from stores in relatively close proximity in an area of Chicago.

The Tylenol line of pain relievers was the $525 million per year business of McNeil Consumer Products, Inc., a subsidiary of Johnson & Johnson. The Tylenol capsules represented 30 percent of McNeil's Tylenol sales and consumers seemed to prefer the capsules because they were easy to swallow. McNeil's marketing studies also indicated that consumers believed, without substantiation, that the capsules worked faster than the Tylenol tablets.

The poisonings, never solved, were the result of the capsule's design which permitted them to be taken apart, tainted, and then restored to the packaging without evidence of tampering. As McNeil and Johnson & Johnson executives met, they were told that processes for sealing the capsules were greatly improved, but no one could give the assurance that the capsules were tamper-proof.

As the executives of the firm met, they realized that the popularity of the capsule would give their competitors, Bristol-Myers (Excedrin) and American Home Products (Anacin) a market advantage. They also realized that the cost of abandoning the capsule would be $150 million just for 1982. Jim Burke, CEO of Johnson & Johnson concluded the meetings by stating that without a tamper-proof package, they would risk not only Tylenol but Johnson & Johnson. The decision was made to abandon the capsule.

Frank Young, then a commissioner with the FDA, stated, "This is a matter of Johnson & Johnson's own business judgment, and represents a responsible action under tough circumstances."[1]

The company quickly developed its new "caplets" — a tablet in the shape of a capsule. Johnson & Johnson then offered consumers an exchange: if they turned in their capsules, Johnson & Johnson would give them a coupon good for a bottle of the new caplets. Within five days of the announcement of the recall and offer of caplets, Johnson & Johnson had received 200,000 responses from consumers. Johnson & Johnson had eliminated a key product in its line — a product that customers clearly preferred in the interest of safety. Professor Otto Lerbinger of Boston University's College of Communication, cited the actions of Johnson & Johnson as a "model of corporate social responsibility."[2]

Then-President Reagan, addressing a group of business executives said, "Jim Burke, of Johnson & Johnson, you have our deepest admiration. In recent days you have lived up to the very highest ideals of corporate responsibility and grace under pressure."[3]

Within one year of the Tylenol poisonings, Johnson & Johnson regained its 40 percent market share for its Tylenol product.

---

1. "Drug Firm Pulls All Its Capsules Off the Market," *Arizona Republic* (Feb. 18, 1986): A2.

2. Pat Guy, and Clifford Glickman, "J & J Uses Candor in Crisis," *USA Today* (Feb. 12, 1986): 2B.

3. "The Tylenol Rescue," *Newsweek* (Mar. 3, 1986): 52.

Discussion Questions

1. Was the risk small that there would be other Tylenol poisonings?
2. Were the shareholders' interests abandoned in the decision to take a $150 million dollar write-off and possibly the loss of $525 million in annual sales?
3. Suppose that you were a Tylenol competitor. Would you have continued with your capsule sales?
4. Was Burke's decision a long-term decision? Did the decision take into account the interests of all stakeholders?
5. What financial arguments could be made against the decision to abandon the capsule?
6. Is balancing of the risks appropriate in this case?

5.16 HALCION: THE SLEEPING PILL OF PRESIDENTS

Mrs. Ilo Grundberg shot her mother eight times on the night before her mother's eighty-third birthday. Mrs. Grundberg then placed a birthday card in her mother's hand.

When she was charged with the murder, Mrs. Grundberg was able to escape prosecution using the Halcion defense. She was using Halcion, the most popular sleeping pill in the world, total sales of $104 million in the U.S. and $133 million abroad in 1991. Mrs. Grundberg said its side effects made her kill her mother. Upjohn, the makers of Halcion, settled out of court with Mrs. Grundberg for an undisclosed amount and denied Halcion had anything to do with the murder.

Prior to the settlement, Mrs. Grundberg's lawyers were able to obtain copies of undisclosed data about Halcion's side effects. Side effects include amnesia, paranoia, depression and hallucinations. In October 1991, Britain banned the drug finding that it "is associated with an inadequate margin of safety in relation to dose and that the risks outweigh its benefits."[1] Ten other countries have banned the drug because of findings of side effects (including those previously listed) and anxiety, extreme excitability and dizziness.

President George Bush disclosed that he took the pill on international trips to help him cope with the rapid changes from time zone to time zone. When reporters commented on his verbal gaffes, and many commentators discussed and attributed them to Halcion, Bush discontinued its use.

The Federal Drug Administration re-examined its approval of Halcion in 1992. An eight-member advisory panel, in a seven to one vote, approved continued use of the drug in May, 1992 but recommended that the drug have a stronger warning label including a recommendation that if symptoms develop, use should be discontinued.

Public Citizen's Health Research Group, a consumer advocate group led by Ralph Nader, stated in the hearings through its director, Dr. Sidney Wolfe, "The drug is intrinsically dangerous. It causes psychiatric disorders. The margin of safety is very, very low."[2] Dr. Mark Novitch, a vice chairman of Upjohn responded, "As usual, it was elegant, but it was half the story."[3]

Upjohn is beginning new tests that will involve 10,000 patients and run eighteen months. Currently, the Physician's Desk Reference states that Halcion should not be given in more than a thirty-day supply and that withdrawal symptoms may result. Other listed side effects include headaches, nausea, confusion, memory impairment, nightmares and depression.

Dr. Theodore Cooper, chairman of Upjohn, has stated, "We would not knowingly put out anything that was not safe and effective."[4]

---

1. Richard Vernaci, "Halcion Drug Safe, Panel Says," *Arizona Republic* (May 19, 1992): A1.

2. *Ibid.*

3. *Ibid.*, A5.

4. "The Price of a Good Night's Sleep," *The New York Times* (Jan. 26, 1992): E9.

Discussion Questions

1. Assume that you are the CEO of Upjohn and you have reviewed the conflicting views on Halcion. You do have FDA approval. What action, if any, would you take?
2. Halcion is the world's most popular sleeping pill and represents $237 million in sales for you. Would it be wrong to jeopardize those sales so long as they are legal?
3. Would you use Halcion? Why or why not?

SOURCES

"Bush Stops Taking Halcion Amid Concern Over Its Use." *Wall Street Journal* Feb. 6, 1992, B6.

Kleinberg, Howard. "Just Say No: Bush Risks Trouble By Taking Halcion." *Mesa Tribune* Feb. 6, 1992, A11.

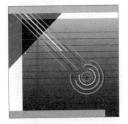

Section C
Product Quality

Quality is the new management buzz word. Managing for total quality is the means for insuring product quality.

5.17 Preventable Potholes

Gerty's Gravel is a highway construction firm founded by Ed Dietrich. Ed began Gerty's after fifteen years of experience with another construction firm. During his work experience, Ed discovered that U.S. highways have a life expectancy of only twenty years and consist of three layers of work. Layer one is two to six feet of compacted original soil. Layer two, which is at the ground level, consists of twelve inches of concrete. The final layer of asphalt is four inches thick.

European highways have a life expectancy of forty years and very different construction. Layer one is five to six feet of backfilled new soil. Layer two is four inches of asphalt separation. Layer three consists of ten inches of gravel drainage. A fourth layer is comprised of ten inches of concrete. The top of the road consists of two layers of asphalt. The fifth layer is four to six inches of asphalt base and the final or sixth layer is three inches of special asphalt.

In addition, Dietrich discovered that research and development by European asphalt firms exceeds U.S. research expenditures per capita by as much as twenty times. For example, in France, a firm has discovered that the road life can be doubled by adding a polymer to the asphalt that is similar to shredded Tupperware at an additional cost of 8 percent.

Dietrich's business strategy is to build a version of the European roads including the addition of the French polymer. Dietrich has a model for building a better road but his costs will be 25–30 percent higher than the firms that continue to bid based on the old U.S. standard. Dietrich also faces the problem that state and local governments award bids to the lowest bidder in spite of the fact that the workmanship for the roads may be sloppy and the materials of lesser quality.

Dietrich has enough experience in bidding and construction to win as many projects as he would like if he ignores the European technology and builds roads the way they have been built in the United States since the 1950s. Dietrich tells his road supervisor, Matt Cochran:

> "The U.S. roads are a mess. The latest figures from the Federal Highway Administration are that 52% of our interstate highways and other major roads are rated "low fair" or rutted, cracked and unfit for high speed travel. That translates to a cost of $120 billion a year for resulting accidents and congestion. I want to build the right kinds of roads but I'll never get this business going if I don't underbid. Believe me, I know all the tricks of getting the prices down. I can outbid anyone. But the road won't last."

In 1991 Congress passed a new highway act that emphasizes maintenance and research and development, but a provision requiring contractors to guarantee their roads was eliminated. The position of the Associated General Contractors is that road warranties would just be an invitation for litigation.

Matt Cochran responds to Dietrich, "Just build the roads. You don't have to give a guarantee. It's what they want — roads, quick and cheap. Besides, who's really hurt by a few potholes here and there?"

Discussion Questions

1. Would it bother you to build cheap roads if you knew there was a better system?
2. You are not legally required to give a guarantee. Does it bother you to sell a shoddy product?
3. Will it be difficult for Dietrich to run a successful business built on underbidding at the expense of quality?
4. Could Dietrich find a market niche for himself based on his dilemma?
5. Do the builders of the quick, cheap roads have moral responsibility for injuries and accidents caused when the roads have problems in a few years?

SOURCE

Van Voorst, Bruce. "Why America Has So Many Potholes." *Time* May 4, 1992, 64–65.

Section D
Customer Privacy

How much should businesses know about you? Should they disclose your name for advertising via direct mail to other firms?

5.18 Credit Card and Buying Privacy

A name can be sold for as little as $35. Some names bring high prices of $200. Those who use a credit card, will find that their names and purchases are grouped, regrouped, sold and resold to companies who are interested in targeting them because of their income, buying habits or location. Without these lists of names, direct marketers are forced to use a shotgun approach that may or may not bring results. But if a marketer knows you own a luxury car, you are a good target for car alarm marketing. If the marketer knows you buy clothes via catalog purchases, you are a good target for a new clothing catalog. For example, American Express breaks its credit card holders into six spending tiers based on card use including "Rodeo Drive Chic," "Fifth Avenue Sophisticated," "Fashion Conscious," and "Value Seeker." The lists were then used for sales promotions by Saks Fifth Avenue, American Airlines, Hertz and Marriott Hotels.

As technology has improved, the ability to collect and refine lists of names as potential customers has grown. Lotus software developed a CD-ROM database called MarketPlace but withdrew it after receiving 30,000 letters and calls from people who did not want to be on the list. Lotus also received objections from the American Civil Liberties Union and Computer Professionals for Social Responsibility. A recent survey by Equifax, one of the country's top three credit reporting agencies, found that 76 percent of the public feels that the sale of personal information about income, home ownership and credit history is unacceptable.

Steve Toman, chairman of the Direct Marketers Association in 1988 warned that those who want to be in the information business have to be psychologically and financially prepared to defend themselves and their product. He warned that, "strict laws in the areas of privacy and ethics could virtually put us out of business."[1]

Regulation has been proposed in California. The Personal Information Integrity Act would require firms to notify individuals within seven days each time information about them is collected or transmitted. Based on the right of correction of the federal Consumer Credit Reporting Act, the proposed legislation would allow consumers the opportunity to correct the information. It is estimated that the legislation would triple the costs of the data collection firms and most direct mail houses would be forced out of business.

Self-regulation is also being used. Equifax is experimenting with a consensual data base. A $10 million project involves a list of people who have expressed a willingness to offer information targeting them for various categories of direct mail marketing. Equifax offers the participants $250 per year in discounts on products for which they are targeted. Equifax has discontinued its practice of selling junk-mailers lists drawn from its confidential credit files, stating that it believed such sales to be "morally wrong."

New York's Attorney General Robert Adams has been very active in the protection of the rights of credit card users and has stated, "A consumer who pays with a credit card is entitled to as much privacy as one who pays for cash or check. Credit card holders should not unknowingly have their spending patterns and life styles analyzed and categorized for the use of merchants fishing for prospects."[2]

Adams' office and American Express Company have entered into an agreement by which American Express will notify customers that their names could be sold for marketing purposes and offer them the option of being excluded from future marketing efforts. As part of the agreement, American Express acknowledged that it was using information about cardholders' lifestyles and spending habits to engage in joint marketing efforts with merchants.

The House Banking Committee scrapped a measure to bar credit bureaus from selling private financial data to direct marketers, but the FTC continues to call the practice illegal. However, proposed amendments to the Fair Credit Reporting Act would require advance disclosure to consumers to give them the right to opt out of lists prepared by the credit bureaus.

Discussion Questions

1. Is the use of the credit card information for the purpose of directing marketing "morally wrong"?
2. Is there a difference between a credit reporting agency selling the information and a credit card company selling the information?
3. What about the people who do not feel their privacy is violated and would welcome the targeted marketing efforts?
4. Presently, is the activity of selling the lists illegal?
5. Should the firms voluntarily impose restrictions or develop new procedures for sales of lists of names?

---

1. "Privacy and Ethics Issues Affect List Industry," *Direct Marketing News* (October 1988): 8.

2. Peter Pae, "American Express Discloses It Gives Merchants Data on Cardholders' Habits," *Wall Street Journal* (May 14, 1992): B4.

SOURCE

"A Tighter Rein on Credit Data for Marketing Urged." *Credit Risk Management Report* May 25, 1992, 2–3.

Bayor, Leslie. "Equifax Addresses Mail Preferences." *Advertising Age* Jan. 14, 1991, 21.

Bird, Laura. "Amid Privacy Furor, Lotus Kills a Disk." *AdWeek's Marketing Week* January 28, 1991, 21.

Coleman, Lynn G. "Biz-to-Biz Software Rises From Grave." *Marketing News* Sept. 2, 1991, 43.

Francese, Peter. "What Business Are You In?" *American Demographics* April 1991, 2.

"Lotus Cancels CD-ROM Project Amid Privacy Concerns." *Direct Marketing* March 1991, 8.

Miller, Cyndee. "Lotus Forced to Cancel New Software Program." *Marketing News* Feb. 18, 1991, 11.

Oliver, Suzanne L. "You've No Place to Hide." *Forbes* Apr. 29, 1991, 86–88.

Posch, Robert. "Worst List Threat of the Decade." *Direct Marketing* March 1988, 124.

Posta, Melissa Della. "California List Business Headed for Extinction?" *Folio: The Magazine for Magazine Management* Feb. 1990, 17.

"Privacy and Ethics Issues Affect List Industry." *Direct Marketing* October 1988, 8.

Radding, Alan. "Lotus Stirs Research marketplace." *Advertising Age* Jan. 14, 1991, 21.

Rappaport, Donn. "Privacy Paranoia: List Owners Need to Regulate Themselves Before the Government Does." *Folio: The Magazine for Magazine Management* October 1990, 101–2.

Ruhe, Linda Savage. "Marketers Hope to Program Buying Habits." *Advertising Age* July 19, 1984, 44.

Schwartz, Marvin. "List Usage Ethics and Marketing Opportunity in Merge/Purge." *Direct Marketing* August 1987, 52–56.

Uehling, Mark D. "Here Comes the Perfect Mailing List." *American Demographics* August 1991, 11–12.

"Equifax Vows to Get it Right." *Business Week* July 13, 1992, 38.

UNIT SIX
BUSINESS AND ITS
STAKEHOLDERS

There are many people affected by the decisions of a business: those who have a stake in the continuing profitable operation of the business. Often a business must examine the interests of those stakeholders before reaching a decision in an ethical dilemma.

SECTION A
SHAREHOLDERS' INTERESTS

The interests of shareholders and the interests of management are not always the same. Whose interest should prevail?

6.1 THE CLEAN OPINION AND THE FAILED MERGER

Associated Industries is a publicly traded (Pacific Stock Exchange) corporation founded in 1956. George Cole is currently CEO of Associated, a firm that manufacturers a variety of industrial products. Cole, age forty-three, joined Associated in 1982 and has a background in marketing.

Selected 1989 unaudited financial data appears below:

SUMMARIZED, NON-AUDITED FINANCIAL INFORMATION FOR 1989:

Net Sales	$52,497,000	Accounts Receivable	$10,116,625
Cost of Sales	39,397,000	Inventory	9,509,375
Net Income	5,370,000	Plant & Equipment	32,125,000

From 1986 to 1988, Associated's net income grew at a 12 percent annual rate. Preliminary negotiations began in 1989 for a friendly takeover of Associated by a large conglomerate. If the merger was successfully completed, Cole would receive a substantial bonus. Cole, of course, was supportive of the merger. The merger was contingent upon continued strong financial performance. Unaudited figures for 1989 showed that Associated's income was up 13 percent.

Brigham Brothers, a large accounting firm, was hired to do the audit of the 1989 financial statements for Associated. The fee Brigham Brothers negotiated with Associated represented 20 percent of the firm's income for the Albuquerque office of Brigham Brothers.

During the course of the audit, both the manager and the assigned partner for Brigham focused their attention on the issue of the possible obsolescence of Associated's best selling products. The product was Associated's electronic switching circuit that allowed for automatic control of switching operations when connected to older, manual electrical switches.

In the audit for 1988, the previous auditor had written a memo noting that research that could possibly lead to a fully integrated electronic switching unit was being conducted at the time by several of Associated's competitors. The memo noted that the research of all the competitors was at the very early stages. The auditors and Associated's management determined that no disclosures about the research were necessary in the financial statements for 1989. Generally, when there are developments that are not yet quantifiable but could have an impact on the company's financial position, the auditor will issue a qualified opinion stating the qualification in the audit letter. Alternatively, management will make the appropriate disclosures in management's discussion and analysis in the financial reports for the company's security filings such as the 10-K (the SEC-mandated annual report).

However, during 1989 and early 1990, updated information on the research and development of the fully integrated switching unit became available.

In discussions with Associated's electronic controls manager, it was confirmed that the competition had designed a technologically superior product. The manager had investigated the designs at a trade fair and found the new designs made the client's product technologically obsolete. However, Associated also had been developing a replacement product. Production of the old design continued, to serve old customers' needs until the commercial success and cost competitiveness of the new technology might be established. Associated's product manager noted "There is little else we can do, right now; we don't have a replacement available now, but we plan to have a competitive replacement available by the end of 1990."

According the to competitors' press releases, new circuits might be expected to sell for approximately $40, a figure below the price at which Associated historically offered their product (that being $50). One firm had accepted limited orders for later delivery at $37. Associated staff felt this was a temporary marketing strategy. Thus, early information suggested the new device would be price competitive when available. It was believed significant pricing changes might be necessary for Associated to sell existing inventory and continue production. Profitability was a question.

The head of Associated's marketing division characterized as premature any significant loss projections on the switching inventory. Although the competition was accepting orders, he estimated that it would take at least eight to ten months for the competition to gear up to full production (because of retooling and production delays). The marketing head stressed, "Many customers either can't or won't wait that long for an item not proven under production conditions." Furthermore, Associated's product manager was skeptical about the adequacy of the competition's testing of the new technological device, believing that the competition might be attempting to prematurely market the device.

Associated had an international marketing team that aggressively marketed its older technology products in developing nations around the world. Experience indicated that there was a healthy third-world market for electronic components, such as the old switching device. Preliminary analyses by Associated's international team indicated five thousand units per month could be expected, conservatively, to sell in these foreign markets, at a price which would yield positive profit margins. Existing market channels and personnel would be used.

Associated had sixty thousand switching units in year-end stock, carried at full absorption cost of $30 each. This was equivalent to six months sales, at ten thousand units per month. Production of the unit was continuing. Over the last three years, the average selling price was $50, and delivery costs about $12.50.

In early 1990, Brigham's audit partner decided there was a lack of sufficiently reliable information to forecast either material inventory losses or significant reductions in future profitability due to changing technology. Accordingly, no write-down of inventory value (with its accompanying reduction of income) was taken for the 1989 financial statements, and no disclosures were made respecting the evolving market environment and its potential impact on future performance.

Subsequently, Associated was not able to dispose of all inventory profitably through domestic and foreign sales. Rather, significant losses ensued as the competition's product entered the market early in large numbers and at a low price. Further, few problems were encountered in early applications of the new technology which appears to have been well pretested. Associated was forced to cease production of the old product early in the following year as domestic sales fell. Further, to sell the inventory on foreign markets, the sales price had to be cut sharply. With the increased costs of foreign shipment, losses per item were sufficiently large that Associated decided to simply scrap much of the remaining inventory. Associated was not able to develop a competitive replacement product in a timely fashion and continued to experience a significant loss of market share. Profits dropped sharply in 1990 and again in the first quarter of 1991. While the merger was successfully consummated in 1990, subsequent inventory loss disclosures led the acquiring corporation to file suit in 1991 against Brigham for issuing an unqualified (favorable, "clean") opinion on 1989 financial statements which were allegedly significantly misstated.

Discussion Questions

1. For each audit, the independent auditor must weigh his/her responsibility to both *future* stockholders, creditors, etc. and his/her responsibility to *existing* stockholders, creditors, and employees. An auditor can issue an unqualified (clean) audit opinion; alternatively, an auditor can issue a qualified audit opinion, taking exception to elements of management's financial statements. The inappropriate issuance of a qualified audit opinion is not without cost; it has severe ramifications and can be self-fulfilling. That is, commentators on the public accounting profession have compared a qualified audit opinion to a quarantine notice nailed to one's front door. Ability to obtain credit in a timely fashion and at a good rate may be impaired; suppliers may extend less favorable terms; new stock offerings may become impossible. As a result, strategic business opportunities may be foregone and severe financial losses may accrue, not only to management, but also to existing investors and employees. The auditor must carefully weight the strength of his/her evidence.

   Did the Brigham auditors make an appropriate decision in not disclosing the issues surrounding the development of integrated switching?

2. Did Cole's interest in seeing the merger through influence the information given by employees to the Brigham auditors?
3. Did Brigham's percentage of income from the audit influence its decision to issue a favorable opinion?
4. Does hindsight bias, knowing the outcome was unfavorable, influence your evaluation of the ethical commitments of management and the auditors? Should they be evaluated from their perspective at the time?
5. Could the disclosure have hurt the firm? Would it have also hurt its creditors?

SOURCE

Hypothetical research case used by Marianne Jennings, Phillip Reckers and John Anderson pursuant to a Peat Marwick research grant, Arizona State University (1992).

6.2 OF GOLDEN PARACHUTES AND ANTI-TAKEOVER PROTECTIONS

Arizona Development, Inc., (AD) is a corporation engaged in residential and commercial development in and around the Phoenix area. AD has been successful in its projects and is the state's fifth largest employer.

Bernard Hudson, forty-four, is the CEO of AD and has been referred to in the *Arizona Business Gazette* as innovative and determined. The paper described him as "having the management skills managerial theorists wish they had thought of." *Phoenix Magazine* has also reported on Hudson and stated, "Hudson surrounds himself with the best and brightest. His CFO is Deborah Nemesis, a Wharton MBA who successfully took the company public in 1986. His VP of marketing, Bob Guthrie, ASU MBA, has used conservation and simplicity as themes to keep sales going during our four-year slump."

Sales of homes for 1991 were down slightly and AD's commercial development was very slow, but AD still showed a small profit. AD was catching the attention of several regional and national developers because of its demonstrated success, but also because AD had a large number of tax write-offs it was unable to take in any one year but could carry forward.

As rumors of a takeover interest appeared in the financial press, Hudson called a meeting with Nemesis and Guthrie. He began the meeting by explaining he would avoid a takeover at any cost. "This is my company. I built it, literally and figuratively, from the ground up. My loyalty is to Arizona and my shareholders. If anyone of these companies takes over, they'll take the tax write-offs, gut the company and move on."

Nemesis responded, "Well, they'll have to pay a premium price for the shares. The shareholders will make tremendous capital gains. Just the rumors of a takeover have sent share prices soaring. We're up today from $19 per share to $32 per share."

Guthrie added, "It's just not clear what the market is going to do. We could maintain the status quo or the bottom could fall out. Arizona just lost the Super Collider project. We could lose everything. Maybe bailing out is a good idea."

Hudson was furious, "This is *my* company. If it goes, it goes. But I'm going with it." Hudson then directed Nemesis to work with the lawyers to develop golden parachutes for all officers, silver parachutes for all managers and tin parachutes for all employees. The parachutes would provide all company employees with severance packages in the event the takeover was successful and terminations of all or some employees resulted. For example, officers would be given a minimum of four times their annual salary. Managers would be awarded two times their annual salary and employees would be given one year's salary. All terminated employees (including officers and managers) would receive one year of medical coverage, paying the same contribution amounts they paid as employees. The parachute packages would reduce earnings by 30 percent if the officers and managers were terminated.

Hudson also directed Nemesis to work with the lawyers to develop a poison pill that would take effect if a takeover was successful. Nemesis and the lawyers developed a plan in which all shareholders would be issued shares immediately, a dividend in the form of a special class of stock. In the event of a takeover, the stock would have to be repurchased at a cost of $35 per share. The effect of the plan was to double the cost of a takeover.

When the parachute plans and the stock purchase plan were drafted with all appropriate details, Hudson presented them to the board for approval. The board members had several questions for Hudson about the appropriateness of the plan. An outside director asked, "Wouldn't the shareholders be better off to take $32 a share in a tender offer? Why are we trying to keep the company and its management?"

Hudson replied, "The shareholders benefit but Phoenix will probably lose an employer and a good corporate citizen. We're the last of the independent builders to survive. Now isn't the time to attach a value per share to this company. It could be worth 3 times $32 a share in five to six years."

Another director responded, "But our responsibility is to shareholders not to the City of Phoenix and not to philanthropy. And part of our responsibility is overseeing compensation. I'm not going to approve huge parachutes to forever deter takeovers."

A third director stated, "What you're asking us to do with this poison pill is saddle this company with debt. Because anyone who takes it over is going to have to carry financing to pay 2 times what it's worth. I'm not going to throw a successful firm into debt."

Hudson replied, "You're not throwing it into debt. The figures are high to prevent a takeover, not encourage it."

The third director added, "What these parachutes do is guarantee money even if you need to go. New owners and managers could never be brought in at these costs!"

Discussion Questions

1. If you were a director, would you approve the parachutes? Why or why not?
2. If you were a director, would you approve the poison pill? Why or why not?
3. If you were Nemesis or Guthrie, would you raise additional objections to the antitakeover provisions?
4. Are there interests other than the shareholders that should be served?
5. If you were an AD shareholder, what would be your position on the takeover?

SECTION B
EXECUTIVE SALARIES

How much is too much? Should shareholders have the right to control the amount paid to executives?

6.3 LEVELS OF EXECUTIVE COMPENSATION: HOW MUCH SHOULD THE BOSS MAKE?

Pay levels for executives have been increasing steadily and rapidly since 1980. Sibson & Company data show that between 1980 and 1990, the average cash compensation for CEOs had increased over 160 percent.[1] The figures for production workers, based on the average hourly wage paid to nonsupervisory manufacturing employees, show that their wages have not kept pace with inflation. CEOs in U.S.-based companies earn 160 times more than the average employee. By contrast, Japanese CEOs earn only 16 times more than the average worker.[2]

Honda Motor Company paid its top thirty-six officers about $10.2 million total for their 1990 compensation. Nissan Motor Company paid even less in 1990 to its forty-eight officers. And because of Japan's 65 percent tax rate, the highest paid officers in these groups would have brought home less than $150,000. By contrast, Lee Iacocca, CEO of Chrysler had direct compensation of $4.65 million during the same period. Also, Iacocca received 62,500 shares of Chrysler stock valued at $718,000. Some other executive compensation levels, noted according to year appear below:

1. Jeffrey Birnbaum, "From Quayle to Clinton, Politicians are Pouncing on the Hot Issue of Top Executives' Hefty Salaries," *Wall Street Journal* (Jan. 15, 1991): A16.

2. Jill Abramson, and Christopher J. Chipello, "High Pay of CEOs Traveling With Bush Touches a Nerve in Asia," *Wall Street Journal* (Dec. 30, 1991): A1.

COMPANY	CEO	PAY	YEAR
American International Group	Maurice Greenberg	$ 1,750,000	1990
Philips Petroleum	C.J. Silas	4,000,000	1990
American Express	James D. Robinson	3,500,000	1990
Textron	B.F. Dolan	2,590,000	1990
Air Products & Chemical	Dexter Baxter	1,090,000	1990
TRW	Joseph Gorman	1,060,000	1990
ITT	Rand Araskog	7,000,000	1990
Reebok	Paul Fireman	14,800,000	1990
		2,000,000	1991
U.S. Surgical	Leon Hirsch	118,000,000	1991
Coca-Cola	Robert Goizueta	86,000,000	1991
H.J. Heinz	Anthony O'Reilly	75,000,000	1991
Telecommunications, Inc.	John Malone	26,000,000	1991
National Medical Enterprises	Richard Eamer	17,000,000	1991
Exxon	Lawrence Rawl	9,300,000	1991
Dial	John Teets	3,600,000	1991
Bell Atlantic	Raymond Smith	2,800,000	1991
IBM	John Akers	2,500,000	1991
General Motors	Robert Stempel	1,300,000	1991
Medco Containment	Martin Wygod	33,749,000	1991
Primerica	Sanford Weill	15,906,000	1991
Philip Morris	Hamish Maxwell	15,677,000	1991
Ralston Purina	William Stiritz	13,813,000	1991
Bristol-Myers Squibb	Richard Gelb	12,658,000	1991
Merrill Lynch	William Schreyer	11,530,000	1991

As a result of the released figures on CEO compensation, large institutional investors and small shareholders as well became outraged and submitted shareholder proposals for the annual meetings of forty-three companies. Those shareholder proposals called for reform in the setting of executive pay such as the New York City Employees Retirement System proposing through it 259,328 shares of Reebok that executive compensation be established by an independent panel. Elizabeth Holztman, a trustee of the New York system said, "It is unconscionable to have sky-high executive compensation that is not related to long-term corporate performance."[3]

The California Public Employees' Retirement System released a list of twelve high-profile companies' executives' pay for 1991 in an attempt to pressure

---

3. "Reebok Comes Under Fire for Executive Pay," *Wall Street Journal* (Mar. 21, 1991): G1.

management of the firms into reform. Calpers, as it is known, had tried to negotiate privately with the firms but was rebuffed in some cases. Calpers' spokesman, Richard H. Koppes, stated, "This year, the kinder and gentler approach doesn't seem to be working. That's why we released the names."[4]

Some shareholders have pointed out conflicts of interest in board compensation committees: CEOs from other firms sit on boards or lawyers whose firms furnish the bulk of the company's legal service sit on compensation committees to determine the CEO's compensation, the same person who hires their firm. Management consultant Graef Crystal explains, "It's a cozy you-scratch-my-back-I'll-scratch-yours arrangement. If you're a CEO, you don't want Mother Teresa or the Sisters of Charity on your compensation committee."[5]

Stanley C. Gault, chairman of Goodyear Tire & Rubber Co., is an executive who has joined with the shareholders in their complaints, "The American public is tired of seeing executives make many, many millions of dollars a year when the stock price goes down, the dividends are cut and the book value is reduced."[6] Some executives have initiated reform in their compensation system out of fear of new federal regulations. On the other hand, executives such as Roberto C. Goizueta of Coca-Cola continue to defend their compensation: "Our stock outperformed the other 29 stocks in the Dow industrial average in the past decade. The end result has been the creation of $50 billion of additional wealth for the share owners of our company in the same time period."[7] When Goizueta defended his compensation at the annual shareholders' meeting, he was greeted by the attending shareholders with applause.

Ben & Jerry's Homemade, Inc., the Vermont ice cream manufacturer, limits its CEO pay to seven times the average worker's salary. Herman Miller, a Fortune 500 company, limits its CEO's pay to 20 times the average employee paycheck, which was $28,000 in 1991. That limit includes both salary and bonus. The average for the other Fortune 500 companies for CEO compensation is 117 times the amount of the salary of the average worker. Max DePress, a member of Herman Miller's founding family and chairman of the company's board says, "People have to think about the common good. Our CEO and senior officers make good competitive salaries when the performance is there."[8] Nonunionized plant workers support the plan, "This is a fair and equitable way to pay ... If they tried to revoke it, people would speak out."[9]

James O'Toole, executive director of the leadership institute at the University of Southern California, says of the Herman Miller plan, "We should follow this model, instead of the bad examples of the 1980s. The purpose of the corporation is much broader than meeting the needs of stock speculators or the power needs of top managers."[10]

---

4. *Ibid.*

5. Thomas McCarroll, "The Shareholders Strike Back," *Time* (May 4, 1992): 46–47.

6. John Byre, et al., "Executive Pay," *Business Week* (Mar. 30, 1992): 52.

7. Jerry Schwartz, "Coke's Chairman Defends $86 Million Pay and Bonus," *New York Times* (Apr. 16, 1992): C1.

8. Jacqueline Mitchell, "Herman Miller Links Worker-CEO Pay," *Wall Street Journal* (May 7, 1992): B1.

9. *Ibid.*

10. *Ibid.*

In summer 1992, a proposed bill introduced in Congress would put upper limits on the tax deductibility of CEO compensation as a means of controlling increases. At the same time, the SEC passed new rules and formats for disclosure of executive compensation in the annual proxy materials. Boards have also begun taking action of their own. Compensation committees comprised of outside directors exist at 80 percent of the institutions surveyed by Dow Jones. These committees have also begun to hire independent consultants for advice on compensation issues.

Discussion Questions

1. So long as a company is performing and providing a return to investors and growth in the value of their investment, should the amount of compensation be an issue?
2. The compensation of executives is a deductible business expense. Are U.S. taxpayers subsidizing the large CEO salaries?
3. Should CEO pay be tied to worker compensation?
4. Should CEO pay be tied to company performance?
5. Who should establish executive pay rates?
6. Should institutional investors and other shareholders have input on executive compensation?
7. Do directors who work for the company as consultants or lawyers have conflicts of interest in setting executive compensation?
8. Would government regulation of executive pay interfere with the free enterprise system?

SOURCES

Lublin, JoAnn S. "Compensation Panels Get More Assertive, Hiring Consultants and Sparking Clashes." *Wall Street Journal* July 15, 1992, B1.

Becker, Gary. "The Problem is Not What CEOs Get — It's Getting Them to Go." *Business Week* Mar. 2, 1992, 18.

Salwen, Kevin G. "Shareholder Proposals on Pay Must Be Aired, SEC to Tell 10 Firms." *Wall Street Journal* Feb. 13, 1992, A1 and A4.

Cowan, Alison Leigh. "The Gadfly CEOs Want to Swat." *New York Times* Apr. 2, 1992, Section 3, 1 and 6.

Dobrzynski, Judith H. "CEO Pay: Something Should Be Done — But Not By Congress." *Business Week* Feb. 3, 1992, 29.

Salwen, Kevin G., and JoAnn S. Lublin. "Giant Investors Flex Their Muscles More at U.S. Corporations." *Wall Street Journal* Apr. 27, 1992, A1 and A8.

"How Sweet It Was." *Time* Feb. 24, 1992, 42.

Wilke, John R. "Reebok Holders Reject Plan for Panel to Set Salaries, But It Gets Sizable Vote." *Wall Street Journal* May 6, 1992, A2.

Byren, John. "What, Me Overpaid? CEOs Fight Back." *Business Week* May 4, 1992, 142–62.

6.4 HIDDEN BONUSES: STOCK OPTIONS FOR OFFICERS

While CEO compensation has been a topic of discussion for shareholders and boards alike, some of the attention is focused on one specific component of CEO compensation: stock options. Although most of the protests have centered on CEO salaries, the result may be an increase in the number of options to divert attention away from salaries while maintaining comparable levels of compensation for CEOs. Options accounted for one-third of all CEO pay in 1991 compared with only 8 percent of CEO pay in 1985.

The wisdom of the switch to stock options as a means of compensation is widely debated. Anthony Luiso of Multifoods Corporation in Minneapolis took stock options in lieu of a salary for five years because stock options link his interests to those of the shareholders. But some option plans allow executives more stock options as the value of the shares declines.

The way the executives make money on stock options is by exercising the stock options at the price at which they were awarded (generally much lower than at the time of exercise), and then selling the shares at the higher market price. Supporters of options say everyone is happy. The executives have increased the value of the shares for both their benefit and the benefit of the shareholders.

In some cases, the value of the options can be five to ten times an executive's annual cash compensation. Anthony J. O'Reilly of H.J. Heinz Company made $71,500,000 in 1992 by exercising stock options. U.S. Surgical Chairman Leon Hirsch received nearly a $120,000,000 option package and AT&T, Equimark, Merrill Lynch, Paramount, Philip Morris and Westinghouse gave out 300,000 shares or more to their CEOs in early 1992. Management consultant, David Swinford maintains in the supply and demand sense that executive talent is not so scarce that it requires this kind of money.

The Securities and Exchange Commission (SEC) has proposed that companies place a value on options when they are awarded to executives as part of a compensation package. Currently, the companies treat the options as if they have no value until they are exercised. The most common packages allow the executives to exercise their options at any time during the next ten years, usually at the price on the day the options are given. Compensation committees of boards hope that the option packages provide incentive for key executives to increase the value of the firm's shares.

The Financial Accounting Standards Board (FASB) has raised the issue that executives' salaries are expenses to the company that must be booked and thereby reduce profits. Options, regardless of their size, are not booked and do not affect earnings. Once the option is exercised it becomes a tax deduction for the corporation. FASB is reconsidering its accounting position and a bill was introduced in Congress in 1992 to require companies to reduce profits by the amount of options granted. FASB's concern is that without some booking of the item, no checks are in place for the levels of compensation.

Also, the SEC adopted rules on disclosure of option packages in the proxy materials for shareholders.

Another problem with options is that executives frequently will not exercise them until they have left the company and the compensation is thus never reported because the executive is no longer an officer of the company and no disclosure need be made on any SEC documents or to shareholders.

Discussion Questions

1. Are options an incentive for executive performance?
2. Is anyone really harmed by large numbers of options being granted to executives?
3. Should there be some financial reporting of the options?
4. Isn't a multimillion dollar salary sufficient incentive for performance?
5. Shouldn't a stock option plan motivate executives to increase share value?
6. Is it always best for the company to increase share value immediately if long-term survival is affected?

SOURCES

Byrne, John. "What, Me Overpaid? CEOs Fight Back." *Business Week* May 4, 1992, 142–62.

Grant, Linda. "Tensions Rising Over Incentives for Execs." *Arizona Republic* May 1, 1992, F1 and F2.

McCarroll, Thomas. "The Shareholders Strike Back." *Time* May 4, 1992, 46–48.

Byrne, John. "Executive Pay." *Business Week* Mar. 30, 1992, 52–58.

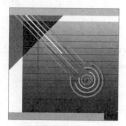

Section C
Corporate Contributions

Businesses as philanthropists look to help communities. But what happens when community members disagree about the value or values of the nonprofit organization?

6.5 The Boy Scouts Of America, U.S. West And Gay Rights

The Boy Scouts of American (BSA) is a private organization founded in 1910. BSA relies on private support from individuals, foundations and corporations. The Scout oath provides:

> On my honor, I will do my best:
> To do my duty to God and my Country,
> To obey the Scout Law.
> To help other people at all times.
> To keep myself physically strong,
> Mentally awake, and morally straight.

BSA has a policy of refusing to admit gays as members or as troop leaders. BSA is facing legal challenges over the policy with the American Civil Liberties Union in a suit filed in Los Angeles by a gay man who applied to become a Scoutmaster. BSA is also facing legal challenges from its policies against admitting women and atheists. In San Francisco, the United Way fund withdrew a $9,000 contribution to BSA and the board of education has banned operation of BSA activities on school property during school hours.

U.S. West, the largest corporation headquartered in Colorado, with annual revenues of $9.7 billion and 14,000 of its 53,000 employees in the state, has been a contributor to BSA of Colorado through its foundation's $25 million budget. U.S. West gave $300,000 to BSA in Colorado in 1990 and 1991.

U.S. West's philanthropic giving concentrates on early childhood development programs, rural economic development and American Indian tribal colleges.

U.S. West, in response to questions employees raised about BSA admittance requirements, has called for a review of its contributions to BSA. An internal memo from U.S. West's public relations board called BSA policies "particularly troubling ... in light of U.S. West's values around pluralism and diversity."[1] The public relations memo recommended that the U.S. West foundation "review its giving practices, working to align its funding decisions with its own policies and with U.S. West's values."[2]

The U.S. West foundation met and agreed to continue to support BSA and released the following statement: "There is no litmus test we can apply to every organization we fund on every issue. We do not have to agree with everything an organization espouses in order to support the good it does overall."[3]

Jim Tuller, treasurer of the Employee Association of Gays and Lesbians, a support group for U.S. West workers responded, "There's a profound sense of disappointment. I'm surprised they made the decision so quickly. I think this was a political hot potato and the company, perhaps, reacted to their switchboard lighting up."[4] Sue Anderson, director of the Gay and Lesbian Community Center in Denver noted, "It's unfortunate they claim to back gay and lesbian employees, but at the same time support an organization that actively works against them. It really sets a confusing standard."[5]

Bill Kephart, director of the Denver BSA Council noted, "We're pleased. You have to appreciate, it's been a very delicate situation for us. U.S. West is an important sponsor for us. We respect that; at the same time we need to stand firm in our position."[6]

BSA continues to face publicity and legal challenges. In the summer of 1992, a twenty-one-year-old Rutgers student and former Eagle Scout filed suit against BSA for revocation of his membership after his admission that he was gay.

Discussion Questions

1. Was U.S. West's BSA donation policy inconsistent with its corporate commitment to plurality and diversity?
2. Should a corporation be free to choose the donees for its philanthropic giving?
3. Will public outcry serve to restrict corporate giving?
4. In mid–1992, Levi Strauss & Company decided to end its financial support ($40,000 to $80,000 annually) to the Boy Scouts of America because the Boy Scouts, exclusion of homosexuals was "at odds" with the company's "core values" and Levi Strauss "could not fund any organization that discriminates

---

1. A. Bettelheim, "Scout Aid May Be Cut," *The Denver Post* (Oct. 31, 1991): 1A.

2. *Ibid.*

3. A. Bettelheim, "U.S. West Won't End Boy Scout Aid," *The Denver Post* (Nov. 7, 1991): 1A and 16A.

4. *Ibid.*

5. *Ibid.*

6. P. Colman, "U.S. West to Keep Funding Boy Scouts," *The Rocky Mountain News* (Nov. 7, 1991): 55.

on the basis of sexual orientation and religious beliefs."[7] Rev. Donald Wildmon, a Methodist minister, responded, "The fact that they would penalize the Boy Scouts for refusing to accept openly practicing homosexuals as scoutmasters shows they no longer want the business of a majority of Americans."[8] Should Levi Strauss and other firms be able to use their donation clout to dictate the policies of their donees?

SOURCES

"Scouts' Gay Ban is Misguided." *The Denver Post* Nov. 3, 1991, 2H.

Knight, A. "U.S. West: Give a Lot, Take a Lot." *The Denver Post* Nov. 10, 1991, 5H.

"Ex-Eagle Scout Sues Group Over Ban on Homosexuals." *New York Times* July 30, 1992, A12.

7. Woody Hochswender, "Boy Scouts Learn Levi's Don't Fit," *New York Times* (June 5, 1992): A12.

8. *Ibid.*

6.6 DAYTON-HUDSON AND ITS CONTRIBUTIONS TO PLANNED PARENTHOOD

Dayton-Hudson Corporation is a multistate department store chain. Its focus is sales of clothing, cosmetics and kitchenware. Dayton-Hudson's charitable foundation has contributed to Planned Parenthood for twenty-two years. In 1990, Dayton-Hudson gave $18,000 to Planned Parenthood but also contributed to Children's Home Society, the Association for the Advancement of Young Women and the Young Women's Christian Association.

Pro-life/anti-abortion groups have been very vocal with respect to corporate foundations that support Planned Parenthood and they have been successful in persuading J.C. Penney Co. and American Telephone and Telegraph to halt funding for Planned Parenthood. Pioneer Hi-Bred International's foundation made a $25,000 contribution to Planned Parenthood of Greater Iowa, and although the money was designated for rural clinics that did not perform abortions, midwest farmers began circulating a flyer headlined, "Is Pioneer Hi-Bred Pro-Abortion?" CEO Thomas Urban canceled funding, "We were blackmailed, but you can't put the core business at risk."[1] When the groups approached the Dayton-Hudson foundation, the foundation board decided to halt contributions.

Pro-choice supporters responded strongly with boycotts of Dayton-Hudson stores, letters to newspaper editors and closed charge accounts. Pickets appeared outside Dayton-Hudson stores and cut up their charge cards for media cameras.

A trustee for the New York City Employees Retirement System, an owner of 438,290 Dayton shares commented: "By antagonizing consumers, they've threatened the value of our investment."[2]

Dayton-Hudson announced that it would resume funding and anti-abortion groups announced plans to proceed with their boycotts.

Discussion Questions

1. Is there any way for a corporation to meet all demands in formulating policies with regard to philanthropic giving?
2. Should contributions be formulated on the basis that they are simply an extension of marketing?
3. Should contributions be consistent with the firm's culture and values?
4. Is giving in to attacks on donations by special interest groups ethical?

SOURCE

Portnoy, F. "Corporate Giving Creates Tough Decisions, Fragile Balances." *The Denver Business Journal* Nov. 15, 1991, 15.

1. Richard Gibson, "Boycott Drive Against Pioneer Hi-Bred Shows Perils of Corporate Philanthropy," *Wall Street Journal* (June 10, 1992): B1.

2. K. Kelly, "Dayton-Hudson Finds There's No Graceful Way to Flip-Flop," *Business Week* (Sept. 24, 1990): 50.

6.7 GIVING AND SPENDING THE UNITED WAY

The United Way is a national charitable organization that evolved from the local community chests of the 1920s. Leaders organized the umbrella charity to fund other charities through a payroll-deduction system.

The payroll-deduction system was an effective means of fundraising for the United Way. Ninety percent of all charitable payroll deductions were for United Way. Campaigns for signing employees up for the payroll deductions included bonuses for 100 percent employee participation. Betty Beene, president of United Way of Tristate (New York, New Jersey and Connecticut) has commented, "If participation is 100%, it means someone has been coerced."[1] Tristate is discontinuing the bonuses and arm-twisting.

From 1970 to 1992, William Aramony, served as president of United Way. He increased United Way receipts from $787 million in 1970 to $3 billion in 1990.

In early 1992, the *Washington Post* reported the following information about Aramony's tenure as president:

- Aramony earned $463,000 per year as salary
- Aramony was flying first class on commercial airlines
- Aramony spent $20,000 in one year for limousines
- Aramony used the Concorde for trans-Atlantic flights
- One of the taxable spin-off companies Aramony created to provide travel and bulk purchasing for United Way chapters purchased a $430,000 condominium in Manhattan, and a $125,000 apartment in Coral Gables, Florida for use by Aramony
- Another one of the spin-off companies hired William Aramony's son, Robert Aramony, as its president.

When the information about Aramony's expenses and salary became public, Stanley C. Gault, chairman of Goodyear Tire & Rubber Co., said, "Where was the board? The outside auditors?"[2] Aramony resigned after fifteen chapters of the United Way threatened to withhold their annual dues.

Robert O. Bothwell, executive director of the National Committee for Responsive Philanthropy, said, "I think it is obscene that he is making that kind of salary and asking people who are making $10,000 a year to give 5% of their income."[3]

In August 1992, the United Way board of directors hired Elaine Chao, the Peace Corps director, to replace William Aramony. Ms. Chao was hired at a salary of $195,000, but no perks.[4]

---

1. Susan Garland, "Keeping a Sharper Eye on Those Who Pass the Hat," *Business Week* (Mar. 16, 1992): 39.

2. *Ibid.*

3. Felicity Barringer, "United Way Head Is Forced Out In a Furor Over His Lavish Style," *New York Times* (Feb. 28, 1992): A1.

4. Desda Moss, "Peace Corps Director to Head United Way," *USA Today* (Aug. 27, 1992): 6A; Sabra Chartrand, "Head of Peace Corps Named United Way President," *New York Times* (Aug. 27, 1992): A8.

Discussion Questions

1. Was there anything unethical about Aramony's expenditures?
2. Was the Board responsible for the expenditures?
3. Is the perception as important as the acts themselves?
4. If Aramony were a CEO of a for-profit firm, would your answers change?

SOURCES

Duffy, Michael. "Charity Begins at Home." *Time* Mar. 9, 1992, 48.

Kinsley, Michael. "Charity Begins With Government." *Time* Apr. 6, 1992, 74.

Allen, Frank E., and Susan Pulliam. "United Way's Rivals Take Aim at its Practices." *Wall Street Journal* Mar. 6, 1992, B1 and B6.

Barringer, Felicity. "Ex-Chief of United Way Vows to Fight Accusations." *New York Times* Apr. 10, 1992, A13.

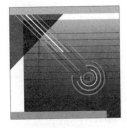

SECTION D
SOCIAL ISSUES

Should business spending and product decisions take into account social goals and impact? Is spending by businesses to solve social problems necessary or just a misuse of business funds?

6.8 THE CHICAGO INNER-CITY SCHOOL EXPERIMENT

A group of Chicago businesses has pooled funds and created a privately owned and operated elementary school in one of Chicago's inner-city neighborhoods. The school is free for children ages two to twelve who reside in the neighborhood. The children are given breakfast, lunch and snacks as well as after-school care.

Teachers in the school are paid 10 percent more than their counterparts in other Chicago public schools. The school is run like a private corporation and the administrators and teachers understand that a lack of improvement in the students can result in termination of employment.

The businesses have created the special school and its philosophy of operation because of their concerns about the quality of education. The business founders maintain that American businesses spend a total of $4 to $5 billion annually in training programs necessary just to bring their workers to very basic skill levels.

These high training costs convinced them of the need to improve public education. Their concept was to test their ideas on teacher pay and accountability in the most challenging environment — that of the inner-city school. Success in this initial project would provide a formula for success in other schools. The founders of this Chicago experiment believe the future success of their businesses is dependent upon the skills of their employees.

Discussion Questions

1. Would Milton Friedman support the school founders in their endeavor as a proper use of shareholder funds?
2. A shareholder of one of the businesses has protested:

    "Why are my funds being used for an inner-city school? We have taxes for that. I invested in a distribution firm, not an education firm. Your job is to earn my dividend, not spend it on things you think are important."

    If you were the director of shareholder relations for the firm, how would you respond to the shareholder?

SOURCES

Kotlowitz, Alex. "A Businessman Turns His Skills to Aiding Inner-City Schools." *Wall Street Journal* Feb. 25, 1992, A1, A8.

"Why Business Should Invest in Literacy." *Business Week* July 20, 1992, 102.

6.9 THE ROCK MUSIC WARNING LABELS

In the summer of 1985, Tipper Gore, the wife of Senator Albert Gore, and Susan Baker, the wife of then-U.S. Treasury Secretary, James Baker, formed a citizens' group called the Parents' Resource Music Center (PMRC). The group's view was that rock music advocates "aggressive and hostile rebellion, the abuse of drugs and alcohol, irresponsible sexuality, sexual perversions, violence and involvement in the occult." Gore began the group as a result of listening to the song "Darling Nikki" from her eleven-year-old daughter's Purple Rain album by Prince. The song is about a girl masturbating with a magazine. Gore then discovered Sheena Easton singing about "genital arousal" and Judas Priest singing about oral sex at gunpoint. She discovered the following lyrics in Motley Crue's top-selling "Shout at the Devil" album: "... now I'm killing you ... Watch your face turning blue."

The strategy of PMRC was to work with record companies to see if a mutually agreeable solution could be devised. PMRC began by holding meetings with the Recording Industry Association of America and requested a ratings system for records, similar to that used for movies, and a requirement of printed lyrics so that disc jockeys would know what is being sent out over the air waves. In the first month after PMRC was organized, it received over 10,000 letters of support and inquiry. PMRC maintains a data base with the following information:

- teenagers listen to their music 4–6 hours per day for a total of 10,000 hours between grades 7 and 12;
- 70% of all violent crimes are committed by youths under the age of 17;
- teenage suicide has increased by 300% since 1955;
- U.S. teenage pregnancy rates are the highest in the world.

When PMRC was not able to reach an agreement with the record industry, Congressional hearings were held on a proposed bill to require labeling on records. Mrs. Baker and Mrs. Gore testified as did Frank Zappa, former member of the Mothers of Invention, and Dee Snider of Twisted Sister. Mr. Zappa stated, "Putting labels on albums is the equivalent of treating dandruff by decapitation." The hearings did not bring any results for either the industry or PMRC.

However, by 1990, there were bills pending in thirty-five state legislatures to require labeling of records. With the backing of PMRC, state groups had proposed the legislation in the states and were lobbying strongly for passage. In Arizona, a reporter for *The New Times* asked a sponsoring Senator (Jan Brewer) to read some of the objectionable lyrics. The reporter recorded the readings, set them to music and played the tapes over the speakers at the Capitol.

In May of 1990, with the state legislative debates on the label requirements still in progress, the Recording Industry Association of America introduced a uniform label for albums with explicit lyrics and expressed hope that the voluntary system would halt legislation pending in the states. The label is black and white and appears on the lower right-hand corner of the album. It reads: "PARENTAL ADVISORY - EXPLICIT LYRICS." The label would be used on albums with lyrics relating to sex, violence, suicide, drug abuse, bigotry or satanic worship. The decision to affix the label is left to the record company and the artists.

The PMRC and the PTA endorsed the new warning system and requested state legislators to consider dropping pending label legislation.

Controversy continues to surround rock music lyrics. In the summer of 1990, a civil suit against the rock group Judas Priest by the parents of a teenager who committed suicide alleged that the song lyrics of the group resulted in murderous mind control and the death of their son. Their subliminal persuasion argument was unsuccessful.

Discussion Questions

1. What ethical issues are involved in the production of songs with explicit lyrics?
2. Will voluntary regulation work for this industry?
3. If you were a record producer, would your company sign artists with explicit lyrics?
4. If you were a record producer, would you feel an obligation to do more than put a warning label on albums with explicit lyrics?
5. You have just been informed that a teenager committed suicide while listening to the music of one of your artists. The music suggested suicide as an alternative to unhappiness. Would you feel morally responsible for the suicide? Should the artist feel morally responsible?

SOURCES

Henry, William A. "Did the Music Say 'Do It'?" *Time* July 30, 1990, 65.

"Record Firm to Back Stores with Legal Aid." *Mesa Tribune* June 5, 1990, A2.

"Warning: Rock Music Ahead." *Time* May 21, 1990, 69.

Foster, Ed. "Music-Label Bill Shelved." *Arizona Republic* Mar. 24, 1990, A1.

Andrews, Robert M. "Records Get Uniform Warning Tag." *Arizona Republic* May 10, 1990, A1.

White, Carrie. "Rating Rock Music." *Mesa Tribune* Dec. 12, 1985, D1.

"Musicians Mock Senators' Wives at Hearing." *Mesa Tribune* Sept. 20, 1985, A4.

Malone, Julia. "Washington Wives Use Influence to Target Sex, Drugs in Rock Music." *Christian Science Monitor* Aug. 23, 1985, 1, 36.

6.10 INSURANCE FOR THE DRIVE-BY VICTIM

Global Life and Indemnity Insurance Company is a California-based insurer. The executives of Global have met to discuss the recent wave of drive-by shootings in certain areas of Los Angeles. In two of the five drive-by shootings, small children were killed.

The executives also discussed Global's plan for insurance for children. The plan, Global's Children of America Policy, allows parents or guardians to purchase up to $5,000 of life insurance for their children with the following payment schedule:

$1 for first six months

$10 for second six months

$20 per year through age twenty-six

$75 per year after age twenty-six[1]

The marketing director proposes that Global's sales force be sent to the neighborhoods where the drive-by shootings occurred. Salespeople will be directed to focus on homes with bullet marks and those areas most infiltrated by gang activity.

Sheila Marquardt, a new vice president for finance, and a member of the discussion group is troubled. As she listens to the marketing director's proposals, her thoughts are that Global will be taking advantage of a parent's fear and capitalizing on a social problem. After Sheila expresses her views, the marketing director responds, "We sold insurance to war brides during World War II, Korea and Vietnam. We helped many of them with financial security. Why is this program any different?"

Discussion Questions

1. Do you share Sheila's concerns?
2. Is the marketing director correct — that the financial compensation is important and helpful?
3. Is selling insurance for inner-city children different from selling insurance for children in other neighborhoods?
4. If you were a salesperson, would you feel comfortable with the proposed marketing program?

---

1. The policy, at this point, builds a cash value.

6.11 SATURDAY NIGHT SPECIALS: THE WEAPON OF CHOICE

In California, there are three gun manufacturers that evolved from the Jennings family. George Jennings founded Raven Arms, Inc., in 1970 and began manufacturing the Raven .25. The Raven is often labeled a Saturday Night Special, a nickname for an inexpensive handgun that costs $13 to make and retails for $59 - $70.

George's son, Bruce Jennings, left Raven to form Jennings Firearms, Inc., in 1978 which manufactures another Saturday Night Special, the Jennings .22 which costs $13 to make and retails for $75 to $89.

George's son-in-law, Jim Davis, left Raven and began Davis Industries, Inc., in 1982. Davis Industries manufactures yet another Saturday Night Special, the Davis .38 that costs $15 to make and retails for $95 to $100.

Based on data from the Bureau of Alcohol, Tobacco and Firearms (from handguns sold after 1986), the leading handguns used in crimes are the Davis, the Raven and the Jennings.

Many criminologists, prosecutors and gun-sale reform advocates maintain that the availability of cheap weapons escalates crime and killing. Josh Sugarmann of the Violence Policy Center, a center studying violence prevention refers to the Saturday Night Specials as follows: "We have a fire burning, and these companies are throwing gasoline on it. These people know what the inner-city gun buyer wants."[1]

Dave Brazeau, the general manager of Raven Arms responds, "If it wasn't a gun, it would just be something else — a rock, a bow and arrow or a baseball bat."[2]

Only a few states ban the cheap gun models. For example, Maryland bans the Jennings .22 and .25 as "unreliable as to safety." South Carolina and Illinois have banned the three companies' brands because the zinc-alloy frames melt at less than 800 degrees.[3]

The Jennings' group of companies is not number one in gun sales (Smith & Wesson Co. is), but the group does account for 22 percent of all handguns and 27 percent of all handguns used in crimes across the country.[4]

The Saturday Night Specials are often sold in bulk in states where gun laws are lax and then smuggled to urban areas for sale. An illegal gun dealer in Harlem commented, "Here where I live, every young kid has a .22 or a .25. It's like their first Pampers."[5]

---

1. A. M. Freedman, "A Single Family Makes Many of Cheap Pistols That Saturate Cities," *Wall Street Journal* (Feb. 28, 1992): A1.

2. *Ibid.*

3. *Ibid.*

4. *Ibid.*

5. *Ibid.*, at A6.

Discussion Questions

1. Would any employees or owners of the Jennings companies be morally responsible for crimes committed with the weapons?
2. Would any gun dealer be morally responsible for a crime committed by someone to whom a gun was sold?
3. The Jennings companies have found a very successful market niche by selling low-cost guns to those who could otherwise not afford them. Is it ethical to capitalize on this market factor?
4. If the price of the weapon were increased, would the Jennings companies' moral responsibility be reduced?
5. If you were a sporting goods store owner or a gun dealer, would you carry Saturday Night Specials?

6.12 THE KILLER NOVEL

Simon & Schuster, Inc., entered into a contract with Bret Easton Ellis for the publication of his book *American Psycho*. Ellis received a $300,000 advance.

As the manuscript was readied for production, several Simon & Schuster editors protested the book's unusually violent sexual content. *Time* magazine, in its review of the manuscript, said its contents had "the most appalling acts of torture, murder and dismemberment ever described in a book targeted for the best seller lists."[1]

Mr. Ellis's first novel *Less Than Zero* was about drugs and sex among the children of the wealthy and was a best seller in 1985. The main character in *American Psycho* is an investment banker/serial killer who mutilates his victims. Those mutilations are described in great detail by Ellis in the book.

Based on editors' objections, Simon & Schuster announced it was canceling the book one month before its scheduled distribution in bookstores. Richard Snyder, Simon & Schuster's chairman, explained it "is not a book that Simon & Schuster is willing to publish, even though Mr. Ellis is a serious author whose work Simon & Schuster has previously published."[2]

Morton Janklow, an attorney and literary agent, commented on hearing of the Simon & Schuster decision, "I'm a great believer in the First Amendment, but this doesn't mean everything that gets written has to be published … This isn't a censorship issue — it's a taste issue."[3]

Discussion Questions

1. If Mr. Ellis's work has merit, should it be published?
2. Were the editors raising an ethical concern when they objected to the book's violent sexual content?
3. Are Mr. Ellis's First Amendment rights violated by the refusal to publish?
4. Would you have made the same decision as Simon & Schuster?
5. Will another publishing firm publish the book? Will the publicity over its content help its sales?

---

1. M. Cox, and L. Landro, "Paramount Unit Shelves a Novel on Serial Killer," *Wall Street Journal* (Nov. 15, 1990): B1.

2. *Ibid.*

3. *Ibid.*

6.13 THE "KILLER CARDS"

Dean Mullaney is a producer of a line of cards similar to baseball trading cards that features FBI agents and criminals. Mullaney's line of cards, and similar ones, have pictures and backgrounds of notorious killers such as Charles Manson, Richard Speck, Jeffrey Dahmer, Ted Bundy and David Berkowitz (aka "Son of Sam").

The cards are sold in candy and comic-books stores and include often graphic descriptions of the killers' actions. Some legislators in New York and other states are concerned about the sale of the cards to minors. Likening the cards to an "R"-rated movie, they are calling for a ban on the sale of the cards to minors.

Mullaney and others cite First Amendment protection, and Mullaney objects, "*Silence of the Lambs* won the Academy Award, but it's not a glorification of cannibalism."

Discussion Questions

1. Should the card manufacturers impose self-restraints on the sale of the cards?
2. Should the card manufacturers stop manufacturing the cards?
3. Should merchants refuse to sell the cards? Refuse to sell the cards to minors? If the merchants don't sell the cards, won't somebody else do it and make the money?
4. Isn't the purchase and use of the cards a matter for parental discretion?

SOURCE

"Dealing from a Crooked Deck." *Time* May 4, 1992, 21–22.

6.14 THE "MOMMY DOLL"

Villy Nielsen, APS, a Danish toy company, has introduced "The Mommy-To-Be-Doll" in the United States. The doll, Judith, is 11½ inches tall with a belly that is removable. When you remove the belly, there is a baby inside Judith that can be popped out. When the baby is popped out, Judith's original stomach pops back into place. The new stomach is very flat and restores Judith instantaneously to her young figure.

Teenage girls are intrigued by the doll, referring it to as "neat." However, Diane Welsh, the president of the New York chapter of the National Organization for Women stated, "A doll that magically becomes pregnant and unpregnant is an irresponsible toy. We need to understand having a child is a very serious business. We have enough unwanted children in this world."[1]

"Mommy-To-Be" comes with Charles, her husband, and baby accessories. An eleven-year-old shopper said, "I don't think she looks like a mommy ... She looks like a teenager."[2]

Discussion Questions

1. Is the doll socially responsible?
2. Would you carry the doll if you owned a toy store?
3. Would you want your children to have the doll?

---

1. "'Mommy' Doll Makes Birth a Snap," *Mesa Tribune* (May 9, 1992): A7.
2. *Ibid.*

6.15 THE SOUTH AFRICAN INVESTMENT

The political climate and social issues of South Africa have presented ongoing dilemmas for U.S. businesses. It was in 1986 that those issues came to a head as governmental policies affected the ability of U.S. firms to conduct business in South Africa. South Africa's apartheid government, seen as a violation of human rights, became a target of U.S. sanctions. In October 1986, Congress, through the override of a presidential veto, banned new U.S. investment and bank loans to South Africa, revoked landing rights for South African Airways in the United States, and prohibited imports of uranium, coal, steel, textiles, military vehicles and farm products.

At the same time, opponents of South African apartheid were successful in convincing colleges and universities and some other holders of stock in firms still operating in South Africa to divest themselves of the firms' stock. Georgetown and Harvard were among the universities to divest themselves of investment in firms with South African ties. At that time, the top 15 U.S. firms operating in South Africa were:

DuPont

RJR Nabisco

Mobil

Chevron

Johnson & Johnson

3M

Bristol-Myers

Hewlett-Packard

Texaco

Abbott Labs

American Home Products

Eli Lilly

Dun & Bradstreet

Pfizer

Boeing

Divestment became more complex as states such as Michigan and New Jersey passed statutes requiring the state employees' pension fund to comply with divestment requirements. In Michigan, the state pension fund found itself selling General Motors Corp. and Ford Motor Co. stock, two of the state's largest employers.

At the end of 1986, firms with South African ties comprised 40.5 percent of the capitalization of the Standard & Poor's 500–stock index. Within two years, after eighty-five U.S. companies divested themselves of South African holdings, the Standard & Poor's capitalization percentage fell to 18.9 percent.

The divestment laws were continually modified, and some states added additional teeth to their South African policies by prohibiting the award of contracts to firms with South African ties.

The South African political climate continued to remain tense during this time period with continual eruptions of violence. By 1986, 2,100 South Africans had been killed in racial violence. Before the commencement of divestment, there were three hundred U.S. firms in South Africa with a total investment of $2.5 billion. The businesses employed approximately 70,000 South Africans, both black and white, a total of less than 1 percent of the labor force. However, estimates are that each employed South African feeds about ten other South Africans as a result of employment.

About half of the U.S. firms (153) in South Africa operated their businesses there using the Sullivan Code. The Sullivan Code was developed by Reverend Dr. Leon Sullivan, a minister in a large Philadelphia Baptist church. The Sullivan Code established six principles for business operation that included the absence of segregation in the workplace, equal pay for equal work, fair employment practices, assumption of social responsibility for improving the lives of black workers, and advancement of blacks in the workplace. The text of the Code appears below:

I. Nonsegregation of the races in all eating, comfort, and work facilities.
II. Equal and fair employment practices for all employees.
III. Equal pay for all employees doing equal or comparable work for the same period of time.
IV. Initiation of and development of training programs that will prepare, in substantial numbers, blacks and other nonwhites for supervisory, administrative, clerical, and technical jobs.
V. Increasing the number of blacks and other nonwhites in management and supervisory positions.
VI. Improving the quality of employees' lives outside the work environment in such areas as housing, transportation, schooling, recreation, and health facilities.

These companies agree to further implement these principles. Where implementation requires a modification of existing South African working conditions, we will seek such modification through appropriate channels.

The following is an excerpt from a letter that was sent to Johnson & Johnson shareholders explaining the company's South African policy and its commitment to the Sullivan Code:

We thought Johnson & Johnson stockholders would be interested in the following brief description of the Company's position on South Africa:

South Africa is in a state of crisis. Throughout the United States, and particularly on our college campuses, apartheid has become an emotional as well as a political issue.

Our position is clear — we abhor and condemn apartheid. We have been in South Africa since 1930 and have a strong commitment to our 1,400 employees, more than half of whom are black. It is not right to abandon them to an uncertain future; therefore, we are opposed to disinvestment.

We have fostered equality in our facilities and pay equal wages for equal work. Our facilities are totally integrated. We place the same emphasis on individual achievement as a basis for advancement.

We continue to devote much of our resources to black education and training, to health care and housing for the disadvantaged, and to the establishment of black-owned businesses. Our employment practices and affirmative-action programs reflect a continuing leadership position in plant communities.

Since 1978 we have subscribed to the Sullivan Principles for improving conditions of South African blacks. We are committed to improving the quality of life for black South Africans. In our efforts to foster peaceful change, we are extending our efforts to include national government authorities.

We oppose measures that would restrict investment by U.S. companies in South Africa. Such actions would hurt rather than help blacks by depriving them of both job opportunities and improved education. The American business community is a force for constructive political, social and economic change in South Africa, including democracy, civil liberties and prosperity. American companies are in key industries. They have visibility and influence well beyond their percentages of employment and investment.

There are times when one has the choice of being part of the problem or part of the solution. Our decision to remain in South Africa is the result of making the latter choice. We believe it is better to face the evil and work towards its eradication than to withdraw from it.

One of the difficulties with the Code was that, in spite of the South African government's acceptance of it, compliance with the Code was supported only so long as it did not violate existing laws. Existing laws, in some instances, required continuing segregation.

The effect of divestment, the racial tension, and the problems U.S. firms encountered in South African operations was evident in the South African economy. In 1986, inflation was at 16 percent and output was dropping about 7 percent per year. There had been no economic growth since 1980, and 1985 saw a 2.5 percent drop in gross national product.

Kellogg Company continued to operate its plant for producing and packaging ready-to-eat cereals. Kellogg adhered to the Sullivan Code and employed, in 1986, 250 blacks and 100 whites at its plant in Springs, some forty miles from Johannesburg. While the Sullivan Code required that companies pay wages 30 percent above the household subsistence level, Kellogg paid 80 percent above the subsistence level. Also, Kellogg became involved in the local community by annually paying funds to subsidize mortgages for new housing for workers. The 18 percent interest rate would have made home ownership impossible for many of the workers without the Kellogg's subsidy. The housing shortage continues to be a problem with some families waiting twenty years on a list for a home.

Kellogg also "adopted" a local elementary school. Through this program, Kellogg paid for physical improvements to the school building, contributed funds and materials for the school and assisted with teacher training.

Other companies were involved in projects to help the economy and the advancement of blacks. Coca-Cola established a $10 million fund for assistance with housing, education and business development for blacks. Control Data closed its in-house print shop and awarded a long-term contract to three black entrepreneurs. General Motors, the second-largest U.S. employer, offered to pay legal expenses for employees who wished to challenge segregation at the beaches in Port Elizabeth.

As U.S. firms debated the issue of whether to stay or withdraw, Phiroshaw Camay, the general secretary of the Council of the Unions of South Africa, stated,

"The people who would be hurt by disinvestment may be a small price to pay to reduce the stress and tension caused by people being killed everyday."[1]

Firms continued to withdraw from South Africa, including Apple Computer, Blue Bell, Singer, PepsiCo, General Foods, Helena Rubenstein, Ford Motor Company and International Harvester.

The political climate of South Africa gradually changed over the next four years, culminating with the release of African National Congress President Nelson Mandela from prison in 1990. Gradually U.S. firms are re-entering the South African markets. Lotus and Microsoft have entered the South African markets with affirmative action plans and programs for training black graduates in the United States to return them to Johannesburg as managers in the operations there. One Microsoft intern, planning to return upon completion of her work in the United States states, "I feel there are many ways to fight the war against apartheid. My way is through education."

In July 1991, President Bush lifted the trade sanctions against South Africa but approximately 140 states and local governments still have contract restrictions on firms with South African investments. Apartheid is described as "crumbling" in South Africa.

Discussion Questions

1. What interests were the firms who had holdings in South Africa in 1986 trying to balance?
2. What interests were investors trying to balance by adopting divestment policies?
3. Was it appropriate for state and local governments to adopt contract restrictions, prohibitions on awarding contracts to firms with South African investments?
4. Would it be wrong to withdraw the efforts such as those of Kellogg and GM?
5. If you were a firm with South African investment in 1986, would you have withdrawn? Would the risk of revolution have influenced your decision?

SOURCES

Brenner, Brian. "Doing the Right Thing in South Africa." *Business Week* Apr. 27, 1992, 60–64.

White, James A. "Divestment Proves Costly and Hard." *Wall Street Journal* Jan. 2, 1989, B1.

Aim, Richard, and Jim Jones. "Fighting Apartheid American Style." *U.S. News & World Report* Oct. 20, 1986, 45–46.

---

1. Jonathan Kapstein, et al., "Leaving South Africa," *Business Week* (Sept. 23, 1985): 104–12.

6.16 THE TOYS PARENTS AND TEACHERS HATE

Kenner Products, Inc., a subsidiary of Hasbro, Inc., developed a new line of action figures called Savage Mondo Blitzers. The toys carry names such as:

Knight to Dismember

Snot Shot

Barf Bucket

Puke Shooter

Butt Kicker

Projectile Vomit

Eye Pus

Kiss My Bat

There are forty characters in the line of action figures. During test marketing, actual sales were double the forecasts by Kenner.

The catalog copy for the toys reads:

"Parents will hate 'em, teachers will despise 'em, but Savage Mondo Blitzers will be the latest rage with kids."

Teachers and students have written to the company to protest the line of toys. Parent-teacher groups have moved to organize boycotts against both Kenner and Hasbro.

Kenner states the line of toys is intended to be "wacky, irreverent and humorous."[1]

A toy buyer commented on the new line, "If parents let their kids watch MTV they're certainly going to allow them to play with Mondo Blitzers."[2]

Discussion Questions

1. Suppose that you are the marketing director for Kenner. The test market for Savage Mondo Blitzers tells you that you have a "slam dunk" in terms of the success of the line. Nonetheless, the toys themselves are disgusting to you and conjure up visions of psychotic killers and bodily functions. Would you be able to continue marketing the line? Would you consider the toys a means of exploiting children?
2. Suppose that you are a toy store owner. Would you have any ethical reservations about selling the line of toys?
3. If you were the children's TV ad director for a local TV station, would you have any ethical reservations about running Mondo Savage Blitzer ads?

---

1. Joseph Pereira, "We've Not Mentioned the Worst, and They're Selling Them to Kids," *Wall Street Journal* (Feb. 28, 1992): B1.

2. *Ibid.*

6.17 THE NFL, ARIZONA AND THE MARTIN LUTHER KING HOLIDAY

It was 1989 and the National Football League (NFL) chose the Phoenix suburb of Tempe as the sight for the Super Bowl XXVII (January 1993). There was one condition attached to the award of the lucrative game ($200 million estimated revenues); Arizonans had to approve a Martin Luther King Holiday set as a referendum on the November 6, 1990 ballot.

Arizona's history with the holiday was long and troubled. In 1986, then-Governor Bruce Babbitt declared a paid King holiday for all state workers. In 1987, shortly after newly-elected then-Governor Evan Mecham was sworn in, the holiday was rescinded by the new governor. Arizona experienced a loss of $30 million in revenue because of boycotts against the state. Other sporting events, conventions and a major league baseball franchise were jeopardized by the lack of a King holiday.

The new governor was then impeached for a variety of reasons and the state legislature approved a holiday. A petition circulated by voters placed the initiative for the holiday on the ballot.

Then-Governor Rose Mofford who rose to the office after the impeachment pledged to clean up the state's image, "We believe it's the right thing to do ... we need to adopt the holiday to show our support for civil rights. We were working on it well before the Super Bowl issue."[1]

The referendum for the King holiday was defeated by 17,226 votes, less than one percent of the 1.8 million votes cast in the 1990 election. After the defeat of the holiday, the NFL owners voted that the 1993 Super Bowl be held elsewhere because they did not feel comfortable holding the Super Bowl in any state that did not have a King holiday.

Discussion Questions

1. Was it ethical for the NFL to use its economic clout to intervene in the Arizona political process?
2. Should the MLK holiday have been an issue in the award of the Super Bowl contract?
3. Is outside intervention appropriate in a state's political process?
4. Is the NFL's position simply good business or is it morally correct?

SOURCES

Bergsman, Steve. "Holiday Flap Still Haunts Arizona." *Hotel & Motel Management* Oct. 17, 1988, 37–38.

Bremner, Brian. "People Who Live in Glass Stadiums." *Business Week* Nov. 26, 1990, 78.

---

1. Renee E. Warren, "No Promised Land in Arizona," *Black Enterprise* (Feb. 1991): 16.

Business Discipline Index

PRODUCT INDEX

TOPIC INDEX

Whistle -Blowing: